Middlemarch in the Twenty-First Century

Edited by

Karen Chase

OXFORD
UNIVERSITY PRESS

2006

OXFORD
UNIVERSITY PRESS

Oxford University Press, Inc., publishes works that further
Oxford University's objective of excellence
in research, scholarship, and education.

Oxford   New York

Auckland   Cape Town   Dar es Salaam   Hong Kong   Karachi
Kuala Lumpur   Madrid   Melbourne   Mexico City   Nairobi
New Delhi   Shanghai   Taipei   Toronto

With offices in

Argentina   Austria   Brazil   Chile   Czech Republic   France   Greece
Guatemala   Hungary   Italy   Japan   Poland   Portugal   Singapore
South Korea   Switzerland   Thailand   Turkey   Ukraine   Vietnam

Published by Oxford University Press, Inc.
198 Madison Avenue, New York, New York 10016

www.oup.com

Oxford is a registered trademark of Oxford University Press.

Library of Congress Cataloging-in-Publication Data
Middlemarch in the twenty-first century / edited by Karen Chase.
p. cm.
Includes bibliographical references and index.
ISBN-13 978-0-19-516995-9; 978-0-19-516996-6 (pbk.)
0-19-516995-6; 0-19-516996-4 (pbk.)
1. Eliot, George, 1819–1880. Middlemarch. I. Chase, Karen, 1952–
PR4662.M483 2006
823'.8—dc22   2005006371

1 3 5 7 9 8 6 4 2
Printed in the United States of America
on acid-free paper

For Michael, who makes ideal the real yoke of marriage,
and for Alex and Sarah, who widen the skirts of light

Acknowledgments

To the contributors of this volume I owe a debt of gratitude for producing such stimulating essays and for their patience with my suggestions and requests. To Elissa Morris I give thanks for encouragement and accommodation from this project's conception through its publication. To Alex Chase-Levenson I give three cheers for his willingness to extend his technological prowess to the correction of the seemingly limitless number of computer errors of which I am capable. I am grateful to Daniel Siegel, who at long-distance, cheerfully talked me through the steps necessary to convert separate files into a seamless manuscript. And for Michael Levenson, who, as always, gave generously intellectual, technical, and emotional support, I reserve my greatest thanks and highest esteem.

A NOTE ON THE TEXT   The Oxford edition of *Middlemarch* is used throughout this collection of essays. References will be cited by chapter and page parenthetically within the text. George Eliot, *Middlemarch* (Oxford: Oxford University Press, 1998).

Contents

Contributors

Nina Auerbach is John Welsh Centennial Professor of Literature at the University of Pennsylvania. Her books include *Women and the Demon: The Life of a Victorian Myth*; *Ellen Terry, Player in Her Own Time*; and *Our Vampires, Ourselves*. She has written a good deal about Victorian women and the social mythology surrounding them, Victorian fantasy, and the Victorian theater, but she has never, until now, written an extended exploration of *Middlemarch*, the novel she loves most.

Dame Gillian Beer was recently the King Edward VII Professor of English Literature at the University of Cambridge. Among her books are *Darwin's Plots: Evolutionary Narrative in Darwin, George Eliot, and Nineteenth-century Novels* (2nd edition, 2000); *George Eliot* (1988); *Open Fields: Science in Cultural Encounter* (1996); and *Virginia Woolf: the Common Ground* (1996). She is currently completing a study of Carroll's Alice books called *Alice in Space*.

Elizabeth Deeds Ermarth is an interdisciplinary scholar who writes on the cultural history and current crisis of representation as a cultural value, with special emphasis on history as an explanatory mechanism. She is author of five books including *Realism and Consensus*; *Sequel to History*; and (forthcoming) *Rewriting Democracy*, and of many articles for *New Literary History*, *History and Theory*, *Time and Society* and other journals. She has held several distinguished appointments including as Presidential Research Professor at Univ. of Maryland, Saintsbury Professor at Edinburgh (UK), and Cox Professor at Univ. of Colorado.

Kate Flint is Professor of English at Rutgers University. She is the author of *The Woman Reader 1837–1914* and *The Victorians and the Visual Imagination*, as well as many articles on nineteenth- and twentieth-century literature, visual art, and cultural history. She is currently completing *The Transatlantic Indian 1785–1930*.

Jakob Lothe is Professor of English literature at the University of Oslo. His books include *Conrad's Narrative Method* and *Narrative in Fiction and Film*. He has edited and co-edited several volumes, most recently *Franz Kafka* and *European and Nordic Modernisms*. He is the author of numerous essays, including contributions to the Cambridge Companions to Joseph Conrad and Thomas Hardy.

J. Hillis Miller taught for many years at the Johns Hopkins University and then at Yale University, before going to the University of California at Irvine in 1986, where is he now UCI Distinguished Research Professor. He is the author of many books and essays on nineteenth and twentieth-century English, European, and American literature, and on literary theory. His most recent books are *Others*, *Speech Acts in Literature*, *On Literature*, and *Zero Plus One*. He is at work on a book on speech acts in the novels and stories of Henry James. A *J. Hillis Miller Reader* is forthcoming from Edinburgh University Press and Stanford University Press.

Daniel Siegel is assistant Professor at the University of Alabama at Birmingham. He is currently writing on condescension and Victorian philanthropy, a topic on which he has published essays in *Victorian Literature and Culture* and *Dickens Studies Annual*.

David Trotter is King Edward VII Professor of English Literature at the University of Cambridge. He has written widely about English and American literature of the nineteenth and twentieth centuries. His most recent book is *Paranoid Modernism*. He is currently writing *A Poetics of Early Cinema*.

Middlemarch in the Twenty-First Century

1
Introduction

KAREN CHASE

◆　◆　◆

WHAT BETTER JUSTIFIES a collection of new essays on an old classic than an acknowledgment of interpretive evanescence? The phrase, "the varying experiments of Time" (prelude, 3) suggests why criticism always benefits from renewal, but it hardly narrows the field. With few editorial alterations, the text of *Middlemarch* remains unchanged: the novel withstands the pressures of time, circumstance, and personality. However, its meaning changes both within the culture and within the consciousness of individual readers. It is for each generation to chart the differences that ensure that the novel will not become a relic, but will continue to exert a pressure on the twenty-first century as vitally as it did in its nineteenth and our twentieth centuries.

Critical reassessments fill the space between "ambitious ideals" of the past and the "breathing forgetfulness" of the present (ch. 20, 181): if Dorothea had been accompanied by a more responsive critic on her Roman honeymoon, she might have been spared her first marital catastrophe. This recognition puts a gloss on Will Ladislaw's critique of Casaubon's datedness. We might say that *Middlemarch* advises us to read it from a contemporary lens lest we find ourselves, like Casaubon, faced with a gap between the object of our study and our perceptions of it. We begin then, with life in time, the life of the novel *Middlemarch*, and within that novel, the representation of life in time.

Who besides Eliot has been better aware of the alteration of objects given a change in perspective? Of course perspective is subject to time as well as space: as the narrator in *Middlemarch* acknowledges, "time changes the proportion of things" (ch. 37, 339–40). Michael Levenson has discussed the transmutations of narrative as it encounters time as duration or time as chronology.[1] For many of us, reading *Middlemarch* is a little of each: the reading moment is always "duration," but the history of our rereadings contributes to the novel's life in time and creates its own chronology. The essays in this volume attach *Middlemarch* to the twenty-first century by way of their aesthetic, ethical, and social concerns, but each reading also dwells within the confines of the pages of the novel and its communities. We move constantly between the early and later nineteenth century and to the start of the twenty-first century, respecting the differences without allowing them to become obstacles in our way.

The distinction between chronology and duration makes for an illuminating counterpoint that allows us to move from the novel's portrait of life in time to our own perception of the novel's life in time. Let me suggest for a moment a new lineage for Eliot's masterpiece. Despite the many claims for a "timeless" passion evinced in its pages, Emily Brontë's *Wuthering Heights* is as time-conscious as a railway schedule. We commonly say that this novel understands passion inside and out, or in the terms above, passion as duration. Less common is the observation that Brontë submits eternal passion to the stringencies of time. Once Catherine Earnshaw dies, Heathcliff's love must endure the slow passage of time, aging, waiting impatiently for a death that will restore it to ghostly eternity. His passion itself, "the desire for reunion with Cathy," is "unchangeable and unchanged," but Heathcliff, who is the bearer of the passion, must grow older even if his passion does not.[2] One of the keenest and most unsettling preoccupations of the novel is the concern with desire that can find no outlet, that cannot reach its object, that forces us to endure a passage of time bringing no relief, which in Heath-cliff's description (and who should know better?) devours our exis-tence, swallows us "in anticipation of its fulfillment"—its fulfill-ment, not ours (256). Heathcliff's passion heralds the demonic, but Brontë's vision pursues another course as well. Through its genera-tional structure, passion unrestrained in the initial cast of characters is famously disciplined, and perhaps diminished, in the second. In this sense what would have been the resolution of age is instead dis-tributedamong the second generation of the Linton and Earnshaw families.

George Eliot, pursuing a similar course, arrives at startlingly different conclusions. Life in time is for her, as for Brontë, best ex-pressed through images of emotions, passions if you will, caught in the passage of time. But for Eliot, passion is a vocation, and vocation itself another name for passion.

> We are not afraid of telling over and over again how a man comes to fall in love with a woman and be wedded to her, or else be fa-tally parted from her. Is it due to excess of poetry or of stupidity that we are never weary of describing what King James called a woman's "makdom and her fairnesse," never weary of listening to the twanging of the old Troubadour strings, and are compara-tively uninterested in that other kind of "makdom and fairnesse" which must be wooed with industrious thought and patient re-nunciation of small desires? In the story of this passion, too, the development varies: sometimes it is the glorious marriage, some-times frustration and final parting. And not seldom the catas-trophe is bound up with the other passion, sung by the Trouba-dours. (ch. 15, 135)

Vocational passion crafts its own attendant actions, generates its own music, and suggests its own forms of triumph and tragedy. As Alan Mintz and Dorothea Barrett have amply demonstrated, voca-tion takes many forms in this novel, as many forms as there are pos-sibilities for action, for of course vocation is just one way to define what it is one does in the world.[3] And if in Eliot vocation is also a form of idealism, that is because of the ardor (another name *Middle-*

march gives to passion) with which it is pursued. But as in *Wuthering Heights*, in *Middlemarch* no passion, desire, or intention can withstand the pressures of time. For instance, vocational passion is no more stable than "the other," romantic passion for which it is often exchanged. The "moment of vocation" (ch. 15, 135) is no less blinding than the eruption of love, and just as liable to disappointment. Eliot paints a grim picture of the waning of vocational purpose: "perhaps their ardour in generous unpaid toil cooled . . . till one day their earlier self walked like a ghost in its old home and made the new furniture ghastly" (ch. 15, 135). *Middlemarch* anatomizes the downward trajectory that characterizes the passionate embrace of some form of action, a wish to do something of consequence in or for the world, as it submits to the movement through time. Dorothea's sensitivity to "all who had slipped below their own intention" (ch. 50, 465) leads to her recognition of the erosions of time on individual intention: "There is no sorrow I have thought more about than that—to love what is great, and try to reach it, and yet to fail" (ch. 76, 719). Will watches Lydgate's ideals disintegrate and takes his friend's example as a warning not to succumb to "that pleasureless yielding to the small solicitations of circumstance" (ch. 79, 736). As we know, some strong individuals can conquer time, as "it always remains true that if we had been greater, circumstance would have been less strong against us" (ch. 58, 551). Lydgate's tragedy is to observe the growing distance between his actions and intentions: "he began to familiarize his imagination with another step even more unlike his remembered self" (ch. 67, 639). Of course others witness the same decline: Farebrother notes "he was getting unlike his former self" (ch. 70, 670), and Will's realization that he could follow Lydgate's downward path leads the narrator to observe "We are on a perilous margin when we begin to look passively at our future selves" (ch. 79, 736). Mr. Brooke's famous dilettantism is itself a kind of vocational passion even though each pursuit he follows falls short of a passionate embrace. We witness the transformation of that vocational conceit from an active pursuit to an act of memory: "I went into that at one time" replaces the actual engagement in politics, reform, literature, art, and so on. Of course we cannot know the extent of his involvement in any of the subjects he claims to have pursued, but in the short passage from 1829 to 1831 we do see his gestures toward national politics and local reforms radically curtailed. In short, for all but the luckiest or most exemplary characters even the passions that do not diminish over time give way to something other than their original object and thus prepare the way for moral decay, mental slovenliness, and emotional anguish.

A few characters manage to uphold their original intentions in spite of the temptations to give way to small changes that gradually make for large gaps between past and present. Rosamond Vincy is frighteningly consistent; time leaves no mark on her. But such consistency in others, such as Caleb Garth, is more reassuring. Farebrother's attraction to Mary makes him temporarily waver when it comes to warning Fred to mind his behavior. But Farebrother's intentions weather the intrusions of time as he realizes "I had once meant better than that, and I am come back to my old intention" (ch. 66, 635–6). Time offers him the opportunity to develop a passion for the work that he never desired to pursue: "I used often to wish I had been something else than a clergyman," he confesses to Lydgate, "but perhaps it will be better to try and make as good a clergyman out of myself as I can" (ch. 52, 480). Is it vigilance or instinct that makes Harriet Bulstrode incline toward her husband in his crisis? Surely it is the former that inspires Dorothea when she masters her rage to reach out once more to her tired husband, or when she overcomes her despair in order to visit her presumed "rival" in order to offer comfort. These characters embrace duration—the concentrated emotion of time—as an occasion to fortify themselves against the temptations of change that chronology thrusts in their paths. They are not necessarily better or happier than others for this difference, but they are creatures of a different pattern. What more bracing than this realization that discipline can be a bulwark against the erosions of time: "we can set a watch over our affections and our constancy as we can over other treasures" (ch. 57, 544)?

FREQUENTLY ELIOT "THROWS INTO RELIEF" a particular trait she wants to emphasize by way of the surrounding contrast. Dorothea's beauty is "thrown into relief by poor dress" (ch. 1, 7); the autumnal day of Dorothea's first visit to Lowick prompts the narrator to remark that her fiancé "had no bloom that could be thrown into relief by that background" (ch. 9, 60) or by the contrast with Dorothea's frequently remarked bloom. In the Vatican, the German artist Naumann admires the "fine bit of antithesis" exhibited by the Quaker-clad Dorothea leaning against the "sensuous perfection" of the marble Cleopatra (Ariadne) (ch. 19, 155), each throwing the other into relief, and suggesting the possibility of commerce rather than contrast in the assessment "sensuous force controlled by spiritual passion" (ch. 19, 156). In similar fashion, I have brought Emily Brontë's *Wuthering Heights* to bear on *Middlemarch*, because it throws into relief Eliot's efforts to discipline romanticism, and also suggests some relation that survives the contrast. We might extend the analogy one step further.

Both novels make use of the marriage plot as the means of addressing the clash—formal and dramatic—between what can still usefully be called romance and realism. The trajectory is worked out in generational terms in the earlier novel. Torn between her love for the rough Heathcliff and the civilized Linton, Cathy marries the latter only to regret the loss of the former. She dies in the failed attempt to unite the two, and eventually both men follow her to the grave. Her daughter, however, perceives how to teach the raw Hareton to be(come) the civilized gentleman. But this is no story of the renunciation of childhood and the realization of maturity. We are warned that Heathcliff is "not a human being" (128), but this is too tame: indeed, Heathcliff might be thought of as the image that best expresses Cathy's yearning for a soul mate. She dies for want of him, and he becomes superfluous—the embodiment of romantic attachment that lingers after the longing for it has extinguished the self. Heathcliff is conjured from the girl's imagination as a figure for romantic love. The novelist searches for a composite that dilutes the extreme but is sustainable outside the realm of imaginative fulfillment. By casting the situation in generational terms Brontë elides the question of progression that has preoccupied critics: how to account for the movement from childhood to maturity, imagination to reality, romance to realism, romantic to Victorian. The novel settles for alternate adolescent fantasies; it relinquishes one, and adopts another, but whether we can call the loss or the gain a growth or development is highly debatable.

Eliot approaches a similar problem from a different angle. Dorothea is inexperienced at the start, but she becomes increasingly childlike as experience strips her egotism and leads her through the "real" to "the ideal . . . yoke of marriage" (ch. 48, 452). In marrying Casaubon, Dorothea seems almost to choose the path of maturity before she has traversed that of adolescence. She begins with renunciation, seeks discipline, and eagerly anticipates "giving up" that which brings her delightful pleasure. In learning to love Will Ladislaw, Dorothea discovers the childhood she eschewed in her earlier years. She does not regress; she merely reverses the order of experience. Dorothea begins as an adult and learns how to be a child; put in other terms, we might say that she allows herself to experience pleasure once she is certain of her ability to do without it. For Dorothea, then, to age is to emerge more childlike than she was at the start. Time works its experiments differently on each character. And on the text itself it has the same "incalculable" effect that Dorothea has on those around her.

Middlemarch is an open text with illimitable interpretations: this is the general perspective adopted by the authors included in this volume. I did not determine in advance that it would be so. But it will be clear to every reader that the authors are enjoying themselves. The readings are never flippant, but they are not reverent either. Irreverence is something this novel sorely needs after more than a century of worship. Reading *Middlemarch* for pleasure is not irreconcilable with reading it earnestly, and criticism can be more vivid when it reads with and against the grain that George Eliot has etched.

Gillian Beer broadens the scope of what investigations of the text's materiality usually consider. Always keeping in view two contemporary audiences, Eliot's and our own, Beer explores the gaps within (and without) the text that initial readers did not experience, or did not experience in the same way that readers today do. Beer feels the novel's contours by the shape of things absent. She fills in the apparent absences, restoring the density that confronted nineteenth-century readers, and making palpable to present-day readers some of the acute emotions that have seemed elusive for want of articulation. Her realization that "what's not in *Middlemarch*" may be more vexing than what is prepares us for a newly oriented engagement with the text. Beer extends an invitation to visit *Middlemarch* in the same way that Alice visits Wonderland. Like Alice, falling down the rabbit hole and simultaneously perceiving the materiality and immateriality of the world she now inhabits, Beer introduces us to a world in which things absent sharpen and define the experience of worldliness itself.

Beer fills the "empty" space we call absence, enabling the shapes of things *not* present to exert a force on the reader's perceptions. David Trotter brings into view regions typically obscured in the provinces of domestic realism. He offers a cartological investigation into these seemingly inaccessible spaces and attempts to locate such ineffables as sexuality and personality within the realms typically concealed by the stylistic conventions Eliot employs. Taking his lead from Eliot's principle that "all form is difference," Trotter explores the variety of shapes and shapelessness that compose the distance between distinction and nebulous mass. There are notable surprises: Casaubon's instability is measured by the tension wrought by a thick constitution cast within a thin, "indistinct" frame; Joshua Rigg and Will Ladislaw mingle incongruously as new species received harshly by an uncomprehending Middlemarch community; and once we plot her movements on a "performative" rather than a "purposive" axis, Dorothea's complicated awakening is more extensive than previously thought. Actions that "carry the force of feeling" beyond that of speech carve forms that become vessels for emotions, enlarging possibilities by imposing new shapes, and destabilizing the present even as they prepare for the future.

Although Eliot is commonly praised for her ability to render homely detail, more often she is remembered for her unflinching scrutiny of the mental universe. Beer and Trotter call into question a strict separation between these two spheres, and Kate Flint also begins by challenging a divorce between mood and matter. Flint explores the dialectic between perceptions and the things perceived. Eliot's embrace of a determinist outlook is then understood as a creative exchange, an animated dance between moods and materials. Flint finds striking convergence between Eliot's grasp of Victorian neuroscience and contemporary research into the properties of pheromones. Her essay helps us to reconstitute the atmosphere in which characters and society take shape.

"[B]ut why always Dorothea?" (ch. 29, 261) the narrator of *Middlemarch* famously checks her own tendency to enshrine her heroine, thus warning readers to be conscious of the distortions of narrative privilege. Nina Auerbach's irreverent reading plucks Dorothea off her throne and locates her alongside the cast of troubling figures that includes Rosamond, Bulstrode, Rigg, and even Raffles. The shock of the reading is that Dorothea's personality gains when it loses its solitary luster. Auerbach's aim is not to bring down the Wendy-bird but to demonstrate the range of "parallel destinies" that prevent both easy contrasts and comforting notions of development. If there is no remove between high and low, exalted and debased, philanthropic and selfish, if the contrast between sunrise and sunset wavers, then we must revise the conventional understanding of Eliot's trust in amelioration, her belief in a struggle toward enlightened sympathy.

Elizabeth Ermarth focuses on Eliot's dependence on identifiable linguistic patterns to redefine the quest or even the possibility for certainty, stability, or authority. The authority of Eliot's narrator has not been easy to unsettle, but according to Ermarth, even the narrator (and certainly all other voices in the novel) participates in the general march toward "reversibility" in her pronouncements. Just as Auerbach questions our assumption of Eliot's confidence in meliorist progress, Ermarth suggests we have too quickly granted to the narrator scriptural authority that the novel resists. In this world of kaleidoscopic pronouncements, the only certainty is in the availability of an alternative perspective. Dorothea believes that Greek or "even Hebrew" (ch. 7, 59) might bring her closer to the truth, or that if Casaubon only knew German, his work would be closer to the "key" he pursues so relentlessly. But Ermarth helps us realize that the great good of linguistic facility is precisely in its responsiveness to otherness, even as it makes impossible the dream of fully realizing "other." The proliferation of languages, like the proliferation of readings, augments but never completes comprehension. Some people know German, Greek, and "even" Hebrew, but for each of us there is a German, a language we do not and cannot possess.

J. Hillis Miller also finds openness rather than finality in this author, once considered relentless in her determinism. Miller upsets any interpretation that places reliance on the stability of George Eliot's perspective, arguing that the only inevitability in the novel is the reader's inability to find completion. Instead, we are released, free to read at will within the indeterminacy of the text. Miller's earlier work showed how the novel deconstructs its own authority, but here the focus is on the rejuvenating effects to which such performative acts give rise. In his most recent reconsideration, Miller shows how the narrator and reader become partners in constructive friction, the result of which is a tension that is neither antagonistic nor competitive, nor even hierarchical. Instead, the contact allows us to "take possession" of *Middlemarch* no less than it possesses us. Casaubon diligently transcribes successive manifestations of myth without realizing that the "key" resides in the diffuse effects generated by the collision between instance and interpretation. With a much lighter touch, Eliot skims the resources of myth as a way of injecting into her novel a form of repetition that remains adaptive to character, circumstance, and the reader's "will." Thus in Miller's artful hands does deconstructive debris prepare the ground for a vital regrowth, no more stable than the last, but promising continual regeneration. Miller identifies Dorothea's appeal in "her immense limitless yes," and the appeal of his own approach is not dissimilar. Part of the excitement his essay generates derives from the realization of the potential for deconstruction to reconstruct, and the proof that affirmation can be predicated by the refusal to blink even, or especially, when the urge is great.

Daniel Siegel takes seriously Ermarth's injunction to think of egotism and altruism as relativizing gestures. His examination of "giving" exposes a complicated dialectic between performative acts of release and the "ethical contours of renunciation." Siegel's central insight—that there is an art to abdication, which involves the deliberate adjustment of relations between profit and loss—makes possible unlikely juxtapositions between characters with vastly different motives. Siegel shows how Featherstone and Casaubon are no less likely intimates for Miss Brooke than Garth or Farebrother, and that though Nicholas Bulstrode and Sir James Chettam suffer unequally, they similarly endure the weight of private emotions condemned by community sentiment. Sometimes characters differ in the timing or staging of actions that are substantively similar. And these slight differences result eventually in narratives of loss or gain. These terms are opaque, since *Middlemarch* itself profits by its elevation of the narrative of loss. Once again we see a world in which characters echo one another oddly, general propositions are subject to astonishing and unexpected reversals, and the deconstruction of effects may well engender affirmation, or, in Siegel's terms, redemption.

Lothe's deft analysis strengthens our visual susceptibility to the novel by tilting with the various ways in which Anthony Page's BBC adaptation of *Middlemarch* engages with the role and function of narrator. Apart from the heavy technique of voice-over, how can film represent the distinctive tones of Eliot's narrator? Lothe shows how this film represents something as abstract as "idealism," or as dense as "realism," how the filmmaker can preserve vision without being shortsighted, and how Page appreciates the literal without forsaking the metaphoric. Like Trotter, Lothe finds drama in gestures that replace speech, and like Auerbach and Siegel he discloses the ironic convergence of contrasting figures, here between Dorothea and Casaubon. Most provocatively, Lothe suggests that in turning novel into film, Page creates something beyond transcription: the film accents the novel's corners, crevices, and shadows. The film "Middlemarch" is not *Middlemarch*; it is a hybrid, both less and more. Lothe's compelling vision comprehends the fullness of its difference.

Ever rigorous and exacting, *Middlemarch* refuses to make promises even in its final pages. After all, "promises may not be kept" (finale, 779) and so are less secure than the elastic and ambiguous but more promising "hopefulness" that is itself a quality of the novel's sadness. The hope lies not in any particular character or reform, nor in the community that exiled its idealists or in the city that swallows them whole. And yet, neither is it part of "a group of airy conditions" (ch. 64, 622) nor a fantasy of an "unreal Better" (ch. 75, 709). Eliot's hope lies not in a determinate outcome so much as in the palpable earthy conditions out of which any good must come: in the sturdiness of "land" as opposed to "speckilation" (ch. 12, 102–3); in the "out of doors" (finale, 784) that Dorothea's unnamed son chooses over a political life; or in the cottage life transformed through Fred and Mary's efforts, which persists despite Dorothea's failure to realize it herself. If diffusion is the image of choice at the end, and incalculable is the measure of effects, then perhaps, incongruously, it is to "good Mr. Brooke's scrappy slovenliness" (ch. 2, 17) that we ought to return for a last nod. Brooke agrees to write Will Ladislaw to prevent Will's visit to Lowick following Casaubon's physical collapse, "But the end of Mr. Brooke's pen was a thinking organ, evolving sentences, especially of the benevolent kind, before the rest of his mind could well overtake them" (ch. 30, 273). Generating plot is a form for hopefulness. Like the famous opening of *Adam Bede*, in which the narrator acknowledges making reality "with this drop of ink at the end of my pen," Eliot reserves for the narrator, whose imagination engages with possibility, the task of producing a benevolence we might call hope, and extending that generally to the imagined world. There is hope, then, in the home epic, told and retold under varying conditions, which evolves scientifically and imaginatively, predictably and unexpectedly. And that hope is refigured in critical discourse, which continually redraws the novel's interpretative geometry according to the designs of its own age. Even the most dour reader conveys the novel's hope simply by reading *Middlemarch* in our own time.

Notes

1. Michael Levenson, "Telling Times: A Rhythm in Life and Literature," Public Lecture, March 21, 2003, Charlottesville, University of Virginia.

2. Emily Brontë, *Wuthering Heights* (1963; Norton, 1972), 88. Further references are to this edition; page numbers will be included parenthetically within the text.

3. Alan Mintz, *George Eliot and the Novel of Vocation* (Cambridge, Mass.: Harvard University Press, 1978); Dorothea Barrett, *Vocation and Desire: George Eliot's Heroines* (London: Routledge, 1980).

2

What's Not in *Middlemarch*

GILLIAN BEER

◆　◆　◆

MY TITLE MAY seem perverse, and is certainly two-edged. The *inclusiveness* of George Eliot's novel *Middlemarch* or, at the least, its capaciousness, is one of the book's most marked characteristics. The novel is usually praised for its copiousness or blamed for its deterministic inclusiveness. It can't include everything, of course: plastic cups and chaos theory are beyond its horizon. George Eliot's narrator insists "that all the light I can command must be concentrated on this particular web, and not dispersed over that tempting range of relevancies called the universe" (ch. 15, 132). Those "relevancies," however, give scope to the book, permeating its apparently constrained subject matter described in the subtitle: "a study of provincial life." Moreover, the book's boundaries are permeable: not only is it highly allusive, but it also calls on a stock of common knowledge—that is to say, knowledge common to its first readers and not to us.

So the question of what's in the text of *Middlemarch* is not a simple one. It involves the contingent reader; it involves particularly a host whose absence we may not notice: those first readers who lived alongside George Eliot and whose needs, desires, assumptions, and knowledge the book resists and leans toward. With the astuteness of hindsight, present-day readers can observe the apparent absence in the book's subject matter of the industrial working classes, of colonialism, and, less obviously, of the death of loved people. The three deaths that propel the plot are all of dislikeable people, and only at the book's end, and distanced, does the reader hear by report of Lydgate's death. But other absences, proximate and remote, shape the book then and now. They shape it differently then, and now.

Middlemarch is a fruitful example both of what we can never know and of how we can augment our reading experience by imagining the initial conditions of reading when the work first appeared. We shall always be tracking, dramatizing, and uncovering features that lay latent for earlier readers. We shall also be missing much that would have been manifest to them. *Middlemarch* is a revealing text in which to explore such issues because of the author's abundant and extraordinarily wide-ranging knowledge, and equally because of the shared knowledge that she does not share with us but takes for granted with her first readers. Here the para-texts can help. Those early readers, lost to us, were the *wes*, the *yous*, of this declarative text. They easily knew things we don't and took part in a dialogic exchange from which we are excluded. And some things were physically present in the early form of the material book *Middlemarch* that are absent now.

I shall here be concerned with the physical form of first publication and the advertisements that surround the text of *Middlemarch*, in order to explore what these juxtapositions may tell us. Advertisements are fleeting para-texts; they are absolutely "of the moment" and so give a window onto the readers by whom this work was first received. I shall be concerned also with topics that engage the imagination of other Victorian novelists—in particular, food and religion—topics that are either relegated or notably excluded from this novel. Further: *Middlemarch*, unusually among George Eliot's novels, is not concerned with the erotic drive between siblings, or across generations of the same family (as is *The Mill on the Floss* or, more indirectly, *Romola* or *Daniel Deronda*). The eschewing of that particular energy needs to be noted but does not seem to be a controlling lack. Adultery, however, is. Though it never quite happens in the book's present time, adultery is a threshold, a brink for the work as well as the characters. It is a possibility so close in fantasy that it measures (and sometimes threatens to obliterate) the gap between the inner and the outer world of present event. Casaubon and Rosamond, in every other way so different, are equally driven by this fantasy. And, from the past, Featherstone's illegitimate son is the motor for the revenge visited on Bulstrode. Adultery, or adulteration, is there, too, in the cheap practices the local factory owners employ in their dying of silks (I shall return to that issue).

But before I turn to those proximities and absences, let's pause on the most obvious "not there": the main thing not to be found in Middlemarch, the town, is *Middlemarch*, the book. That is to say that the book outgoes, inordinately even, the town community that is its ostensible topic. The disparities between topic and writing are striking. The town of Middlemarch is provincial, the writing of *Middlemarch* is urban, cosmopolitan even. The concerns of the people are local, of the writing polymathic (Casaubon is, in this, awkward kin to the writer, as George Eliot well knew). The writing gains a temporal march on its subject: it is endowed with the additional knowledge gained between around 1830, the setting of the work, to around 1870, the time of its publication. These time disjunctions are the chosen conditions of the novel; but its enterprise is, very often, to temper them, and to get away from the developmental or evolutionary hierarchies that such an organization seems to assert. It implies questions such as: have things "improved" between 1830 and 1870 (come to that, between 1870 and 2005)? Or are we watching the higgledy-piggledy motion of growth rather than a teleological building of ethics?

The tension between Middlemarch the town and *Middlemarch* the book is not static but supple. How much have things changed? How capable are they of change?—these are the questions implicit in the taut ironies enacted between setting and first readers. The month–by–month political events of the late 1820s and early 1830s are accurately and inconspicuously alluded to in the novel, forming a national calendar for the intimate and local happenings.[1] They also produce wry comparisons for the reader early in the 1870s: the bank crises of the late 1820s, described in the particular case of Bulstrode, are brought close for the first readers by the—undescribed—1866 panic and City crash. The coming of the first Reform Bill in 1832 is presaged in the characters' lives, while Eliot's 1870s readers were responding to the second Reform Bill. The shifts (or the lack of them) in the position and education of women in the intervening period are caustically indicated. The undescribed period between 1832 and 1871 is, in fact, never absent from *Middlemarch*: it is, rather, the invisible structuring arc of the book and the source of many of its most telling ironies. It is also the shared zone of George Eliot and most of her first readers: the common time of their adulthoods.

The very first form in which the work appeared was as eight books, and *book* does mean book. "Miss Brooke," "Old and Young," "Waiting for Death," "Three Love Problems," "The Dead Hand," "The Widow and the Wife," "Two Temptations," "Sunset and Sunrise": each appeared first as a separate paperback, then was bound as a separate hardback volume with sage green covers. The title of each book appeared on the spine beneath *Middlemarch*. And in every volume the text is surrounded by advertisements.

These—quite decorous—advertisements bear some intriguing relations to the topics of the work: they promote jewelry, chocolate, pens, fabrics, dyes, medicines, candles, indigestion cures, mourning clothes,[2] and even (self-reflexively) the *Wise, Witty, and Tender Sayings in Prose and Verse, Selected from the Works of George Eliot* by Alexander Main. The publisher Bentley buys space for his latest list (this in a Blackwood publication). The advertisements give much less room for scandal than do those surrounding Dickens's novels, for example the monthly parts of *Bleak House*, with its images of unclad mermaids and advertisements for what seem, discreetly, to be abortion pills. The advertisements surrounding the books of *Middlemarch* are intensely verbal, with only a few images. Each volume has at the front an advertisement for the jeweller Streeter and at its end one for French chocolate: "Chocolat de la Cie. Coloniale."[3]

The juxtapositions between advertisement and text may seem generalized, simply reproducing the accoutrements of bourgeois life rather than knowingly placing a product to agree with the text.[4] George Eliot certainly did not set out to accommodate them as she wrote, well in advance of any publication, nor did she and Lewes (so

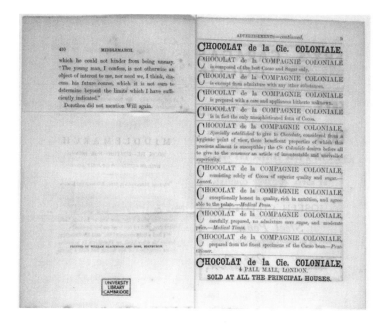

far as we know) make them more relevant in further episodes. However, neither (clearly) did they veto the appearance of advertisements that seem quite at odds with the tenor of the work. In the four-volume version of the novel published later in the same year these advertisements are not included.

The advertisements often open up issues also engaged with in the novel, and in some cases the unironic juxtaposition of text and advertisement seems positively scandalous now. Lydgate, for example, the modern doctor of the 1830s, would still have had much to do against medical quackery in the 1870s, as we see when we read the advertisement for the astonishingly omni-competent "Allcock's Porous Strengthening Plaster":

A Curative Host in itself: superior to any electric or galvanic chain-band or belt, or Spanish fly blister, or any blister, or any rubefacients or stimulating liniments whatsoever. The best and most successful remedy in all cases of Weak Muscles, Nervous Affections, Bronchitis, Sciatica, Tic Doloureux, Rheumatism, Local Pains, Inflammation of the lungs, Severe Coughs, Asthma, Lumbago, Diarrhoea and Consumption.

Among the testimonials cited in the advertisement is this one:

> He affirms that *headache* is cured by one worn just below the breastbone; that one placed over the navel will cure hysterics, as well as dysentery and affections of the bowels. Even *chronic costiveness* he found to be greatly relieved by wearing one over the bowels.

Had Casaubon but known!—his chronic costiveness might have vanished. The absurd and total barrier between what is present in the text and what is beside the text sparks various thoughts of what could have been, had the characters had access to the advertisements. It is also curious to reflect that *Felix Holt*, in George Eliot's novel of that name, refuses to follow in his father's footsteps producing quack medicine. Yet here, only a few years later, we have just such medicines advertised in the work of Holt's inventor.

The advertisements flout the insights of the novel while provocatively demonstrating the degree to which the novel itself draws on a common material world shared, apparently un-self-consciously, by George Eliot and her first readers. After the initial reader reached the final moving cadences of the work—"that things are not so ill with you and me as they might have been, is half owing to the number who lived faithfully a hidden life, and rest in unvisited tombs"—the page was turned to:

> Keating's Cough Lozenges. Under Patronage of Royalty. Daily Recommended by the Faculty.
>
> In *Incipient Consumption*, *Asthma*, and *Winter Cough*, they are unfailing. Being free from every hurtful ingredient, they may be taken *by the most delicate female* or *the youngest child*; while the *Public Speaker* and *Professional Singer* will find them invaluable in allaying the hoarseness and irritation incidental to vocal exertion, and also a powerful auxiliary in the production of *Melodious Enunciation*.

Like a commentary, even a satire, the advertisement brings to mind Dorothea's melodious voice, Bulstrode's public speaking, Rosamond's delicacy: all, it seems, to be controlled by Keating's cough lozenges. And if the reader has been reading the novel aloud, they will indeed be called for as the end is reached.

Cough lozenges and chocolate are frequent in these pages that surround the main text: chocolate in all its forms, sometimes bringing the Colonies close to the text as at the desolating end of book 2: "Dorothea did not mention Will again" (ch. 22, 211). The facing page sings the praises through a series of repeated refrains of "Chocolat de la Cie. Coloniale." Nancy Henry has recently given an account of George Eliot's connections to the colonies in *George Eliot and the British Empire* (Cambridge: Cambridge University Press, 2003): this chocolate advertisement registers a telling blindness to juxtaposition shared by George Eliot with her readers, just as present-day readers often flip across the ideological implications of advertisements at odds with their personal views. Those personal views are yet at the mercy of the shared social assumptions of the time.

Perhaps most intriguing of all, for its connection with hidden recesses of the work, is the advertisement for "Judson's Simple Dyes" where the testimonial asserts:

> The process being so clean and simple, there appears no reason why every lady should not be her own dyer, or why dyeing day should not, in every well-regulated family, be as common, and much more agreeable, than washing day. The thing would be worth trying from motives of economy; and much more real amusement would result from it than from many of the melancholy recreations to which young ladies of the present day are condemned.

Fabric is the key metaphor of the novel: "this particular web" is not so much spider's web as cloth, social fabric, and the tissues of the body, and it is a metaphor for fundamental enquiry: "What is the primitive tissue?" But here we come to the question of what may be present in the novel's "thick description" that is invisible to present-day readers but perhaps obvious to the first readers. That is, it raises

the question of what *was* in *Middlemarch* that is now unavailable to present readers without special prompting.

Are industrial workers excluded from this work?—that is a generally held current critical opinion. But in the nearby villages are the handloom weavers and in Middlemarch itself the dyers: Mr Vincy, mayor of Middlemarch ("a very good fellow") is also, as Mrs Cadwallader says, "one of those who suck the life out of the wretched handloom weavers in Tipton and Freshitt. That is how his family look so fair and sleek" (ch. 34, 307). The cloth these weavers produce is dyed by some new methods. And the new dyes rot the silks.

The new dyes are from manganese, as is several times mentioned in the novel. Sure enough, there were manganese mines in the Midlands in the 1820s and 1830s (though more in north Wales). In the town discussions of Bulstrode's downfall a worker speaks: "a firm-voiced dyer, whose crimson hands looked out of keeping with his good-natured face" (ch. 71, 678). Manganese, which had earlier been used to make glass, was now producing bright new color dyes. Just touched in at intervals across the whole spread of the novel are these references to manganese: Featherstone and Bulstrode have both made money from the mines (ch. 32, 288; ch. 56, 520). That is where much of the money that may or not be left to Fred Vincy comes from. "The great Plymdale dyeing house" has a profitable business relation to Mr. Bulstrode. And Mr. Bulstrode is "a sleeping partner in trading concerns, in which his ability was directed to economy in the raw material, as in the case of the dyes which rotted Mr. Vincy's silk" (ch. 56, 581). The weaving and dyeing imagery moves through many levels, suggesting the fabric of society and how it rots or is close-knit.

The introduction into the novel's economy of the new techniques for producing dyes from manganese makes it clear that, though never placed at the center of concern for any of the prominent characters in the novel, the workers in the mines and the dyeing houses and at the hand-looms are crucial to the town of Middlemarch, its economy, and its psychic health. These industrial workers are present in the plot and in the discourse of the novel—and their presence may have been more readily recognized by the first readers, scanning the advertisement for Judson's Simple Dyes. The advertisement is in tension with a prior assumption that dyeing is dirty and dangerous factory work; that is exactly why it seeks to present dyeing instead as a genteel and domestic undertaking.

The advertisements (now always absent from the text and already gone from the four-volume edition of the novel published in the same year) form a surface of common expectation and need between writer and first readers. But precisely because they frame needs, advertisements highlight lack and yearning as much as satisfaction. They highlight for us those areas of awareness that were then dulled by familiarity. They can also pinpoint areas of change that we shall ordinarily miss but that were shared without comment by Eliot and her first readers.

The hand-sewing in the novel—decorative by Rosamond and utilitarian by Mary Garth, and from which Dorothea is exempted by her short sight—is juxtaposed in this first presentation of the novel with the advertisement for the Guelph Sewing Machine. Sewing machines, first invented in the late 1840s, moved into mass production only in the 1860s and early 1870s. Guelph was a Canadian manufacturer whose machines were the latest thing in England in 1871. Outside Eliot's cognizance here, this advertisement points a further contrast between the conditions of life in the 1830s and the 1870s.

A somewhat similar point of contrast would have been present in the familiar sensory experience of the first readers of the novel and is probably implicit in George Eliot's descriptions of the dress and the landscapes in the novel; it is expressed textually for us by the advertisement for Judson's simple dyes. In the interval between the novel's setting and its writing and publication the color world of garments and painting had been transformed by the invention of aniline dyes and chromolithography, with their much more garish tones. In the world of the 1830s the ochre and earth tones of Dutch painting, and of the Norwich school, would still have been the usual palette of perception, but by the 1870s the world "had turned into a more lurid spectacle."[5]

Each of these books was reviewed individually as it appeared, over the span of a year, at first bimonthly and then monthly, from December 1871 to December 1872.[6] The pauses between publication

gave space for communal reflection and conversation, also lost to us now. Many commentators then emphasized the work's pessimism, and that effect is indeed intensified by the slow pacing and the uncertainty of outcome, in which the readers set to work, imagining troubled futures. It is intensified also by those reaches of the work that spend many pages on medical politics and on evangelical history, away from the most engaging characters. The spacing out of the work in this way (as I have experienced in a class where we read one book only at a time, stretched across a term) also extends and justifies the book's title: *Middlemarch*.

The work is profoundly concerned with the social fabric of an entire town, rather than with the lot of the individuals whom we so warmly recollect. Looking back, the young characters—particularly Dorothea, Lydgate, Rosamond, and Will, Mary Garth and Fred Vincy—cluster our concern on their lives. In the slower process of absorption book by book, with intervals between, further characters share the foreground, and establish the underground connections that will at intervals erupt or remain forever latent: the banker Bulstrode, of course, but also the auctioneer Trumbull, the doctors—Sprague, Chichely, and Minchin—and their medical wrangles, the tenant farmer Dagley and his wife, Farebrother, Mrs Cadwallader, and incomers like Raffles, emerging from the most buried layers of the past elsewhere.

So the darkness that Victorian readers descried in a text that tends now to be seen as pastoral emerged from structured absences that they could fill with knowledge and conjecture: these are the arc of 1832 to 1872 spanning[7] the shared adulthood of George Eliot and many of her readers. They are also the communal and personal present enacted for those diverse initial readers between the publication dates of the separate books, loading them with premonition and enquiry.

But there were other absences that bore more disturbingly on those readers than on most of us. What, for example, is implied in the cry of a young man, described in one of the first American reviews of the entire work, nine hundred–odd pages long. We are told by *Scribner's Monthly* of this "thoughtful and sensitive young man, who rose from the perusal of *Middlemarch* with his eyes suffused with tears, exclaiming: 'My God! And is that all?' "[8] Despite its massive length he experiences attrition. God is absent from *Middlemarch,* and when the work first appeared that cry of dereliction was often heard. Many of George Eliot's contemporaries were perturbed by the work's determined avoidance of transcendence. The *Spectator*'s reviewer of book 4 ("Three Love Problems") in June 1872 entitles his essay "The Melancholy of *Middlemarch*" and remarks that despite "the frequent springs of delightful humour"

> At the end of almost every part and every chapter, if not nearly every page, there comes an involuntary sigh. George Eliot never makes the world worse than it is, but she makes it a shade darker. She paints the confusions of life no worse than they are, but she steadily discourages the hope that there is any light for us behind the cloud. She is large in her justice to the visible elements in human nature, but she throws cold water with a most determined hand on the idealism, as she evidently thinks it, which in-

terprets by faith what cannot be interpreted by sympathy and sight. (*Critical Heritage*, 298)

That refusal of faith in "a light behind the cloud" takes *Middlemarch* further away from the possibilities of divine redemption than even the muted and opaque affirmation in Tennyson's *In Memoriam*:

> What hope of answer, or redress?
> Behind the veil, behind the veil. (56)

In *Middlemarch*, answers or redress exist only in the present world, in interchange between human beings. Though answers and redress are half-promised in the writing's supple ordering of multiple narratives and discourses, the invitation to the reader is to be joined to the community and yet sceptical of it always. It is this invocation of design, and yet the refusal to implant a pattern that will lead out of the maze, that so discomfited many of the first readers. George Eliot neither claims the position of an all-powerful theistic Designer, nor is she the haphazard wild poet who delights in the random, working "without a conscience or an aim" (*In Memoriam* 34). The conscientiousness and the spring of release in the novel takes always the guise of a leveled insight, without recourse to faith or to any other transcendental signifier. But that insight itself constantly shifts linguistic registers and does not avoid contradictions. She therefore jars her early readers with the book's closeness to a religious language that yet absolutely debars recourse to faith. Her word is *trust*: the assurance that sustains human—and only human—contact.

The clergyman of the novel is Mr. Farebrother, and his name says much. He is entirely on the level of weak, steadfast humanity: a man of failings and foibles (his gambling, his lack of resolve under political pressure) but capable of loving self-sacrifice (his recognition that Mary loves Fred and that he should not press his own suit). Mr. Farebrother is fair and brotherly in an entirely human ethical dimension. The spiritual is absent from this book.

That principled denial of religious comfort in *Middlemarch* the novel has become almost invisible to many readers now, so fully does it concur with the bent of secular assumptions. But the force of resistance in Eliot's exclusion of such comfort accounts for much of the pain as well as the power working within the novel. Moreover, its determined secularism in the portrayal of provincial life denies to 1870s readers even the imagined golden age of undisturbed belief supposedly existing in the 1830s, in the heyday of natural theology, and before the intervening tumult of enquiry that disturbed their own times.

That cry of "Is that all?" was heard (and continues still to be heard) among some of George Eliot's friends within the women's movement who were dismayed by the acquiescence at the end of the novel: no great plans, nothing come to fruition except some personal happiness. Dorothea Brooke cannot sustain an individual challenge to society at large. The heroines of success are absent. Dorothea is no Florence Nightingale or Barbara Bodichon, certainly no Annie Besant. Dorothea does not survive as a woman of exceptional achievement in the outer world, though the range of her aspirations has been inhabited by the reader throughout the book. She does not, either, become a writer, one strategy by women writers for sustaining women's powers: no Aurora Leigh, no heroine of *The Beth Book*.

Dorothea, like all the other characters, is obliged to endure her own typicality. She turns out to be more like other conditioned women of George Eliot's time than could have been foreseen. Mary Garth does write a book, which is attributed to her husband (but then, so is his to her). George Eliot keeps the range of her own work beyond the capacities—or the opportunities—of her characters. Heroines of success are nowhere here; or, success is perverted, as conquest, so that we see Rosamond after Lydgate's death gaining all that she desires: status, admiration, wealth, and a carriage. Her perfect conformity to the shape in which her society casts woman's achievement here brings its own rewards, ironized.

The novel's beginning and its ending are organized in terms of exclusion, negation, and impossibility. Whereas Saint Theresa founded and controlled an entire order, since her time

Many Theresas have been born who found for themselves no epic life wherein there was a constant unfolding of far-resonant action; perhaps only a life of mistakes, the offspring of a certain spiritual grandeur ill-matched with the meanness of opportunity. (prelude, 3)

On the novel's last page we are told that "A new Theresa will hardly have the opportunity of reforming a conventual life, any more than a new Antigone will spend her heroic piety in daring all for the sake of a brother's funeral: the medium in which their ardent deeds took shape is forever gone" (finale, 785). Instead George Eliot turns, at last, to an image of immense importance in many of her other novels: the river, flowing toward the sea. For Maggie, Romola, and Daniel Deronda, the flux of water, the seaming of consciousness and the unconscious, leads on to change and crisis. But in *Middlemarch* water, at least in metaphor, expresses containment: the "brown pond" where the cygnet must continue to live. Dorothea imagines in advance that Casaubon's experience is like "a lake compared with my little pool!" (ch. 3, 23) but she finds that the promised sea of marriage is merely an "enclosed basin": "Having once embarked on your marital voyage, it is impossible not to be aware that you make no way and that the sea is not within sight—that, in fact, you are exploring a closed basin" (ch. 20, 184). Only in the book's final paragraph does the pond or basin open to irrigate the land. Instead of leading to a defining moment of identity, as in George Eliot's other works, here the river is dissipated and nameless: "Her full nature, like that river of which Cyrus broke the strength, spent itself in channels which had no great name on earth" (finale, 785). Dorothea Brook: identity sapped; autonomy broken. Yet her name hints the flow of her being. "The effect of her being on those around her was incalculably diffusive": a tracery of unnamed affect.

George Eliot's narrative method seems to induce relatedness. It may, indeed, conceal for the reader the absence of social contact between the various characters within the work. We know them; few of them know all the others. Social shadows fall across any possible contacts. The doctor, the banker, and the clergyman know secrets and can move relatively freely. But each of them has his own secrets too, and the violation of the core of privacy within the individual is perilous. The community of Middlemarch shares a fear of movements that "lead to everything" (as Mr. Brooke says of science), above all of social movements that reorder relations and undermine hierarchies: "the great safeguard of society and of domestic life was, that opinions were not acted on" (ch. 1, 9). Revolutions do not quite happen here: "inconsistency and formlessness" muffle the drive toward concerted action, yet may also harbor seeds of change.

George Eliot worked with the subtle shifts and siltings of power, including movements of power between writer and reader. She spots how the hermeneutic zeal of the commentator or interpreter may be a self-regarding tribute to that reader's own ingenuity as much as to the authority of the writer. While she was composing this novel she wrote in a letter to her friend Sara Hennell: "I am studying that semi-savage poem, the *Iliad*. How enviable it is to be a classic. When a verse in the Iliad bears six different meanings and nobody knows which is the right, a commentator finds this equivocalness in itself admirable!"[9] George Eliot certainly made full use of "equivocalness" in *Middlemarch*. Equal voices inhabit many of her sentences, refusing to establish secure authority, inviting the reader to align herself or himself and then to take a new position, making each of us aware of how unwary such alignments are as we read: making us reassess what's in, what's out, what we harbor that we would expel as perfidy if uttered aloud by another person.

The treacheries as well as the communality of "we" and "our" are fundamental to the investigation performed by *Middlemarch*. "We" and "our" implies always that there are those who are outside, or left out, just as much as it persuades of "our common humanity." That question of what's left outside the circle is one of the conscious ways in which "what's not in *Middlemarch*" provokes the reader.

But there are peculiar omissions in the novel that seem less conscious, chief among them the absence, for large part, of food and drink. The effect—I would suggest—is to persuade the reader of Dorothea's delayed discovery of her own sexual passion. If one compares the novels of Dickens or Thackeray, or indeed Eliot's own earlier novels such as *Adam Bede* or *Silas Marner*, it becomes the more apparent that food has little presence in *Middlemarch* save as a source of unease. People in *Middlemarch* hardly ever sit down to table together—or if they do it is for a little genteel tea and toast. Appetite is almost entirely absent. Dorothea "dreads the corrosiveness of Celia's pretty carnally-minded prose" when Mr. Casaubon is coming to dinner after being accepted as her future husband. Celia does not yet know of Mr. Casaubon's status. Celia asks "Is any one else coming to dine beside Mr. Casaubon?"

> "I hope there is some one else. Then I shall not hear him eat his soup so."
> "What is there remarkable about his soup-eating?" [asks Dorothea]
> "Really, Dodo, can't you hear how he scrapes his spoon. And he always blinks before he speaks." (ch. 5, 45)

So it is not that Mr. Casaubon slurps his soup even—the body is absent, there's no emphasis on ingestion here. Instead it's the insensitivity of his ears: he scrapes the plate. He dislikes music. He cannot take in others' experience, or share it. This dissociation from appetite might be taken as a particular comment on Mr. Casaubon's lack of "good red blood in his body," as Sir James Chettam puts it; to which Mrs. Cadwallader replies: "No. Somebody put a drop under a magnifying-glass, and it was all semicolons and parentheses" (ch. 8, 65).

But it is not only Mr. Casaubon who is disassociated from food. Caleb Garth is frugal and concerned with reading and writing—with business and interchange—not breakfast: "Mr. Garth was forgetting his tea and toast while he read his letters." When Mr. Farebrother hears that he is to have the Lowick living "His mother left her tea and toast untouched." Lydgate notices accoutrements and conversation, not food:

> He would have behaved perfectly at a table where the sauce was served in a jug with the handle off, and he would have remembered nothing about a grand dinner except that a man was there who talked well. But it had never occurred to him that he should live in any other way than what he would have called an ordinary way, with green glasses for hock, and excellent waiting at table. (ch. 36, 327)

Lydgate's acceptance of these bourgeois necessities marks him out as one readily deflected from reform, just as his straightforward acceptance of hospitality (the jug with the handle off) in a poor household shows his courtesy. Food is not important in these descriptions. At the period of crisis within her marriage Dorothea becomes almost anorexic. She decides not to eat with Casaubon. Then the message comes that "Mr. Casaubon had sent to say that he would have his dinner in the library. He wished to be quite alone this evening, being much occupied."

> "I shall not dine then, Tantripp."
>
> "Oh, madam, let me bring you a little something?"
>
> "No, I am not well. Get everything ready in my dressing-room, but pray do not disturb me again." (ch. 42, 400)

Not eating is a register of emotion, sure enough, but the abstemiousness of consumption by all these different characters throughout the novel is rivaled—outgone—by the narrative meagerness of description. It seems to be a positive sign to be too preoccupied to notice what you are eating. The early immaturity of Ladislaw is signaled by his extremes with food: alternately starving himself and eating lobster. Such excess is rare, and blameable, in this novel. The surrounding advertisements for Fry's and for the "Companie Coloniale" advertise the delights of chocolate: "Fry's" pure coca nib deprived of the superfluous oil," the Companie Coloniale "prepared with a care and appliances hitherto unknown." These delights, assumed to be so comforting and sustaining to the reader, are not admitted within the boundaries of the novel.

This lack of interest in food, among the characters and even in the text of *Middlemarch* itself, is rare among Victorian writers. It helps to account for the way in which the reader accepts the very slow awakening of Dorothea's sexuality in the book—the almost infinite delay before she cries out (and then in anguished retrospect) "Oh, I did love him." Appetite, the carnal, has been exiled from the fabric of the work and kept distant from Dorothea. We are told early on of the overlaps between diverse kinds of passion in a metaphor of communal eating, but the vocabulary is monochrome: "Our passions do not live apart in locked chambers, but, dressed in their small wardrobe of notions, bring their provisions to a common table and mess together, feeding out of the common store according to their appetite" (ch. 16, 156).

This effect is made the more striking by the brief appearance at last of innocent appetite at the end of the last chapter before the finale, when Fred and Mary, their love at last declared, linger outside. The chapter ends:

> The spirit of joy began to laugh more decidedly in Mary's eyes, but the fatal Ben came running to the door with Brownie yapping behind them, and bouncing against them, said—
>
> "Fred and Mary! Are you ever coming in?—or may I eat your cake?" (ch. 86, 778)

Even here, in comedy, the satisfaction of appetite is delayed. One may contrast not only Dickens but, more tellingly perhaps, Thackeray, for whom food is the medium of present experience and the measure of its ephemerality. Taste is intensely of the moment; time melts in the mouth. Even when they are partaking of as light a meal as those that George Eliot's narrative favors, people in Thackeray "*munch* a shred of toast" . . . "*chip* a second egg." When Rawdon Crawley is about to fight a duel with Lord Steyne and weeps for his little boy, Mr. Macmurdo orders breakfast for him as a comfort: "What'll you have, Crawley? Some devilled kidneys and a herring—lets say."

Meat goes off, memory perishes, the heat goes out of dishes and the past: that poignant recognition of the corruptible in appetite, emotion, human life, so strong in *Vanity Fair* is absent, or eschewed, in *Middlemarch*. Adulteration—(prominent in the language of the advertisements that at first surrounded the novel)—is expressed not through food but through cheap manganese dyes that rot the silks they color. And adultery proves to be a false label for the charged emotions experienced by the characters. Indeed, as I suggested earlier, adultery is the brink for the book as well as its characters: carnal categories cannot tell us anything accurate or interesting about peoples' experience, it seems.

Yet the work, as I have emphasized, is embedded in the material conditions of bourgeois life of its first readers (sewing machines, indigestion pills, baldness remedies, fabrics, dyes, candles, medicines, hotels, chocolate), which surround the text, not quite in it but certainly of it. These advertisements as often encode distress as they do greed. They remind us, particularly the poignant medical claims, of the drive of human hopefulness, always essential to the play of narrative as well. The book respects that force, the energy of hope, but curtails it too, in the cautious negatives and conditionals of its final sentences, concluding that the fact that things "are not so ill with you and me as they might have been, is half owing to the number who lived faithfully a hidden life, and rest in unvisited tombs" (finale, 785).

The unhistoric and the unwritten, the unknown people who have read the book before us, temper the hubris of epic scope. *Middlemarch* makes its claim to inclusiveness by demurring at any all-embracing explanation, by offering us at last the sense of things left out: an elegy for all those unknown others by whom at any time the single reader is surrounded.

Notes

An earlier version of this essay was presented at the 2002 conference of the Korean Nineteenth Century Studies Association, "The Location of Cultures in Fiction," Oct. 26, 2002, held in Seoul, South Korea. I am grateful to Professor Julie Choi for that invitation.

1. E.g., "Mr. Brooke's estate, presumably worth about three thousand-a-year—a rental that seemed wealth to provincial families, still discussing Mr. Peel's late conduct on the Catholic question, innocent of future goldfields" (ch. 1, 9). In March 1929 Peel changed sides to pro-emancipation.

2. It was common for novels in the 1870s to include publishers' lists but not as common for them to include other advertisements. The practice of including advertisements was also a source of jokes: for example, *A Pack of Scribbles Written By Members of the Inns of Court. A Christmas Book at Christmas Time* (London: T. Cautley Newby, 1868) says in its preface that it includes no advertisements because "people at Christmas time don't want to be reminded of dyspepsia by a flaring announcement of Swalloway's Pills." The 1868 Christmas number of the *Quiver* has eight pages of advertisements.

3. The illustrations to this essay are from the eight–volume first publication of *Middlemarch* (London: Blackwood's, 1871–72) and are reproduced by kind permission of the Syndics of Cambridge University Library.

4. Thomas Richards in *The Commodity Culture of Victorian England: Advertising and Spectacle 1851–1914* (Stanford: Stanford University Press, 1990) does not refer to *Middlemarch* among the "domestic novels" he briefly describes. His interests lie elsewhere.

5. Personal communication from Professor Tim Barringer, 9 April 2004. See also "Aestheticism's True Colors: The Politics of Pigments in Victorian Art, Criticism, and Fashion," in Talia Schaffer and Kathy Alexis, eds., *Psomiades* (Charlottesville: University of Virginia Press, 1999), 172–91.

6. See Carol Martin, *George Eliot's Serial Fiction* (Columbus: Ohio State University Press, 1994), especially chap. 5, "*Middlemarch*: a Bimonthly Serial," ch. 7, "Filling in the Blanks: Readers Respond to the Serialization of *Middlemarch* and *Daniel Deronda*," and app. 1.

7. Lord John Russell's reform bill is referred to obliquely in order to set the exact time, March 1831, in national as well as local and personal terms, at the start of chapter 46, for example: "By the time that Lord John Russell's measure was being debated in the house of Common, there was a new political animation in Middlemarch, and a new definition of parties which might show a decided change of balance if a new election came" (431).

8. *Scribner's Monthly* 21 (1881), 791, cited in David Carroll, ed., *George Eliot: The Critical Heritage* (London: Routledge, 1971). Further citations of this work will be included in the text.

9. *Selected Letters*, ed. Gordon Haight (New Haven: Yale University Press, 1987), 342.

3

Space, Movement, and Sexual Feeling in *Middlemarch*

DAVID TROTTER

◆　◆　◆

IN CHAPTER 9 OF *MIDDLEMARCH*, Dorothea Brooke, accompanied by her uncle and sister, visits her future home at Lowick Manor.

> The building, of greenish stone, was in the old English style, not ugly, but small-windowed and melancholy-looking: the sort of house that must have children, many flowers, open windows, and little vistas of bright things, to make it seem a joyous home. In this latter end of autumn, with a sparse remnant of yellow leaves falling slowly athwart the dark evergreens in a stillness without sunshine, the house too had an air of autumnal decline, and Mr Casaubon, when he presented himself, had no bloom that could be thrown into relief by that background. (ch. 9, 67–8)

Mr Casaubon, rather alarmingly, is in camouflage. He seems unable, or unwilling, at this crucial moment in his life, to stand forth, to assume a shape. It is not that he is invisible but that he remains, even upon presentation of himself, utterly indistinct.

We might gain some sense of what indistinctness meant to Eliot from a late and unpublished essay, "Notes on Form in Art" (1868). The essay includes an account of form in general, as manifest in life as well as in art.

> Form, then, as distinguished from merely massive impression, must first depend on the discrimination of wholes and then on the discrimination of parts. Fundamentally, form is unlikeness. . . . Even taken in its derivative meaning of outline, what is Form but the limit of that difference by which we discriminate one object from another?—a limit determined partly by the intrinsic relations or composition of the object, and partly by the extrinsic action of other bodies upon it.[1]

Form, in life as in art, makes itself known, first, by external difference, or unlikeness; and second, by the degree of organization of internal complexity. No object can be considered to have form unless it reveals both its difference from other objects and a sufficient diversity of parts to require the exercise of an ordering principle. Mr Casaubon's inability to assume a distinct shape suggests that he has already failed on the first count. Whether or not he will succeed on the second remains to be determined.

Eliot, of course, subsequently goes to extraordinary lengths, in some of the most acute and intensely felt passages in her novel, to credit him with an internal complexity that deserves sympathetic understanding. But it may be too late. We need to take full account of the damage done to Casaubon by his enduring indistinctness. The damage is done by the contrast established in chapter 9 between Casaubon and Will Ladislaw. As the party proceed toward the church, Celia takes advantage of Casaubon's momentary absence to remark that she has seen "some one quite young coming up one of the walks": not a gardener, as Mr Brooke proposes, but a gentleman with a sketchbook (ch. 9, 70). Celia's deliberate and reiterated emphasis on youth establishes the gentleman with a sketchbook as a potential rival to Casaubon. On their return from the church, the visitors make a circuit toward a fine yew-tree. "As they approached it, a figure, conspicuous on a dark background of evergreens, was seated on a bench, sketching the old tree" (ch. 9, 72). Unlike Casaubon, this figure immediately stands out. It manifests that difference that is the first condition of form. Only when the two sisters have taken in the form thus made does Eliot allow Casaubon to identify the gentleman with the sketchbook as his second cousin, Will Ladislaw. He impresses upon them his youthful desirability twice over, and on the second occasion for a significant interval, before it can be diminished by a name.

Eliot's guide in aesthetic matters in general, and quite possibly the provocation to study of form in nature and in art, was John Ruskin.[2] I do not mean to propose a source either for her essay or for her novel in Ruskin. But I do think that there is much to be learnt indirectly about the novel, in particular, by considering, for example, his meditation on the difference between seaweed and ribbons, in *The Seven Lamps of Architecture* (1849):

> The loosest weed that drifts and waves under the heaving of the sea, or hangs heavily on the brown and slippery shore, has a marked strength, structure, elasticity, gradation of substance; its extremities are more finely fibred than its centre, its centre than its root: every fork of its ramification is measured and proportioned; every wave of its languid lines is lovely. It has its allotted size, and place, and function; it is a specific creature. What is there like this in a riband? It has no structure: it is a succession of cut threads all alike; it has no skeleton, no make, no form, no size, no will of its own. You cut it and crush it into what you will. It has no strength, no languor. It cannot fall into a single graceful form. It cannot wave, in the true sense, but only flutter: it cannot bend, in the true sense, but only turn and be wrinkled. It is a vile thing; it spoils all that is near its wretched film of an existence. Never use it.[3]

For Ruskin, as for Eliot, form involves difference and a high degree of organized complexity: strength, structure, elasticity, and gradation of substance. Strength and structure do not imply rigidity. Ruskin approved of languor; he might even have approved of Will Ladislaw, a creature specific enough, and yet built on decidedly languid lines. The ribbon, by contrast, is a "vile thing" lacking both external difference and internal complexity. Formlessness, in Ruskin's view, was matter for social and moral as well as aesthetic discrimination. Ribbons, after all, were likely to be worn by woman of a certain class and a certain susceptibility. Ruskin cannot have thought Dickens's *Barnaby Rudge* any less "monstrous" for the deplorable fact that it included "a certain quantity of ordinary operatic pastoral stuff, about a pretty Dolly in ribands, a lover with a wooden leg, and an heroic locksmith."[4]

What is at stake, in chapter 9 of *Middlemarch*, is a woman's choice in marriage. The concept of form has allowed Eliot to be extraordinarily frank in assessing the prospects of the two men who want to marry Dorothea Brooke. Mr Casaubon, considered either as a member of the human race, or as a man, has no distinctive shape. He does not stand out. In the short term, mutual delusion may conceal this disability. For Casaubon, however, the game is already up. He will not reproduce himself. Hard though Eliot subsequently tries to rehabilitate him, she cannot undo the impression created with such meticulous brutality in chapter 9. Casaubon is a born loser. He does not stand a chance against Will Ladislaw. The disability apparent before a marriage made possible by mutual delusion becomes doubly apparent after it. In chapter 21, in what should have been the full flush of honeymoon, Casaubon returns from a day in the Vatican library to find Dorothea and Will Ladislaw engaged in lively conversation. His immediate response is a surprise "quite unmixed with pleasure": he knows perfectly well that he is in the presence of a rival whose superiority in the longer term is no longer in question. "Mr Casaubon was less happy than usual, and this perhaps made him look all the dimmer and more faded; else, the effect might easily have been produced by the contrast of his young cousin's appearance." Eliot takes the opportunity to emphasize Will's "sunny brightness," and the dynamism of the utterly distinctive shape he cuts: "Surely, his very features changed their form; his jaw looked sometimes large and sometimes small; and the little ripple in his nose was a preparation for metamorphosis." Ladislaw is Ruskin's seaweed in human guise, his shapeliness exhibiting "a marked strength, structure, elasticity, gradation of substance." To Dorothea, and perhaps to Eliot herself, every wave of his languid lines is lovely. "Mr Casaubon, on the contrary, stood rayless" (ch. 21, 196).

Frankness was in the air, in 1871, when Eliot took the decision to incorporate a burgeoning story about one "Miss Brooke" into a novel which until that point had mainly featured Vincys and Featherstones. Darwin published *The Descent of Man and Selection in Relation to Sex*, which expands upon the theories advanced in *The Origin of Species*, and upon their consequences, for an understanding of the evolution of humankind. The struggle that shapes sexual selection, he had explained in *The Origin of Species*, is not for existence in relation to "other organic beings" or to "external conditions" but, rather, "between the individuals of one sex, generally the males, for the possession of the other sex." Victory, here, depends less on "general vigour" than on the development (by the male of the species) of an array of "special weapons"; while for the unsuccessful competitor, the outcome is not death but few or no offspring.[5] The "sexual struggle," he argued in *The Descent of Man*,

> is of two kinds; in the one it is between the individuals of the same sex, generally the males, in order to drive away or kill their rivals, the females remaining passive; whilst in the other, the struggle is likewise between the individuals of the same sex, in order to excite or charm those of the opposite sex, generally the females, which no longer remain passive, but select the more agreeable partners.

The Descent of Man offers, among other things, a detailed and graphic account of the secondary sexual characteristics (the special weapons) developed by the males of many species in order either to overcome other males or to charm the more agreeable among the females; and of the uses to which these characteristics have been put, by insects, animals, and human beings. The uses, one might note, are conscious uses.

> When we behold two males fighting for the possession of the female, or several male birds displaying their gorgeous plumage, and performing strange antics before an assembled body of fe-

males, we cannot doubt that, though led by instinct, they know what they are about, and consciously exert their mental and bodily powers.[6]

Primitive cultures would appear to have constituted for Darwin a benchmark of the sexual struggle at its most ferocious. "How low in the scale of nature the law of battle descends," he remarked in *The Origin of Species*, "I know not; male alligators have been described as fighting, bellowing, and whirling round, like Indians in a war-dance, for the possession of the females."[7] In *The Descent of Man*, looking high rather than low in the scale of nature, he was in no doubt that "as savages still fight for the possession of their women, a similar process of selection has probably gone on in a greater or less degree to the present day." Indeed, he seemed to think that modern men and women, too often swayed by "mere wealth or rank," could by conscious sexual selection do rather more than they were in the habit of doing, not only for the "bodily constitution and frame" of any offspring they might have but for their intellectual and moral qualities as well.[8] To be sure, the rather more no longer included, as it might once have done, the elimination of rivals. Eliot, too, was clear on this point. Sir James Chettam, finding that Dorothea has chosen Casaubon, "was not so well acquainted with the habits of primitive races as to feel that an ideal combat for her, tomahawk in hand, so to speak, was necessary to the historical continuity of the marriage-tie" (ch. 6, 57). Understood as a whole, however, the novel suggests very strongly that the pursuit of sexual rivalry, if not through war-dances and tomahawks, then through a display of plumage—and "strange antics" to go with it—remained an important part of modern life. It was Darwinism, with its emphasis on variability as the key both to natural and to sexual selection, that shaped Eliot's understanding of form in life. Mr Casaubon's lack of difference ought to rule him out as a mate for the strongly differentiated Dorothea. Where women are concerned, Eliot wrote in the prelude to *Middlemarch*, the "limits of variation" are really much wider than any one would imagine from the sameness of their coiffure and "the favourite love-stories in prose and verse" (4).[9]

Eliot's consistent frankness in *Middlemarch* about the basis of sexual selection has cut remarkably little ice with her critics. The almost universal assumption is that the novel's portrayal of sexual love is neither convincing nor emancipatory. The objections leveled against it are that Will Ladislaw represents an implausible object of desire; and that Dorothea Brooke remains damagingly unaware of, and thus unable to control, her own sexuality. They have been framed, oddly enough, in terms of the very Darwinism whose presence in the text the critics seem unwilling to acknowledge. On the one hand, we are told, in effect, that Ladislaw will lose out in the sexual struggle because his plumage is inadequate (inadequate in the minds of generations of readers, if not in that of the author); on the other, that Dorothea does not know how to set about choosing for herself an agreeable partner.

Why, Carol Siegel asks in the course of a forceful restatement of the first of these complaints, does marriage to Will Ladislaw not prove a "satisfying solution" to Dorothea Brooke's problems? The problem with Will, Siegel continues, is that his "presence" in the narrative "promises so much" and yet "yields so little." Both the promise, and the ultimate failure, lie "in the register of the erotic." Siegel puts the blame squarely on the conventions of domestic realism. There is an awareness of the erotic as a possibility in *Middlemarch*, she argues, but it comes "from the text itself, from the places where the erotic inheres not in physically accessible space but in memory and speculation, in half-told stories such as that of Will's grandmother, Julia, and in evocation of other literary texts, such as Shakespeare's sonnets." Will Ladislaw's presence in the text as an erotic being is only ever intertextual; he masquerades as the "delightful androgyne whose love inspires and elevates the soul of his admirer 'like to the lark at break of day arising' (sonnet 29)."[10] Siegel demonstrates in convincing detail that reference to Shakespeare enabled Eliot to make Ladislaw attractive; at least up until the point at which he dwindles into a prospective husband. The Dorothea who breaks off their first embrace to say that she will take trouble to learn what everything costs (ch. 83, 762) does not appear to have her eye on delightful androgyny. Intertextuality, in Siegel's view, is where the fun is, or once was; the resumption of domestic realism has put an end to all that. What is curious about her argument is that it separates the "text itself" from the conventions that are generally thought in large measure to constitute it: those of domestic realism. I shall argue here that a great deal transpires, including much that ought to count as erotic, in the "physically accessible space" that it is domestic realism's business to represent.

Sally Shuttleworth's objection is that the novel grants Dorothea a "strongly passionate sexual nature" and then forbids her to understand its "workings." It insists throughout on the desirability of integrating intellect with ardor, but then makes an exception where sexuality is concerned. Shuttleworth shows that Eliot's understanding of the relations between mind and body was shaped by the psychological theories of Herbert Spencer and G. H. Lewes. These theories were developed within an evolutionary framework. Both Spencer and Lewis believed that the history of the human race revealed a gradual development from simple to complex structures of thought and feeling, and that the index to this development was the growth of moral consciousness.

When preparing the final volume of Lewes's *Problems of Life and Mind* for publication after his death, Eliot added a passage whose burden was that the growth of moral consciousness would in due course produce "in many highly wrought natures a complete submergence (or, if you will, a transference) of egoistic desire, and an habitual outrush of the emotional force in sympathetic channels." Eliot, Shuttleworth remarks, would appear to have Dorothea firmly in mind here.[11] The passage reads like a commentary on Dorothea's response to the sight of Will Ladislaw kneeling at Rosamond Lydgate's feet. Fury at Will and scorn for Rosamond gradually recede as, in the early hours of the morning, she gazes out of the window at the world beyond the entrance-gates of Lowick Manor. "She was a part of that involuntary, palpitating life, and could neither look out on it from her luxurious shelter as a mere spectator, nor hide her eyes in selfish complaining" (ch. 80, 741). Dorothea would appear to have evolved beyond all kinds of "egoistic desire," including that which informs sexual selection: her anger at Will had been quite specifically an anger at his display of himself, his obtrusion into her life, his refusal to stay among the crowd (ch. 80, 740). This degree of evolution contrasts strikingly with the childishness often attributed to her at moments of sexual crisis: when she and Will finally acknowledge their love for one another, they stand at the window "with their hands clasped, like two children" (ch. 83, 761); when they embrace for the first time, she sobs out in a "childlike way" her readiness to do without new clothes and to learn what things cost (ch. 83, 762). Dorothea either remains in ignorance of her own sexuality or thinks and feels too much to want to exploit it.

When adult sexuality is represented in *Middlemarch*, Shuttleworth maintains, it seems to require the terms not of psychology but of psychiatry: to have sexual thoughts and feelings is to go mad. As she notes shrewdly, Dorothea gazing out at the world beyond the entrance-gates is shadowed by an "obverse image" from the psychiatric literature of the period: that of the hysteric. Her exchanges with Rosamond reduce her to a "palpitating anxiety" (ch. 81, 749): now it is a mind on the edge of breakdown that palpitates, rather than the world, and it does so in misery. Lydgate, who attends Dorothea after Casaubon's death, feels sure that she has been suffering from "the strain and conflict of self-repression" (ch. 50, 462). As Shuttleworth points out, his diagnosis draws on "theories of hysteria as a form of repression, and particularly sexual repression." The novel suggests that he may have reason to associate Dorothea with the insane women of the psychiatric literature. When Casaubon, having heard from Lydgate that he is likely to die, rejects her solicitude, her reaction is furious. "In such a crisis as this," we are told, "some women begin to hate." Dorothea does not, quite. "But the struggle changed continually, as that of a man who begins with a movement towards striking and ends with conquering his desire to strike" (ch. 42, 400). As Shuttleworth shows, there is enough incipient murderousness in Dorothea for Lydgate to associate her with Laure, the actress with whom he had once been in love, and who had murdered her husband.[12]

Shuttleworth and Siegel differ in topic and approach. But they share an assumption: that domestic realism is not up to the task of representing sexuality. In Shuttleworth's view, the portrayal of sexual love in *Middlemarch* is shaped through and through by the "contradictions and ellipses" in the psychological and psychiatric discourse of the time. Domestic realism cannot be said to supplement or to revise that discourse. When it comes to sexual feeling, the novelist has (even) less to offer by way of wisdom than the psychiatrists. If literature does have something to offer, it is not through domestic realism but through the disruption of domestic realism by melodrama. According to Shuttleworth, the "melodramatic history" of Laure "disrupts the onward flow of the tale of Middlemarch life" and "acts to trouble and destabilize the ensuing narrative."[13] In what follows, I shall argue that it is precisely to the onward flow of the tale of Middlemarch life—a life made manifest in "physically accessible space"—that we should look for a representation of sexual feeling.

When Mr Casaubon presents himself, on the occasion of Dorothea's first visit to Lowick Manor, the "background" against which he fails to stand out is that constituted by the house itself, by architecture. The house, however, is as indistinct, as hard to make out, as its owner. It lacks expressive shape. Where, the narrator asks, are the children, the open windows, and the vistas that would transform a commonplace building into a home? The shape lacking at Lowick would be the product of good architecture and good sexual selection. Without such shapeliness, Ruskin had insisted in *Sesame and Lilies* (1865), a home is not a home. No longer distinct from the outer world, it becomes no more than "a part of that outer world which you have roofed over, and lighted fire in."[14]

Karen Chase and Michael Levenson have recently uncovered the fantasy of architectural form that lay at the center of Victorian conceptions of domestic life. They focus on *The Gentleman's House* (1864), a lavish and influential treatise by the architect Robert Kerr. Kerr was a "consummate professional," Chase and Levenson observe, who "brought the technical language of architecture into the general conversation."[15] The subtitle of his book is "How to Plan English Residences, from the Parsonage to the Palace." The topic he had in mind was the accomplishment through architecture of domestic harmony, at the parsonage level and above.

There is a certain triumphalism in Kerr's account of the evolution of the gentleman's house from the eleventh-century Anglo-Saxon hall, comprising one room only, a space shared promiscuously by human and animal, high-born and low-born, men and women, to the complex structures made possible by modern design and engineering. The history of architecture, in short, could be understood as the history of the introduction and development of a concept of form. Form is difference, distinctness. "The spirit of manufacture, from which home is to be a refuge," Chase and Levenson remark, "enters the house in a disciplined squad of modern domestics, whose role is to protect home life from the disruptions they exemplify."[16] Form is also a high degree of organized internal complexity. Modern architecture, Kerr claimed, is

> a science of delightful intricacy, which, when duly applied, even on the smallest scale, constitutes an edifice a thing of complete organisation, in which every part is assigned its special function, and is found to be contrived for that and no other; the express purpose of the whole being that exquisite result which is signified by our scarcely translatable phrase—*home comfort*.[17]

Form, as Eliot had written in 1868, "must first depend on the discrimination of wholes and then on the discrimination of parts."[18] In Kerr's ideal home, the lower-class parts (for the use of the servants) are to be discriminated from the upper-class (for the use of the family), and the male from the female. Chase and Levenson point out that his model dwelling divides "along a vertical axis that bisects domestic space, running from the saloon through the fountain to the garden thoroughfare." With one or two exceptions, everything to the right of the imaginary line is primarily for the use of men, and everything to the left primarily for the use of women: "the gentleman's house thus achieves that rational differentiation of the sexes to which it had long aspired."[19] Form arose out of differentiation, and gave rise in turn to comfort.

Kerr might well have thought the cottages Dorothea Brooke would like her uncle to build by way of improving his estate beneath his attention. But it is worth nothing that the authority to whom Dorothea appeals (ch. 3, 29), John Claudius Loudon, had designed cottages that, although simple in structure, exhibit differentiation along gender lines. For example, male and female children have separate bedrooms that are approached by separate routes.[20] There is form, in these dwellings, and with it the possibility of comfort. The dwelling described in the greatest detail in *Middlemarch*, Lowick Manor, lies somewhere between the parsonage and the palace. It, too, exhibits differentiation along gender lines. That its formal complexity will ever produce comfort seems doubtful.

The library, Kerr maintained, "is primarily a sort of Morning-room for gentlemen rather than anything else. Their correspondence is done here, their reading, and, in some measure, their lounging;—and the Billiard-room, for instance, is not unfrequently attached to it. At the same time the ladies are not exactly excluded." It is rather hard to imagine Casaubon playing billiards; but the ground-floor library is certainly his domain, a place of business and of scholarship (from which Dorothea will not be exactly excluded). His "views of the womanly nature" (ch. 9, 69) are sufficiently broad to include provision of a boudoir for his wife: a blue-green room on the upper floor with a view down an avenue of limes. According to Kerr, the boudoir "is a Private Parlour for the mistress of the house . . . as the personal retreat of the lady, it leaves the Drawing-room—and the Morning-room if any—still occupied by the family and guests."[21]

In *Middlemarch*, marital disputes provoke a retreat into mutually exclusive gendered space. On the morning after their return from the disastrous honeymoon in Rome, Mr Casaubon is to be found in his library interviewing the curate, while Dorothea, upstairs in the boudoir, gazes out on "the still, white enclosure which made her visible world" (ch. 28, 257). The sight of the miniature of Will Ladislaw's grandmother, a woman who "had known some difficulty about marriage," sets Dorothea glowing again. At the further thought of the vivid conversations she had held with Ladislaw in Rome, guilt overwhelms her, and she hurries out of the room "with the irresistible impulse to go and see her husband and inquire if she could do anything for him" (ch. 28, 258–9). A sharply polarized space has become for Dorothea an arena for the compulsive rehearsal of anxieties concerning her choice of a mate.

In chapter 42, after Casaubon has been informed by Lydgate that he is likely to die, and that his wife knows this, Dorothea goes out into the garden to console him, and is bitterly repulsed. As they reenter the house, Dorothea disengages her arm from his. The direction he subsequently moves in will express his feelings about her.

> He entered the library and shut himself in, alone with his sorrow.
> She went up into her boudoir. The open bow-window let in the serene glory of the afternoon lying in the avenue, where the lime-trees cast long shadows. But Dorothea knew nothing of the scene. (399)

Each has retreated into "inward misery" (ch. 42, 399), and at the same time into what one might think of as an extremity of gender identification: all male, all female.[22] The issue rendered critical by this going to extremes is stark enough. The chapter had begun with Casaubon's realization that "against certain facts he was helpless: against Will Ladislaw's existence, his defiant stay in the neighborhood of Lowick, and his flippant state of mind with regard to the possessors of authentic, well-stamped erudition: against Dorothea's nature, always taking on some new shape of ardent activity" (ch. 42, 391–2). The game is up, or almost up. It is not too late to plan a posthumous revenge. Dorothea, meanwhile, gripped by "rebellious anger" (ch. 42, 399), seems momentarily, as we have seen, on the verge of hysteria. Polarization has destroyed the variability that distinguishes her from other women. Once again, though, a reflux of feeling sends her out of the room in search of her husband (ch. 42, 401).

Dorothea's blue-green boudoir has been the subject of a great deal of commentary. Is it the kind of space that becomes for the heroines of other Victorian novels a critical and enabling point of view on the world?[23] It is in the boudoir, in chapter 80, after a night of agony brought about by the sight of Will Ladislaw at Rosamond Lydgate's feet, that Dorothea looks out at the traffic on the road beyond the entrance-gates and feels "part of that involuntary, palpitating life" (741). This time, she leaves the room not guiltily to console her husband but with unshakeable conviction, like one of the new breed of female philanthropists and rescue-workers, to "save" a fallen woman (742).[24] This time, the retreat into "inward misery" has proved a turning-point, as she finally transcends the egoism of desire. It might also be the moment at which, to pursue Carol Siegel's line of argument, intertextuality finally transcends domestic realism: the culmination of a counter-narrative that reproduces the progress made, from dejection through bitter resentment to acceptance, by another forestry-bound protagonist, in Coleridge's poem "This Lime-Tree Bower, My Prison"?[25] Dorothea, as Will Ladislaw had been moved to remark, *is* a poem (ch. 22, 209).

My feeling is that domestic realism keeps a pretty tight grip on the mapping of space in *Middlemarch*; rather, the mapping of space is the grip it keeps on the novel. The boudoir and the library, although on different floors and offering different outlooks, exist in relation to one another on a grid intelligible in the light of Robert Kerr's architectural fantasy. What the novel tells us, however, is that the most decisively gendered spaces on the grid are dead spaces. Mr Casaubon lives for the most part in his library, and the room becomes associated with the heart disease first manifest within it. Dorothea finds solitude in her boudoir, but little relief from her heart's dis-ease. Even the stories arising out of the miniature of Ladislaw's grandmother will remain sterile unless acted upon. The conclusion Dorothea draws from her look out of the window is that she should stop looking out of the window. "Moving through space is less important for Jane [Eyre], than witnessing an expanse."[26] The opposite is true, I hope to show, for Dorothea. The form produced by the gendering of space in Lowick Manor is too much form of the wrong kind.

The "new shapes" of "ardent activity" that so trouble Casaubon emerge in spaces that do not yet bear the marks of a gendered habit of occupancy. After his seizure, Casaubon, who has been forbidden to work in the library, receives visitors in a previously undescribed room on the upper floor. In the opening chapter of book 4 ("Three Love Problems"), Mr Brooke, the Chettams, and Mrs Cadwallader arrive to observe Simon Featherstone's funeral from the window of this room, while Casaubon, who at present has little taste for funerals, slips away, in defiance of doctor's orders, to the library. This displacement within the gendered household grid produces if not a

new angle of sight, then the abrupt admission, as into a camera obscura, of new shapes. But for her visitors, Dorothea too would have
been shut up in the library, and unable to witness a scene which,
aloof though it is from the "tenor of her life," makes a deep impression (ch. 34, 305). "This dream-like association with something alien
and ill-understood with the deepest secrets of her experience
seemed to mirror that sense of loneliness which was due to the very
ardour of Dorothea's nature" (ch. 34, 306).

Dorothea experiences a double alienation. The "something alien
and ill-understood" is both her own sexuality and the world she
looks out at and down on from the upper-floor windows of Lowick
Manor. "And Dorothea was not at ease in the perspective and chillness of that height" (ch. 34, 306). Her protest, in effect, is against too
much external difference: that conscience should look out at and
down on sexual feeling as the gentry look out at and down on the
laborers in the field. However, the very mirroring of one alienation
in another suggests that the form produced by architecture, at least,
is permeable. The terms in which that permeability is described are
worth noting.

> "How piteous!" said Dorothea. "This funeral seems to me the
> most dismal thing I ever saw. It is a blot on the morning. I cannot
> bear to think that any one should die and leave no love behind."
>
> She was going to say more, but she saw her husband enter and
> seat himself a little in the background. The difference his pres-
> ence made to her was not always a happy one: she felt that he
> often inwardly objected to her speech.
>
> "Positively," exclaimed Mrs Cadwallader, "there is a new face
> come out from behind that broad man queerer than any of
> them: a little round head with bulging eyes—a sort of frog-
> face—do look. He must be of another blood, I think."
>
> "Let me see!" said Celia, with awakened curiosity, standing be-
> hind Mrs Cadwallader and leaning forward over her head. "Oh,
> what an odd face!" Then with a quick change to another sort of
> surprised expression, she added, "Why, Dodo, you never told me
> that Mr Ladislaw was come again!"
>
> Dorothea felt a shock of alarm: every one noticed her sudden

paleness as she looked up immediately at her uncle, while Mr
Casaubon looked at her. (ch. 34, 307–8)

Dorothea perceives the lack of love at Featherstone's funeral as a
blot on the morning, a stain; a thought interrupted by her husband's entrance into the room. The thought is taken up, in effect, by
Mrs Cadwallader, who has spotted a different kind of blot, a "frog-
face" among the mourners. Mrs Cadwallader is the spokesperson
for the perspective and chillness granted by social "height." She has
already complained about the rich Lowick farmers, who are in her
view "monsters" because there is no way to class them (ch. 34, 306).
The frog-face is a further monstrosity, a genetic blot. We might re-
call, at this point, that Mrs Cadwallader has been characterized from
the outset as the voice not only of social status—"her feeling towards the vulgar rich was a sort of religious hatred" (ch. 6, 55–6)—
but also, in her perpetual concern with "the Miss Brookes and their
matrimonial prospects" (ch. 6, 56), as the voice of sexual selection.
Celia Brooke has no sooner confirmed the frog-face's oddity than,
substituting as it were one lens for another in the camera obscura,
she spots something even odder: Will Ladislaw's presence among the
mourners. The second discovery bears, of course, upon the "deepest
secrets" of Dorothea's experience. It reintroduces into Lowick
Manor a difference brought about not by architecture but by variation within the species: the difference between Will and the husband
who cannot avoid noticing her sudden, demonstrative paleness.
The paleness is also a blot of a kind, a stain.

The permeabilities registered with quite astonishing subtlety in
this scene are evidence that the production of new forms—of forms
demonstrating variability—may require a certain engagement with
formlessness. One of its effects is to identify Will Ladislaw with
Joshua Rigg, the man with the frog-face, and Featherstone's illegitimate son and, it turns out, heir.[27] Mrs Cadwallader supposes that
Rigg must be of "another blood" (ch. 34, 308); before long, Ladislaw's
habit of stretching himself at full length on the rug in houses where
he feels at home will raise suspicions concerning his "dangerously
mixed blood" (ch. 46, 435).

Joshua Rigg's queerness is a matter of class. The problem lies not so much in his "high chirping voice" and "vile accent" (ch. 35, 319) as in the status Featherstone's money will enable him to claim, a status he is not felt to have earned either by birth or by endeavor. Indeed, he has already begun to merge into a class above the one he was born into. His "nails and modesty," we are told, "were comparable to those of most gentlemen; though his ambition had been educated only by the opportunities of a clerk and accountant in the smaller commercial houses of a seaport" (ch. 41, 387). Joshua Rigg is a clerk masquerading as minor gentry: the epitome of social mobility.

The petty bourgeoisie in general, and clerks in particular, had long been the focus of a Cadwallader-like religious hatred of the vulgar rich, of those who had gotten above themselves.[28] The hatred arose during the transition from the Hungry Forties, when the perceived threat came from a turbulent working-class, to the prosperous Fifties, when the perceived threat came from an emergent mass culture. The anxiety it expressed was an anxiety about imitation. Joshua Rigg threatens only when he starts behaving like a gentleman, with regard to fingernails and modesty. Such behavior disguises the external difference that gives one shape to a gentleman and another to a clerk. Imitation produces a formlessness that the religious hatred of social aspiration grasped as monstrosity: as strange blood, as an unclassifiable frog-face.

Joshua Rigg's fictional ancestor is Uriah Heep, in Charles Dickens's *David Copperfield* (1849–50). Heep, a man of conspicuously humble birth, begins as an articled clerk to lawyer Wickfield's articled clerk, but aims higher. He means to become Wickfield's partner, and if possible his son-in-law; and he recognizes David, who has himself been brought low in the world but is making up ground rapidly, as a rival in both respects. His aim is to resemble David, and then to take his place. The aspiration it encodes is rendered as a physical formlessness or monstrosity that from the outset arouses in David a profound loathing. His face may not be frog-like, but his touch most certainly is.[29] Uriah—like Joshua Rigg in Mrs Cadwallader's eyes—is repellent first, and harmful second. His loathsomeness precedes anything that could possibly be construed as wrongdoing. The differences the two men erase by imitation are restored in and through the disgust their monstrosity arouses.

Dickens tended to arrange spectacular purgative expulsions for his petty-bourgeois imitators. The scene in *David Copperfield* in which Mr Micawber exposes Heep's treachery, like the scene in *Bleak House* in which Mr Bucket sends the Smallweeds and Chadbands packing, is almost euphoric in its sense of a wrong righted and an unmanageable feeling got rid of.[30] Eliot, by contrast, seems altogether relaxed about Joshua Rigg. Rigg sells the property he has inherited and returns to his seaport to run a money-changer's shop. He had meant, when he had property, "to do many things, one of them being to marry a genteel young person; but these were all accidents and joys that imagination could dispense with" (ch. 53, 488). Eliot did not share Dickens's fear that the petty bourgeoisie would seize power. For her, Rigg is of genetic rather than social or political interest.

Peter Featherstone had wanted a copy of himself.

> The copy in this case bore more of outside resemblance to the mother, in whose sex frog-features, accompanied with fresh-coloured cheeks and a well-rounded figure, are compatible with much charm for a certain order of admirers. The result is sometimes a frog-faced male, desirable, surely, to no order of intelligent beings. (ch. 41, 386–7)

The frog-features have the merit, from a scientific and literary point of view, of providing evidence of the variation of species. Rigg is, for better or worse, different (from those born and bred in Middlemarch). Eliot's interest lay not in the bad features but in the process of variation that gave rise to them, and that might just as well give rise to good ones. Will Ladislaw's features, too, are unmistakably the product of variation. Indeed, they express variability: the little ripple in his nose, we remember, seems like "a preparation for metamorphosis" (ch. 21, 196). Will's main trait, Chase observes, "is his ability to vary his traits."[31]

Will Ladislaw and Joshua Rigg converge once again in chapter 47, when Will attends a service at Lowick church in the hope of seeing Dorothea: that is, in order to display himself. Against the background of stolid parishioners, Rigg's frog-face seems like "something alien and unaccountable" (443). As Jackson notes, the phras-

ing connects this abrupt manifestation back to the scene at Featherstone's funeral, in chapter 34, when Dorothea had found the "deepest secrets of her experience" mirrored in "something alien and ill-
understood" in the world outside (306).[32] It may be that in order to
renew both self and society one has to in some measure to engage
with that which does not at first appear to have a form except in
pure difference. Returning to his seaport, and money-changing,
Rigg remains, like Will Ladislaw, a figure of shape-shifting, of metamorphosis.[33] Mrs. Cadwallader, so alert to intruding frog-faces, had
in that earlier scene associated Will's fitness for sexual selection with
a certain indeterminacy of rank and function. "A very pretty sprig,"
said Mrs. Cadwallader, drily. "What is your nephew to be, Mr
Casaubon?" (ch. 34, 309). His fitness, as Chase points out, will depend
not only on his looks but on his ability to assume the responsibilities
of an "ardent public man" (finale, 782). Formlessness deliberately assumed may yet become the basis of a new and better kind of form.
"The free play in Will's life as a dilettante is the freedom to accept
metamorphosis until its work is done."[34]

Movement

In *Middlemarch*, it is not space that constitutes new form—the form
made possible by metamorphosis—but movement through or into
space: a space that is itself constituted, or reconstituted, by movement. In assessing the force of movement, we need to start where
the novel does, with that difference between Dorothea and Celia
that, as Helena Michie has persuasively demonstrated, structures
the first half of the novel.[35]

> When the two girls were in the drawing-room alone, Celia
> said—
> "How very ugly Mr Casaubon is!"
> "Celia! He is one of the most distinguished-looking men I ever
> saw. He is remarkably like the portrait of Locke. He has the same
> deep eye-sockets."
> "Had Locke those two white moles with hairs on them?"

"Oh, I daresay! when people of a certain sort looked at him,"
said Dorothea, walking away a little. (ch. 2, 19)

Celia, as Michie puts it, views the world through a "corporeal lens." She lets us see the flaws and infirmities Dorothea has chosen not to notice. The contrast between the sisters is a contrast not only between modes of appearance and conduct but between modes of perception. It enables Eliot to "resolve the literary problem of representing a heroine who is simultaneously innocent and desirable, sexually repressed and highly erotic." For a while, at least. As Ladislaw looms larger and larger in Dorothea's life, so Celia recedes. "At this point of exchange between Celia and Will, when the impulse of disruptive sexuality is passed from sister to lover, Celia becomes frozen into an almost parodic rendition of herself."[36]

We need, however, to note not only what the sisters see and say but what they do. Celia's commentary on Mr Casaubon's moles makes it clear that she knows he is not a fit mate for Dorothea. Dorothea, infuriated by the commentary, *does* something. She speaks in anger, and then, apparently as the outcome of speech, or of the feeling that has animated speech, walks away a little. That walking away a little is performative rather than purposeful. She is not going anywhere. It supplements speech, and it fills a lack in speech. It does what speech cannot do: occupy, or take possession of, space. It enacts force: the force of feeling; the force of Dorothea's knowledge, already, in excess or contradiction of the words she has spoken, of Mr Casaubon's disability. The force will stay with her, while Celia becomes frozen into a parody of herself: characterized increasingly by the "comfortable staccato" of her voice, or by movement that is never anything other than merely purposeful (ch. 50, 459–60).

The contrast established in this scene between Dorothea and Celia is a contrast established by the skillful deployment of one of the basic techniques of domestic realism: the provision of speech-tags ("she said," "he exclaimed," and so on) that embed what the characters say in the environment (the space and time) delineated by the narrative voice. For the most part, in nineteenth-century fiction, speech-tags served the relatively straightforward purpose of identifying the speaker. Some novelists, however, did put them to a particular use. Dickens, for example, in his early novels, developed the habit of interrupting his characters at intricate length.[37] In *Middlemarch*, Eliot constructed out of speech-tags a bridge between what is said and an action that exceeds or contradicts what is said; rather, she does so, as is domestic realism's privilege, in relation to some characters but not in relation to others. The syntactic pattern established in Dorothea's response to Celia's commentary on moles persists throughout the novel. It enables some characters to occupy space in a way that others do not. Those characters make their presence felt by the follow-through of speech into movement, of word into deed. For them, space becomes an arena for the display of plumage; that is, of vigor, of sexual fitness.

The only other character who moves as Dorothea moves, with feeling but without purpose, as a supplement to the lack in speech, is Will Ladislaw. They are alike in the shape of their movements even when they are alike in nothing else. That compatibility serves, one might hazard, as the novelist's account of the basis of appropriate sexual selection. In chapter 22, as the Casaubons are preparing to leave Rome, Will visits Dorothea to say farewell, at a time when he knows Casaubon will not be there. His use of the arena available to him begins to explain why Casaubon might be thought to stand "rayless" beside him. His first performance for Dorothea's benefit is a protest against her melancholy. " 'You are too young—it is an anachronism for you to have such thoughts,' said Will energetically, with a quick shake of the head, habitual to him" (206). The thoughts, as he immediately makes clear, are those relating to the "stone prison" that awaits her at Lowick. They also relate, evidently, to the difference between an ancient husband and his youthful wife (and her equally youthful admirer). It is the former who must be reckoned the anachronism. Will eclipses his rival momentarily by that quick shake of the head, by the force of the carry-through from word into deed. He fears that he may have "gone too far" (ch. 22, 206). But Dorothea, attending rather to the tone of his utterance than to its content, and possibly not unappreciative of the movement that accompanies it, answers with a "gentle smile" (ch. 22, 207). Before long the smile will be reinforced by a "remonstrant energy" the equal of his (ch. 22, 207), and by movement. " 'And there is one thing even now that you can do,' said Dorothea, rising and walking a little way under the strength of a recurring impulse" (ch. 22, 210). That "one thing" is to stop criticizing Casaubon's scholarship. Will's criticisms, of course, have always been an assault on the basis upon which Dorothea selected a husband. He would do well to pay less attention to her request than to the rising and walking away a little that accompanies it.

In *Middlemarch*, the syntactic pattern evident in the initial deployment of speech-tags itself constitutes, as the novel develops, narrative pattern. In chapter 37, after returning to Middlemarch to act as Mr Brooke's secretary, Will visits Dorothea at Lowick, and they immediately resume the conversation they had held in Rome (341). Once again, he protests against her imprisonment (342). Once again, he shakes his head backward, and then lays into Casaubon's practice as a scholar. Dorothea responds with rather more than a gentle smile.

> "I should like you to stay very much," said Dorothea at once, as simply and readily as she had spoken in Rome. There was not the shadow of a reason in her mind at the moment why she should not say so.
> "Then I will stay," said Ladislaw, shaking his head backward, rising and going towards the window, as if to see whether the rain had ceased. (345)

Siegel understands the punning on "will" as a connection to Shakespeare's sonnets: as evidence that Ladislaw's very being is intertextual.[38] But the conventions of domestic realism also play their part, here. They connect what Ladislaw says ("Then I *will* stay") not to Shakespeare but to a certain occupation of space, a performance: a shake of the head backward, and a movement with only the slightest pretense of ostensible purpose ("as if to see whether the rain had ceased").[39]

In chapter 39, Dorothea surprises Mr Brooke and his secretary at work in the library at Tipton Grange. On her announcement, Ladislaw "started up as from an electric shock, and felt a tingling at his finger-ends" (363). His response prompts the narrator to some thoughts about variability in sexual selection: about the subtle effects that "make a man's passion for one woman differ from his passion for another as joy in the morning light over valley and river and white mountain-top differs from joy among Chinese lanterns and glass panels" (364–5). Dorothea's allure is clearly not of the Chinese-lantern-and-glass-panel variety. It provokes him, once Mr Brooke has left the room, to more than words. " 'I may not have another opportunity of speaking to you about what has occurred,' said Will, rising with a movement of impatience, and holding the back of his chair with both hands" (366). What he has to tell her is that Casaubon, consumed by sexual jealousy, has barred him from Lowick. The bitterness of their rivalry can no longer be concealed. It arouses in Will a new display: an impatient arising.

Since its theme is courtship, the narrative pattern constituted by these performances asserts itself only when Dorothea and Will are alone together; when they are in company, for example at Lydgate's house (ch. 43, 407), or in church at Lowick (ch. 47, 444), both feel constrained. After Casaubon's death, Will calls at Lowick Manor to say goodbye. Dorothea elects to see him in the drawing-room:

> The drawing-room was the most neutral room in the house to her—the one least associated with the trials of her married life: the damask matched the wood-work, which was all white and gold; there were two tall mirrors and tables with nothing on them—in brief, it was a room where you had no reason for sitting in one place rather than in another. (ch. 54, 508)

This lack of association, this lack of a reason to sit in one place rather than another, releases the room from the immobilizing effects of gender polarization. Neutrality makes courtship conceivable again. Indeed, Will only just saves himself from falling at Dorothea's feet.

> "I shall never hear from you. And you will forget all about me."
> "No," said Dorothea, "I shall never forget you. I have never forgotten any one whom I once knew. My life has never been

crowded, and seems not likely to be so. And I have a great deal of space for memory at Lowick, haven't I?" She smiled.

"Good God!" Will burst out passionately, rising with his hat still in his hand, and walking to a marble table, where he suddenly turned and leaned his back against it. The blood had mounted to his face and neck, and he looked almost angry. (ch. 54, 511)

The speech-tag, itself unusually animated ("burst out"), is the bridge to an embedding description of most unusual length and particularity. Will rises, and walks away, and stands upright, the blood mounted to his face and neck. His arousal, here, may be the closest the Victorian novel ever came to describing an erection. Not having to sit in one place rather than another allows you to make yourself fully felt.

There is to be one further farewell, in chapter 62, in the library at Tipton Grange. Will is reminded of their meeting in Rome, Dorothea of the time he came to say goodbye to her at Lowick. His getting up and going to the window is itself reminiscent of a previous encounter in the library at Tipton (593). The novel has established a network of courtship scenes in which the drama of sexual selection takes place. Will and Dorothea perform for each other, but there can be no doubt that (as Darwinian theory would lead one to expect) his performance is the more brazen. It is also the more consistent. Will's arisings are to some extent habitual. They punctuate, for example, his painful interview with Bulstrode in chapter 61 (584–6). Even on that occasion, however, what provokes them is the need to keep his honor unblemished if he is to stand a chance with Dorothea (586). They are *for* Dorothea, then, if not always provoked by her.

There follows the mutual self-revelation, at Lowick. It crosses Dorothea's mind that she cannot receive Will in the library, "where her husband's prohibition seemed to dwell" (ch. 83, 757). The prohibition has already been lifted, I would suggest, through her frank acknowledgement of the fitness of her chosen mate.

There was nothing that she longed for at that moment except to see Will: the possibility of seeing him had thrust itself insistently between her and every other object; and yet she had a throbbing excitement like an alarm upon her—a sense that she was doing something daringly defiant for his sake. (ch. 83, 758)

Their encounter is constituted by a by now familiar pattern of expressive but purposeless movements. The movements lift the spell: they take possession of the space once possessed by Casaubon. There is a certain brutality in this, and the brutality provides an unspoken context for the first embrace, which critics and readers have found so disappointing (ch. 83, 762). The embrace is, admittedly, detumescent. But one wonders whether Eliot, having been so Darwinianly frank throughout the novel, having in this scene allowed Will and Dorothea to make their presence fully felt by movement through and into space, really needed to do anything more.

Notes

1. "Notes on Form in Art" in *Selected Critical Writings*, ed. Rosemary Ashton (Oxford: Oxford University Press, 1992), 354–9, pp. 355–6.

2. "The truth of infinite value that he teaches," she had written in a review of volume 3 of *Modern Painters* in 1856, "is *realism*—the doctrine that all truth and beauty are to be attained by a humble and faithful study of nature": *Selected Critical Writings*, 248.

3. *Seven Lamps of Architecture*, popular ed. (London: George Allen, 1906), 202–3. *Works*, library ed., ed. E. T. Cook and Alexander Wedderburn, 39 vols. (London: Longmans, Green, 1907), 8:148–9.

4. "Notes on the Present State of Engraving" (1872), in *Works*, 22:467.

5. *The Origin of Species* (London: Dent, 1971), 87.

6. *The Descent of Man and Selection in Relation to Sex*, 2nd ed. (London: John Murray, 1894), 614, 211.

7. *Origin*, 87.

8. *Descent*, 596–7, 617.

9. Pointing out the Darwinian provenance of the term "variation," Gillian Beer goes on to argue that the emphasis on plurality rather than singleness is "crucial to the developing argument of *Middlemarch* which, with all its overtly taxonomic ordering, has as its particular deep counter-enterprise the establishment of individual diversity beneath ascribed

typologies": *Darwin's Plots: Evolutionary Narrative in Darwin, George Eliot and Nineteenth-Century Fiction* (London: Routledge, 1983), 149–54.

10. " 'This Thing I Like My Sister May Not Do': Shakespearean Erotics and a Clash of Wills in *Middlemarch,*" *Style* 32 (1998), 36–59, pp. 39–42, 53.

11. "Sexuality and Knowledge in *Middlemarch,*" *Nineteenth-Century Contexts* 19 (1996), 425–41, pp. 427–9.

12. "Sexuality and Knowledge in *Middlemarch,*" 431–2.

13. "Sexuality and Knowledge in *Middlemarch,*" 436, 433.

14. "Of Queens' Gardens," published with "Of Kings' Treasuries" as *Sesame and Lilies* (1865), in *Works,* 18:122.

15. "Robert Kerr: *The Gentleman's House* and the One-Room Solution," in *The Spectacle of Intimacy: A Public Life for the Victorian Family* (Princeton: Princeton University Press, 2000), 156–78, p. 157.

16. "Robert Kerr," 165.

17. *The Gentleman's House,* 3rd ed. (London: John Murray, 1871), 12.

18. "Notes on Form," 355–6.

19. "Robert Kerr," 163.

20. *Encyclopaedia of Cottage, Farm, and Villa Architecture and Furniture,* new ed. (London: Longman, Brown, Green, and Longmans, 1846), 9–11, 1135–45.

21. *Gentleman's House,* 116, 114.

22. A similar retreat afflicts the Lydgates. The failure of their marriage is due, Karen Chase points out, "to their mutual willingness to play out the fate of their gender assignments"; *George Eliot's "Middlemarch"* (Cambridge: Cambridge University Press, 1991), 65. The difference is that those assignments are not played out *in literary space.*

23. I am thinking of Jane Eyre "shrined" in the "double retirement" of a window seat; *Jane Eyre,* ed. Margaret Smith (Oxford: Oxford University Press, 1993), 8. See Karen Chase, *Eros and Psyche: The Representation of Personality in Charlotte Brontë, Charles Dickens, and George Eliot* (London: Methuen, 1984), 85–91. Few novels, Chase remarks, are as "spatially *articulate*" (59) as *Jane Eyre*; *Middlemarch* may be one of them.

24. David Trotter, "Some Brothels: Nineteenth-Century Philanthropy and the Poetics of Space," *Critical Quarterly* 44 (2002), 25–32.

25. Shifra Hochberg, "The Vista from Dorothea's Boudoir Window and a Coleridgean Source," *English Language Notes* 29, 3 (1992), 41–6. The scene may also have a visual source or "intertext." See Joseph Nicholes, "Dorothea in the Moated Grange: Millais's *Mariana* and the *Middlemarch* Window-Scenes," *Victorians Institute Journal* 20 (1992), 93–124.

26. Chase, *Eros and Psyche,* 88.

27. The point is made by R. L. P. Jackson in a perceptive discussion of

the scene: "A History of the Lights and Shadows: The Secret Motion of *Middlemarch*," *Cambridge Quarterly* 26 (1997), 1–18, p. 13.

28. I describe this hatred and its implications at greater length in *Paranoid Modernism: Literary Experiment, Psychosis, and the Professionalization of English Society* (Oxford: Oxford University Press, 2001), chap. 3.

29. *David Copperfield*, ed. Nina Burgis (Oxford: Oxford University Press, 1983), 307–8.

30. *David Copperfield*, 610–21; *Bleak House*, ed. Nicola Bradbury (Harmondsworth, England: Penguin Books, 1996), 943–8. There are similar scenes in Thackeray: for example, *The History of Pendennis*, ed. J. I. M. Stewart (Harmondsworth, England: Penguin Books, 1972), 714–9.

31. *George Eliot: "Middlemarch"* (Cambridge: Cambridge University Press, 1991), 69. I am greatly indebted to her account of Ladislaw's career as the novel's "most serious use of Darwinian insight into the understanding of character within history": 67–72.

32. "A History," 13–4.

33. Franco Moretti points out that in Jane Austen's novels, which he sees as, among other things, an imaginary act of nation-building, narrative complication always takes place not in the "introverted, rural England" where the heroines were brought up and where they will live with their husbands but in cities like London and Bath, or in seaports: *Atlas of the European Novel 1800–1900* (London: Verso, 1998), 18–9.

34. *George Eliot's "Middlemarch,"* 70–1.

35. *Sororophobia: Differences among Women in Literature and Culture* (Oxford: Oxford University Press, 1992), 40–50.

36. *Sororophobia,* 42, 46.

37. Mark Lambert, *Dickens and the Suspended Quotation* (New Haven: Yale University Press, 1981).

38. " 'This Thing,' " 52.

39. I have chosen in this essay to concentrate on domestic realism's most basic techniques in order to enlarge our sense of its "core" capabilities. Some of the other techniques at the disposal of its most sophisticated British exponent are the subject of Garrett Stewart's incisive essay on the "overlap" between strategies for representing sexuality and strategies for representing death in her last novel: " 'Beckoning Death': *Daniel Deronda* and the Plotting of a Reading," in Regina Barreca, ed., *Sex and Death in Victorian Literature* (Basingstoke, England: Macmillan, 1990), 69–106. A Stewart-like reading of *Middlemarch* would usefully complicate the one I offer here. There are hints toward it in Jackson, "A History," 11–3; Michie, *Sororophobia*, 47–8; and Shuttleworth, "Sexuality," 432–5.

4

The Materiality of *Middlemarch*

KATE FLINT

◆　◆　◆

READING IS A physical activity. More than the response to the words on the page, more than the firing of the imagination—whether to produce pictures in the mind's eye, to assimilate and argue with points of view, or to engage with imaginary characters—it entails a particular individual's engagement with a particular object in a specific space or sequence of spaces.

The original readers of *Middlemarch* would have encountered the novel in eight chunky, paper-covered volumes, published by William Blackwood and Sons—books 1–6 appearing at two-month intervals between December 1871 and October 1872, and the final two numbers appearing in November and December of that year. Once they opened the mid-green covers, they would have been in no doubt that they were living in a material world, for, as Gillian Beer explores elsewhere in this volume, the text of the novel was sandwiched between advertisements—for jewelry and patent cigar cases; the Granville Hotel with attached ozonized iodine baths, All-cock's Porous Plaster, and Brandreth's pills; nonguttering candles, and the Crown Hair Restorer; toilet soaps, choice perfumes, and chocolate. These are advertisements aimed at those at once anxious about their bodies and interested in adorning them. Only the recurrent advertisement on the back cover from Blackwood's suggests that they might be interested in indulging their minds, as well. Here could be found publicity for the one-volume Uniform Edition of Eliot's works (in which *Middlemarch* itself was to appear in May 1874) and for Alexander Bain's *Wise, Witty, and Tender Sayings in Prose and Verse. Selected from the Works of George Eliot*: a volume that both acted as homage to the author's thought and rhetoric and indicated a further level of commodification of her prose than that represented by the circulation of her novels and poetry alone (see Price).

Yet to approach *Middlemarch* from the point of view of material culture is to engage, necessarily, with far more than the book's initial physical appearance, or, for that matter, with George Eliot's and G. H. Lewes's interest in numbers of copies sold, in the rapidity with which it was published in Germany (in both an English edition and in translation), or in the fee of twelve hundred pounds that *Harper's* paid Eliot for reprinting the novel in America—although their journals and letters certainly bear witness to their alertness to *Middlemarch*'s identity as an object of sale, purchase, and consumption. My concern here will be primarily with the world of things that the novel represents: with the potential of material objects to bear witness to the processes of social history that underpin the world of the text, even though those may go largely unremarked upon by the narrator, and with the ways in which they are made to relate to the perceptual and emotional habits and responses of those who own, wear, desire, observe, or dispose of them. If the novel has tended to be regarded as a critique of those who are overmaterialist—Eliot certainly having little time for those "many crass minds in Middlemarch whose reflective scales could only weigh things in the lump" (ch. 16, 145–6)—this does not mean that we should pass lightly over her treatment of the visible, tangible world. Rather, we need to give full attention to what Andrew Miller, in his sustained examination of "*Middlemarch* and the solicitudes of material culture" in *Novels Behind Glass: Commodity Culture and Victorian Narrative*, describes as Eliot's method of moving "away from a narrowly materialist understanding of goods; instead of translating goods into their exchange value . . . she rewrites them as aesthetic objects" (216), pressing them to her own novelistic ends. While, as Miller notes, Henry James may have complained that Eliot "proceeds from the abstract to the concrete" (Carroll, 498), the process that he correctly locates in her fiction is one whereby she creates "in the aesthetic structure of her text, a source of value and significance other than that of commodified things" (217).

But considering the materiality of *Middlemarch* involves going way beyond this. It means looking closely at Eliot's linguistic practices. For, in addition to her deployment of the social connotations embedded in household objects, her own rhetorical habit of analogy ensures that she is continually turning the conceptual into the material. And in doing so—as when she writes of the way in which so many would-be independent-minded, ambitious people end up "coming to be shapen after the average and fit to be packed by the gross" (ch. 15, 135)—she reveals a good deal about how the dominant discourse of a society permeates not just the minds of its imagined inhabitants but the ways in which it is described, as well. Eliot originally came from a social environment very like that delineated in the novel, and hence writes of it with an understanding at once amused and critical of the nuances that physical objects carried within it, but by the time she came to write this novel, she had a sustained and close familiarity with current scientific discourse. This emphasized not just the material particulars of the world, and of the role of the senses in registering them, but the differing fibers that went to make up the human body as a whole. In what follows, I shall be exploring the ways in which the body's material constitution was, for Eliot, inseparable from her understanding of the world it inhabits.

The society of Middlemarch is bound up with the material in the most literal of senses. The town's economy, like that of its outlying villages, relied heavily on the textile industry—specifically, the weaving of silk ribbons. In this, it very closely resembled the Coventry of Eliot's childhood, which had experienced considerable prosperity in the second decade of the nineteenth century but which was, by the time in which the novel is set, already suffering economically from the more rapid introduction of steam-driven looms else-

where in the country (notably Derby)—something strongly re-
sisted by a number of the hand-loom weavers. Nonetheless, by 1836
there were fifty-three power-looms in Coventry, run by two of the
largest manufacturers. To give an idea of the numbers of workers involved: in the 1830s, Coventry was at the center of a weaving area of
thirteen thousand looms supporting thirty thousand people; in
Foleshill, to the north of Coventry—the weaving village on which
Tipton may well have been based, and which was very close to
where Eliot lived from 1841 to 1849—there were around 2,540
weavers and their assistants, and a further four thousand or so inhabitants, since this was fast becoming a suburb of Coventry (see *Vic-
toria County History,* vol. 8).

This is the increasingly industrial and urban background against
which a man like Mr Brooke, coming from a long-established background where wealth and status depends on land, not fabric,
announces that he is proud to have no "yard-measuring or parcel-
tying forefathers" (ch. 1, 7). By a not dissimilar process of association, Dorothea's separateness is established through her inability to
"reconcile the anxieties of a spiritual life involving eternal consequences, with a keen interest in guimp and artificial protrusions of
drapery" (ch. 1, 8). But the textile industry lies behind many other
lives, particularly that of the Vincy family. Mr Vincy's financial anxieties are never far from the surface (and we know that "when he was
disappointed in a market for his silk braids, he swore at the groom"
[ch. 36, 321]); Rosamond is underwhelmed by the Middlemarch
young men, who "could speak on no subject with striking knowledge, except perhaps the dyeing and carrying trades" (ch. 27, 251).
Mr Vincy may have a stronger notion of professional propriety than
some of his competitors, remarking that "it is not for the glory of
the Middlemarch trade, that Plymdale's house uses those blue and
green dyes it gets from the Brassing manufactory" that rot the silk
(ch. 13, 121); but his sense of honor is made relative by one of the
novel's rare acknowledgments of the weavers who make his profits
possible. Mrs Cadwallader follows up Mr Brooke's reference to Mr
Vincy as being from "a very decent family—a very good fellow . . . a
credit to the manufacturing interest" by describing him as "one of
those who suck the life out of the wretched handloom weavers in

Tipton and Freshitt. That is how his family look so fair and sleek" (ch. 34, 307). If the weavers themselves are not given a voice by Eliot, this pointed barb remains in our minds when Brooke makes the inept electioneering speech in which he lamely announces his disconnection from the community as a whole by admonishing that "It won't do, you know, breaking machines: everything must go on—trade, manufactures, commerce, interchange of staples—that kind of thing—since Adam Smith, that must go on" (ch. 51, 474).

Yet rather than encountering Middlemarch and its surrounding parishes as sites of labor in the textile industry, one sees them, rather, as sites of display for its products. Dress is important in the novel as a social indicator, as is needlework: Rosamond, nearing her marriage, remarks with extreme condescension—as she contemplates her immediate need for "cambric frilling"—that "Mary Garth might do some work for me now, I should think. Her sewing is exquisite; it is the nicest thing I know about Mary" (ch. 36, 324). Rosamond herself is, of course, the novel's most notorious clothes-horse—and the fact that this is increasingly dwelt upon after her marriage, whether she appears in a "cherry-coloured dress with swansdown trimming about the throat" (ch. 46, 436), or "drapery of transparent faintly-tinted muslin" (ch. 58, 557), is used to accentuate the expense that a desire to show oneself off fashionably brings with it. It would be a mistake to blame her entirely in this respect, however: Eliot demonstrates the ingrained nature of social assumptions when it comes to sartorial display when she remarks that "Lydgate believed himself to be careless about his dress, and despised a man who calculated the effects of his costume; it seemed to him only a matter of course that he had abundance of fresh garments—such things were naturally ordered in sheaves" (ch. 58, 552–3). Relatively early on, and indeed in relation to Lydgate, we are warned against judging overmuch from the outside, since a man may be "known merely as a cluster of signs for his neighbours' false suppositions" (ch. 15, 133); and Letty's reminder that "in the East the men too wore petticoats" (finale, 780), thus undermining assumptions about gender roles based on dress, acts in the novel's finale as a further pointed reminder about the unreliability of judgments based on clothing. Nonetheless, throughout the novel, Eliot presents us with a society that employs and interprets costume as a signaling de-vice—even after death. Featherstone's pallbearers on horseback wore "the richest scarves and hatbands, and even the under-bearers had trappings of woe which were of a good well-priced quality" (ch. 34, 304). The townspeople try to gauge whether or not Mrs Bul-strode yet knows of her husband's disgrace from the headgear she and her daughters wear to church—their new Tuscan bonnets, her bonnet trimmed with a pale lavender feather: sure enough, when the moment comes, she takes off all her ornaments, puts on a plain black gown and bonnet-cap: "her way of expressing to all spectators visible or invisible that she had begun a new life in which she em-braced humiliation" (ch. 74, 707). The device of distinguishing be-tween Rosamond and Dorothea's value systems, as well as class, is made plain enough by Eliot when she garbs the latter in "thin white woollen stuff soft to the touch and soft to the eye . . . always in the shape of a pelisse with sleeves hanging all out of the fashion" (ch. 43, 406). Even Dorothea herself uses dress symbolically, albeit to signify new resolution to herself rather than to society at large, when she abandons her full mourning before bravely setting out, after her restless night, to visit the Lydgates' home—"the tradition that fresh garments belonged to all initiation, haunting her mind" (ch. 80, 742). She may not, however, be entirely innocent—albeit uncon-sciously—of a pointed barb against Rosamond when hesitantly ex-plaining to Will the financial grounds on which they may marry: " 'We could live quite well on my own fortune—it is too much—seven hundred-a-year—I want so little—no new clothes—and I will learn what everything costs' " (ch. 83, 762). Certainly the reader can be in no doubt that the text is proclaiming Dorothea, in materi-alist terms, to be a complete inversion of Mrs Lydgate.

The concern with consumption that is manifested in the novel quickly extends beyond clothing to the settings in which dress is to be displayed. While *Middlemarch* contains few set-piece descriptions of interiors—with the exception of the subtle shifts of atmosphere within Dorothea's blue-grey boudoir at Lowick, to which I will re-turn—the topic of furnishings keeps recurring, even if attitudes toward furniture are made to matter far more than the objects themselves. It is perhaps worth pausing for a moment to consider why Eliot should have passed over giving lengthy accounts of decor. It may be a part of her general reluctance to appear, to be judged, as a woman novelist; of fulfilling the assumptions voiced by Lewes in a review article nearly twenty years earlier, when he wrote: "we may be prepared to find women succeeding the finesse of detail, in pathos and sentiment, while men generally succeed better in the construction of plots and the delineation of character" (1852: 133): the kind of gendered categorization, on Lewes's part, that forms the foundation of the arguments developed by Naomi Schor in her influential book *Reading in Detail*, where she explores the implications of the socially presumed "link between particularity and femininity. . . . Both as a social being and as an individual, woman is seen as more embedded in the concrete and the particular than men" (16).[1] This is, however, a generalization that *Middlemarch* disrupts—not just, obviously, in the person of Dorothea and in the narrator's habits of thought, but in the ways in which numerous men are shown to be tied down by a desire for quantifiable substantiality (the successful grocer Mr Mawmsey's desire for certainty that "something measurable had been delivered" (ch. 45, 418) coloring his judgment about the medical abilities of a doctor who will not dispense drugs himself), or, for that matter, may be praised because of their attention to productive detail, as with Caleb Garth's faith in "getting a good bit of contriving and solid building done" (ch. 40, 377).

Only months before Eliot started writing *Middlemarch*, Charles Eliot Norton visited her and Lewes, writing subsequently to his friend George William Curtis that Lewes

> has what it is hard to call a vulgar air, but at least there is something in his air which reminds you of vulgarity.
>
> He took us into the pleasant cheerful drawing-rooms which occupy one side of the house, where Mrs Lewes received us very pleasantly . . . Lunch was set in the study, a cheerful room like the others, lined with well-filled bookshelves, save over the fireplace where hung a staring likeness and odious, vulgarizing portrait of Mrs. Lewes. Indeed all the works of art in the house bore witness to the want of delicate artistic feeling, or good culture on

the part of the occupants, with the single exception, so far as I observed, of the common lithograph of Titian's "Christ of the Tribute Money." (*Letters* 5:8)

Eliot might well have been dismayed had she read this correspondence: their home had recently been redecorated by the architect Owen Jones, and she had been extremely pleased that Jones "has determined every detail so that we can have the pleasure of admiring what is our own without vanity" (*Letters*, 4:124). *Middlemarch* shows her well aware of the power that furnishings hold over the emotions and imaginations of her characters, particularly those who are too apt to be swayed by surfaces, and think too little about the risk of being vain. As Ellen Bayuk Rosenman puts it, with her eye on *Middlemarch*, "To furnish one's home or to dress simply, no matter how conscious the effort or how becoming the effect, is to display one's lack of vanity, one's indifference to making an impression, and therefore one's moral superiority to fashionable people" (51). The antithesis of such an attitude can, of course, be found in the home of the newly married Lydgates, and here one might well bear in mind Eliot's remark about domestic ornamentation when reviewing Jones's *Grammar of Ornament* for the *Fortnightly Review*: "The subtle relation between all kinds of truth and fitness in our life forbids that bad taste should ever be harmless to our moral sensibility or our intellectual discernment" (124). Notoriously, Lydgate's intellectual distinction "did not penetrate his feelings about furniture, or women" (ch. 15, 141)—this coupling, and the relative position of the two terms, has rightly been frequently noted. We are warned from his introduction onward that he "did not mean to think of furniture at present; but whenever he did so, it was to be feared that neither biology nor schemes of reform would lift him above the vulgarity of feeling that there would be an incompatibility in his furniture not being of the best" (ch. 15, 141)—indication that for Eliot, it would have very likely have seemed "vulgar" to have been overconcerned with those very furnishings that Norton was so quick to label with this epithet. It was not that she paid no attention to her household goods: when she wrote to Maria Congreve in November 1868, she gave a vivid, if not immediately inviting, indication of the state of the Lewes's spare room: "The bed is no softer and no broader; but will you not be tempted by a new carpet and a new bit of matting for your bath?—perhaps there will even be a new fender?" (*Letters*, 4:487) The fender makes a cameo appearance in the auctioning of the Larchers' goods, where Mr Trumbull tickles his audience's imagination as he fantasizes about the improbable antiquity, and multifarious uses, of a fender "of polished steel, with much lancet-shaped open-work and a sharp edge" (ch. 60, 568). When Mrs Mawmsey objects to its sharpness on the practical grounds that a child could cut its head open on the object, Trumbull tries another tack: " 'Gentlemen, here's a fender that if you had the misfortune to hang yourselves would cut you down in no time—with astonishing celerity—four-and-sixpence—five—five-and-sixpence—an appropriate thing for a spare bedroom where there was a four-poster and a guest a little out of his mind—six shillings' " (ch. 60, 568).

Furniture, in other words, plays a central role when it comes to the envisaging of domestic futures: its materiality broadcasting one's social status. As Rosamond and Lydgate's romance develops, she fantasizes about the house at Lowick Gate that she hopes he will buy, "and she imagined the drawing-room in her favourite house with various styles of furniture" (ch. 27, 251). Lydgate's imagination works in a more negative fashion, perhaps as a result of his wider exposure to different degree of privation. Anticipating living in "what he would have called an ordinary way, with green glasses for hock, and excellent waiting at table" (ch. 36, 327), he simply cannot see himself carrying on his profession in "such a home as Wrench had—the doors all open, the oil-cloth worn, the children in soiled pinafores, and lunch lingering in the form of bones, black-handled knives, and willow-pattern" (ch. 36, 333). Even after his marriage starts to founder on the figurative wreckage of expensive dinner-services, the Wrenches, who "make economy look ugly" (ch. 64, 610) remain a benchmark of what he would, fastidiously, rather avoid. For as Lydgate quickly learns, and Rosamond conspicuously fails to internalize, imagined furniture, and the life-style that would go with it, is rather different from the thing itself. To privilege the visible display of taste and status above financial prudence is to court disaster. This may be seen as a sustained example of a major lesson that the novel seeks to impart throughout: that value is connected to labor, and to the expenditure of well-directed personal effort, rather than of cash. Productivity, that is, is valued above speculation: this applies alike to Will's early generalizations about the role of the poet (" 'But you leave out the poems,' said Dorothea. 'I think they are wanted to complete the poet' " [ch. 22, 209]), or to the "poetry" that Caleb Garth finds in such evidence of fruitful labor as a roaring furnace, "the crane at work on the wharf, the piled-up produce in warehouses" (ch. 24, 235–6).

Yet however alert George Eliot might have been to the world of inanimate things, and to the emotions and values that get projected onto them, the material with which she ultimately shows the greatest concern is that which makes up the human body. Nowhere is this clearer than when Lydgate outlines the driving force behind his scientific research for this body's foundational "primitive tissue." A scientifically alert reader, as subsequent commentators have pointed out, would already recognize this physiological quest as being dependent upon a false hypothesis: that all structures start from a common basis, "as your sarsnet, gauze, net, satin and velvet from the raw cocoon" (ch. 15, 139). Lydgate is heavily influenced by the anatomist and physiologist Marie François Xavier Bichat, some of whose ideas Lewes summarizes at the opening of *The Physiology of Common Life* (1859), without himself buying into the idea of a single point of organic origin: that

> the heart, for instance, is an organ constructed out of muscular tissue, connective tissue, nervous tissue, and adipose tissue— each of these tissues manifesting the same properties in the heart which it manifests in every other organ; just as the various substances out of which a ship is constructed—wood, hemp, copper, iron, tar, &c.—preserve their characteristic properties, though the wood may be rudder, deck, or mast, and the iron anchor, nail, or cable. (1:3)

Lewes's analogies were strong in Eliot's mind a decade later: she transposes them to a more domestic context when outlining Lydgate's foundational beliefs in "certain primary webs or tissues" (ch. 15, 138), suggesting a body that resembled a house built up from "wood, iron, stone, brick, zinc, and the rest" (ch. 16, 149). But even if Eliot deliberately used outmoded hypotheses concerning physiological structure as a symbolic analogy for Lydgate's capacity for intense, yet misguided, enthusiasm, her own fascination with the body's material properties runs throughout *Middlemarch*. On one level, this fascination is manifested at the level of extended metaphor. If the personal dramas of the characters unfold in a number of clearly demarcated rooms—the library and boudoir at Lowick; the Lydgates' drawing room; the wainscotted parlor at Stone Court—so are bodies themselves seen as rooms and furniture. While Casaubon might try and shut up his bitter response to criticism of his scholarship in "a dark closet of his verbal memory" (ch. 29, 263), closets do not exist without rooms, nor rooms without houses. Similarly, "Our passions do not live apart in locked chambers, but, dressed in their small wardrobe of notions, bring their provisions to a common table" (ch. 16, 156): a compressed intimation of how interior feeling and external display—or emotions and the language in which they are expressed—not only cohabit but mutually sustain one another. If, on occasion, the live body freezes into ornamental statuary— after Dorothea hears that Casaubon has a potentially fatal condition, she "sat as if she had been turned to marble" (ch. 30, 271); after Casaubon's death, Dorothea and Will sit helplessly when it seems that Will must leave town, and it "seemed to him as if they were like two creatures slowly turning to marble in each other's presence" (ch. 54, 511)—we are nonetheless continually prompted to recognize that even the apparently inanimate conceals the pulsating, and inseparable, demands of body and mind. Thus even in these moments of crisis, Dorothea's "life within her was so intense" (ch. 23, 221); Will is painfully alert that "their hearts were conscious and their eyes were yearning" (ch. 54, 511). Lest we should miss the point, the naturalist clergyman Farebrother later reminds Dorothea (as he makes her contemplate the uncomfortable possibility that Lydgate may not be the man she has taken him to be) that " 'character is not cut in marble—it is not something solid and unalterable. It is something living and changing, and may become diseased as our bodies do' " (ch. 72, 692).

In her everyday life, Eliot could apparently draw a clear distinction between the life of the mind and the emotions on the one hand and the sensations of her physical frame on the other. In her journal for January 1, 1873, Eliot noted that the eighth and last book of *Middlemarch* had been published at the beginning of December, and remarks with great pleasure that no former book of hers had been received with as much enthusiasm, and that she had

> received many deeply affecting assurances of its influence for good on individual minds. Hardly anything could have happened to me which I could regard as a greater blessing than this growth of my spiritual existence when my bodily existence is decaying. The merely egoistic satisfactions of fame are easily nullified by toothache, and that has made my chief consciousness for the last week. (*Journals*, 143)

Yet as even this passage, with its uncertain tone, wavering between the metaphysical and a wan attempt at humor, amalgamates body and consciousness in a way that exemplifies the argument made by Maria H. Frawley *in Individualism and Identity in Nineteenth-Century Britain*: that Victorians validated bodily suffering "not simply for its enobling potential"—that would perhaps be a hard case to make even for severe toothache—"but also for its unique capacity to express the power of subjective experience" (61). Despite—or maybe because of—her own uncomfortable consciousness of her corporeality ("I object strongly to myself as a bundle of unpleasant sensations with a palpitating heart and awkward manners," she wrote to Maria Congreve on December 30, 1867 [*Letters*, 4:413]), Eliot was, on the evidence of her journal and correspondence, constantly monitoring the state of her own body during this period, alert to the interplay between the state of physical well-being and her own moods. In *Middlemarch*, she demonstrates the two-way nature of this transaction when she shows how mental stress registers on the human frame. Mrs Bulstrode's sorrow, as she learns of her husband's past, "was every day streaking her hair with whiteness and making her eyelids languid" (ch. 85, 773); Lydgate, metaphorically "bruised and shattered" by his marital problems, with a literal "dark line under his eyes" (ch. 69, 660), is both offering medical opinion and being autobiographical when he advises Bulstrode that " 'One sees how any mental strain, however slight, may affect a delicate frame' " (ch. 67, 640). "It is a consequence of the wonderful complexity of our organism, in which each part plays upon another," writes Lewes in *The Physiology of Common Life*,

> that remote and unsuspected influences produce important results. Mental agitation will suddenly arrest or increase the secretions; imperfect, or too abundant secretion will depress, or confuse the mind. An idea will agitate the heart, and disturb the liver; a languid liver will disturb the serenity of the mind; a worm in the intestine will produce melancholy, and even madness.— So indissolubly is our mental life bound up with our bodily life. (2:106–7)

Strikingly, in *Middlemarch*, Eliot's sustained consciousness of the symbiotic relationship between body and mind is expressed in the way in which she suggests that ideas and feelings—as well as experience itself—can have an impact so violent that their effect can only be conveyed through the language of acute physical pain, even though there may be no outward sign of inward agony. This may be no more than Celia's anticipation of the discomfort that too much thought and self-analysis can bring with it—"Notions and scruples were like spilt needles, making one afraid of treading, or sitting down, or even eating" (ch. 2, 19–20)—yet if she is here expressing anxiety that her sister is self-damaging through her overscrupulous attitudes, Dorothea herself has no hesitation in dramatizing the degree with which she believes social principles should be internalized, advocating both self- and class mortification when she tells Sir James Chettam that she thinks "we deserve to be beaten out of our beautiful houses with a scourge of small cords—all of us who let tenants live in such sties as we see round us" (ch. 3, 29). But in this novel, the most intense agonies are reserved for affective relationships. Thus Lydgate finds that the need of accommodating himself to Rosamond's inflexible nature "held him as with pincers" (ch. 65, 627); Rosamond herself, witnessing Will's stormy displeasure with

her, found that "all her sensibility was turned to a bewildering nov-
elty of pain; she felt a new terrified recoil under a lash never experienced before" (ch. 78, 733)—reproaches that remained "like a
knife-wound within her" (ch. 81, 750); Will himself, in the crucial,
tense scene with Dorothea in the library at Lowick, a minute or so
before they finally commit themselves to one another, feels "as if
some torture-screw were threatening him" (ch. 83, 761).

In part, the visceral responses that this imagery prompts is related to Eliot's own rhetorical habit of analogy: it is easier both to
imagine and understand something, the text recurrently implies, if
one can give it definite shape and form. The startling moments of
metaphorical violence called up by these instances enact the rever-
sal of a feature that George Levine has isolated as a hallmark of realist fiction: passages that "assert that fiction should shift its focus
from the extreme to the ordinary, and that to do so is morally in-
structive," even if "to do so is also to violate the dominant conventions of fiction" (17). Yet whether sensationalism occurs in the
shocks that a plot may deliver, or in the metaphors through which
wordless mental agony is conveyed to the reader, the body, as the
locus of sensation, remains a constant and necessary given. The way
in which Eliot, and Lewes—in company with many of their scientifically oriented contemporaries—saw both emotion and intellect as
a physiological fact gives the processes of thought an undoubted
materiality, located within the "Cerebrum," whose appearance and
construction Lewes beautifully describes in terms of the most sensuous of fabrics: "The convolutions of the Cerebrum are everywhere
similar and continuous, like so many folds in a piece of velvet"
(Lewes, 1859, 2:82).

Moreover, throughout the novel, Eliot envisages the process of
thought as taking on a solidity of being, too. Thus Casaubon—in
what turns out to be, in fact, one of his most poetically eloquent ut-
terances—remarks that his "mind is something like the ghost of an
ancient, wandering about the world and trying mentally to reconstruct it as it used to be" (ch. 2, 16); Rosamond sees little distinction
between envisaging her engagement to Lydgate and the actual fact:
"That they were some time to be engaged had long been an idea in
her mind; and ideas, we know, tend to a more solid kind of existence,

the necessary materials being at hand" (ch. 27, 255). A materially conceived idea, however, proves to be quite different from the thing itself, as she discovers when the Lydgate with whom she had been in love transmutes from "a group of airy conditions" to a set of "every-day details which must be lived through slowly from hour to hour, not floated through with a rapid selection of favourable aspects" (ch. 64, 622). Yet the dramatic antitheses that animate the consciousness are not just between inner imaginings and external reality, as is demonstrated by the mental convolutions that Bulstrode undergoes when the sick Raffles is in his house, and conscience wrestles unsuccessfully with pragmatic desire. While he might pray, and thereby attempt "to condense words into a solid mental state, there pierced and spread with irresistible vividness the images of the events he desired" (ch. 70, 662). The power of unbidden thought is here described in the language of compelling physical invasion: elsewhere, the mind's contents appear to be ranged in more organized, or at least preformed, fashion, one reflective of modern cultural forms of imaging the world. The memory is capable of shifting "its scenery like a diorama" (ch. 53, 490); Will, at his lowest, seems to see his future as "in a magic panorama" (ch. 79, 736). Even private mental processes, in other words, cannot be separated from the social forms of image-making: our internal vision may follow the patterns of framing scenes that are drawn from outside experience. For all that Will (albeit in a rather unproductive phase of his life) may remark to Naumann that " 'the true seeing is within' " (ch. 19, 179), Eliot herself is in no doubt that such imaging is reliant upon our socialized patterns of interacting with the material world.

The substantiality of ideas may itself be read as an extended metaphor for the physiological and psychological fact not only that body and mind are inseparable but that the properties of the mind itself depend on the materiality of the body. As we have seen, Eliot appears to have followed Lewes very closely in his sustained insistence on their symbiotic relations, and, while I have been drawing on *The Physiology of Common Life* by way of locating Lewes's ideas, one must recognize that the couple's interest in the physiological workings of the mind was a continuing and active one. This impression is confirmed by the entries in Lewes's journal for March 20–26, 1869, when they were in Florence, and they went "to a séance at the laboratory when [Moriz] Schiff exhibited the instrument for measuring the rapidity of thought" (*Letters*, 5:21), and for April 14, 1870, when the couple were staying in Vienna: "Lesson on the Brain to Polly" (*Letters*, 5:90). Again and again in *Middlemarch*, the ways in which an individual registers an impression is described in terms that draw attention to the interweaving of their state of mind with the responses of their bodily frame. So when Fred Vincy is, at last, showing that he is capable of applying himself to some hard work, the narrator shows the effect on the fabric of Caleb Garth's consciousness—"I am not sure that certain fibres in Mr Garth's mind had not resumed their old vibration"—of thinking that Fred might make a suitable partner in his work, hence husband for Mary (ch. 56, 527); less comfortably, when Celia tells her sister about the codicil to Casaubon's will, Dorothea is conscious that she "was undergoing a metamorphosis in which memory would not adjust itself to the stirring of new organs" (ch. 50, 461). Fred Vincy similarly experiences the simultaneity of physical shock and mental awakening when Farebrother tells him that he wants him to prioritize the happiness of Mary's life, and Eliot, slightly coyly, remarks that "Some one highly susceptible to the contemplation of a fine act has said, that it produces a sort of regenerating shudder through the frame, and makes one feel ready to begin a new life. A good degree of that effect was just then present in Fred Vincy" (ch. 66, 636). More striking still are those instances of human connection that are described as in the nature of a potentially dangerous charge. These may be the effects of place—as with the "vast wreck of ambitious ideals, sensual and spiritual, mixed confusedly with the signs of breathing forgetfulness and degradation" that is modern Rome, and that at first "jarred" Dorothea "as with an electric shock" (ch. 20, 181)—or they may be interpersonal. When Ladislaw is helping Mr Brooke arrange his documents and Dorothea is announced, "he started up as from an electric shock, and felt a tingling at his finger-ends" (ch. 39, 363); when he and Dorothea are engaged in an awkward, emotion-filled conversation in the library at Lowick, and Sir James is announced, it "was as if the same electric shock had passed through her and Will" (ch. 54, 513); when Ladislaw goes to The Shrubs, on Bulstrode's invitation, for a private interview, and learns that their histories may be in some way interwoven, "Will felt something like an electric shock" (ch. 61, 583).

Yet Eliot envisages the individual's interaction with the world as a kind of two-way current. Certainly, the senses receive information that may influence an individual's state of mind—their degree of calmness or optimism, anxiety or energy. Lydgate finds that Rosamond's choice of tunes "fell in with his mood as if they had been melodious sea-breezes" (a response that Eliot instantly shows up as facile by calling him an "emotional elephant" [ch. 45, 429]); Mr Brooke is, understandably, thrown out of his uncertain electioneering stride by the cruelly mocking "parrot-like, Punch-voiced echo" of his inadequate speech being returned to him (ch. 51, 474). Sensory perception, moreover, operates at a metaphorical as well as a literal level. Will is alert to this when he acknowledges what Casaubon feels about him:

> Prejudices about rank and status were easy enough to defy in the form of a tyrannical letter from Mr Casaubon; but prejudices, like odorous bodies, have a double existence both solid and subtle—solid as the pyramids, subtle as the twentieth echo of an echo, or as the memory of hyacinths which once scented the darkness. (ch. 43, 408–9)

As Janice Carlisle astutely notes, in *Common Scents*, her study of the work performed by smells in mid-Victorian fiction, this "series of analogies neatly links questions of social distinctions with erotic memories" (47). Yet at the same time that we receive information from our environment—information that may be stored up for future figurative usage, as here—Eliot is also interested in a more symbiotic, two-way process, in which it is hard to distinguish the receptors from their surroundings, or, for that matter, the literal from the metaphoric. Time and again, this interest concentrates on the figure of Dorothea in her blue-green boudoir: here, for example, she looks at the "uniform whiteness and low-hanging uniformity of cloud" outside her window in winter, which not only affects her visual perception, causing the furniture to shrink and the tapestry stag to look even more ghostly than ever, but which seeps into her sense of her position: "The duties of her married life . . . seemed to be shrinking with the furniture and the white vapour-walled land-scape"; the "low arch of dun vapour" outside is also the "stifling oppression" of the gentlewoman's world (ch. 49, 456). Even more striking is the occasion when Casaubon, receiving bad medical news, desires to be alone, and Dorothea, feeling redundant, retires to her boudoir, and "threw herself on a chair, not heeding that she was in the dazzling sun-rays: if there were discomfort in that, how could she tell that it was not part of her inward misery?" (ch. 42, 398) On yet another occasion, the breezeless, "changeless" summer scene outside "seemed to represent the prospect of her life, full of motive-less ease" (ch. 54, 508).

If one way to understand what Eliot is doing here is by invoking the concept of the pathetic fallacy, a more complex possible way into understanding this type of knowledge is explored by Teresa Brennan in her posthumously published *The Transmission of Affect*. Brennan's work is part of today's current tendency to see the work-ings of the mind as intimately tied in with the workings of the body: neuroscience has returned psychoanalytic study, at least in some quarters, to the same physiological basis that preoccupied its mid-nineteenth–century forerunners. Brennan is especially concerned with understanding that process which she describes as "social in origin but biological and physical in affect" (3): how we pick up on the atmosphere of a room or the mood of another person, and how what is happening outside of us registers itself on our own bodies; how, as she puts it, "we are not self-contained in terms of our ener-gies. There is no secure distinction between the 'individual' and the 'environment' " (6), nor "between the biological and the social" (7). For the process by which "one person's or group's nervous and hor-monal systems may be brought into alignment with another's" (9)—the process that neurologists call "entrainment"—involves above all smell. Conscious smell may be at work in fiction and in life—one might instance Rosamond wrinkling her sensitive nose at the way Fred eats red herrings in the morning, or the associations that the Crown Perfume Company, who advertised in books 5 and 6 of the part-issues of *Middlemarch*, may have hoped to summon up through perfumes with such names as "Meadow Queen," "Wild Flowers of India," and "Jockey Club." But what Brennan is concerned with is "unconscious olefaction." She uses the example of pheromones—molecules that signal aggression, or sexual attraction, or depression, and that are airborne and communicate chemical information that allows states of feeling to be transmitted, even when no verbal conversation takes place. "There is," Brennan reminds us, "no field of human action that does not involve hormonal messages" (9). Eliot herself is powerfully alert to how the general motion of matter may be paralleled with the motion of feeling, and does so in a way that quietly suggests how erotic dynamics—or their erosion—are also at stake. Thus she notes how Casaubon's "discontent passed vapour-like through all [Dorothea's] gentle loving manifestations, and clung to that inappreciative world which she had only brought nearer to him" (ch. 42, 392).

Brennan's particular fascination lies not just with the transmission of invisible bodily messages but with why we may resist as well as absorb them, and what this process may have to say about the boundaries of identity. Yet well before the discovery of pheromones, the concept that Lewes termed "unconscious sensibility" was under investigation, and the terms of this investigation were also firmly rooted in biology. Lewes, in chapter 8 of *The Physiology of Common Life*, entitled "Feeling and Thinking," tells us that "We shall do well to hold fast by the maxim that to have a sensation, and to be conscious of it, are two different things" (2:38). For we continually live in what Lewes—anticipating the more influential terminology of William James—called "a vast and powerful stream of sensation" (2:49). In other words, the reader's daily experience is continually composed of sensations, and his or her states of mind proceed from this fact. Lewes demands that we be alert not just to the information that reaches us through the operation of particular senses but that we acknowledge that we are all the time receiving information from the outside world, and that the quality of what we receive—even though we may not be conscious at all of our environment, unless we give it particular attention—will, nonetheless, affect our mood, and our very sense of being. Affect is constantly in process:

> The ebullient energy which one day exalts life, and the mournful
> depression which the next day renders life a burden almost intol-
> erable, are feelings not referable to any of the particular sensa-
> tions; but arise from the massive yet obscure sensibilities of the
> viscera, which form so important a part of the general stream of
> Sensation. (2:47–8)

It was this condition to which Lewes gave the title "Unconscious
Sensibility": this is what happens when, for example, Dorothea goes
for a walk after first meeting Casaubon, and, already in a highly
awakened state, "she looked before her, not consciously seeing, but
absorbing into the intensity of her mood, the solemn glory of the
afternoon with its long swathes of light between the far-off rows of
limes, whose shadows touched each other" (ch. 3, 25).

Dorothea has, of course, a long emotional journey from this moment to the less self-deluding emotions of the novel's close. The language of *Middlemarch*'s concluding paragraphs is very familiar, and
they revisit the novel's constant theme of the interpenetration of
self and environment. "There is no creature," Eliot writes, "whose
inward being is so strong that it is not determined by what lies outside it" (finale, 784–5). Customarily, this has been taken as a commentary on the inextricability of the individual and the social life; a
generalization that finds its place alongside the sentence in *Felix Holt*
that explains that "there is no private life which has not been determined by a wider public life."[2] Yet the text of *Middlemarch* shows the
applicability of this remark at the micro- as well as the macrocosmic
level. Rooms, furniture, clothing, the view from a window, the
weather: all exert their influence on a character's state of mind, on
his or her "determining acts." But the sensations flow in two directions. Dorothea's effect on those around her was, as we all know,
"incalculably diffusive" (finale, 785). This is the terminology not just
of moral influence but of the developing field of molecular physics,
with its new exploration of the revived Lucretian notion that "the
molecules of all bodies are in motion, even when the body itself appears to be at rest"—to quote the article "Molecules," summing up
recent theoretical developments, that James Clerk-Maxwell was to
publish in *Nature* in 1873: the effects of molecular research may be

traced through to—among many other things—the idea of the pheromone. But they may also be found in *Middlemarch*. At the moment when Will is electrically energized by hearing Dorothea announced in Brooke's library, "Any one observing him would have seen a change in his complexion, in the adjustment of his facial muscles, in the vividness of his glance, which might have made them imagine that every molecule in his body had passed the message of a magic touch. And so it had" (ch. 39, 363). At the novel's close, Dorothea, in other words, is linked by Eliot's language both to social effectiveness and to the wider, unstoppable processes of any individual's interaction with the environment: a recognition of universal physical principles that, in turn, enforces the impact of Eliot's theme of each one of us taking on the responsibilities attendant on our capacities for sympathy and influence.

What *Middlemarch* ultimately accomplishes, then, is to offer a clear rebuff to any temptation, whether in her time or ours, to separate the world of things from the life of the mind. Eliot does so in a way that goes far beyond any broad generalization that, necessarily, the material world is always going to be perceived by an individual with a uniquely constructed subjectivity. She consistently acknowledges that interpretation of objects may depend upon the socialization of this perception: that furniture, dress, and table crockery are all subject to the projection of collective assumptions and values, and in doing so, she shares in one of Victorian fiction's most notable attributes, even as she treats caustically those who privilege possessions over people. But much more interesting, experimentally, and idiosyncratically, Eliot emphasizes, again and again, that it is the body's own material constitution that guarantees this inseparability of world and being.

Notes

1. For further discussion about the connection between femininity and detail in relation to nineteenth-century fiction, see Langbauer; Langland; and Miller, 189–218.

2. George Eliot, *Felix Holt, the Radical* (Oxford, Oxford University Press, 1980), 43.

References

Brennan, Teresa. *The Transmission of Affect*. Ithaca: Cornell University Press, 2004.

Carlisle, Janice. *Common Scents. Comparative Encounters in High-Victorian Fiction*. New York: Oxford University Press, 2004.

Carroll, David. *George Eliot: The Critical Heritage*. New York: Barnes and Noble, 1971.

Eliot, George. *The George Eliot Letters*. Ed. Gordon S. Haight. 9 vols. New Haven: Yale University Press, 1954–78.

————. "Grammar of Ornament." *Fortnightly Review* 1 (1865), 124–5.

————. *The Journals of George Eliot*. Ed. Margaret Harris and Judith Johnston. Cambridge: Cambridge University Press, 1998.

Frawley, Maria H. *Invalidism and Identity in Nineteenth-Century Britain*. Chicago: University of Chicago Press, 2004.

Levine, George. *The Realistic Imagination*. Chicago: University of Chicago Press, 1981.

Lewes, George Henry. "The Lady Novelists." *Westminster Review* 58 (1852), 129–41.

————. *The Physiology of Common Life*. 2 vols. Edinburgh: Blackwood, 1859–60.

Maxwell, James Clerk. "Molecules." *Nature* 8 (1873), 437–41.

Miller, Andrew. *Novels behind Glass: Commodity Culture and Victorian Narrative*. Cambridge: Cambridge University Press, 1995.

Rosenman, Ellen Bayuk. "More Stories about Clothing and Furniture. Realism and Bad Commodities." In Christine L. Krueger, ed., *Functions of Victorian Culture at the Present Time*. Athens: Ohio University Press, 2002.

Schor, Naomi. *Reading in Detail: Aesthetics and the Feminine*. New York: Methuen, 1987.

5

Dorothea's Lost Dog

NINA AUERBACH

✦   ✦   ✦

OROTHEA BROOKE HAS always irritated me; in fact, she
makes my flesh creep. My allergy to this saintly, statuesque
heroine, whom everyone else seems to adore, should disqualify me as
a lover of *Middlemarch*, but I hope it won't: when I first read the novel
as a junior in college, its greatness made me shiver, but I shivered at,
and with, poor Casaubon, struggling with an intractable book and a
hectoring wife, and I do still. After all, Casaubon alone among the
novel's characters is doing something he doesn't have to do. He has
money, land, and a respectable position. Working on the shapeless
Key to All Mythologies is a labor of sheer love. He flays himself on
with the grotesque obsession that is another face of faith, while
Dorothea glorifies herself by flailing about crying "What can I do?"

I admit to a quirky bias against this floridly self-mortifying girl.
She begins the novel by highhandedly rejecting two things I cherish:
her dead mother's jewels and Sir James Chettam's offering of "a tiny
Maltese puppy" (ch. 3, 28). She is prevailed on to accept some of the
jewels, pretending to see them as pieces of Heaven rather than what
they are, but she's adamant about the Maltese, claiming grandly

that "creatures . . . bred merely as pets" are soulless and parasitic; besides, she adds, she would be "afraid of treading on it; I am rather short-sighted" (ch. 3, 28).

As part-owner of a little Maltese dog and sole owner of a trove of family jewels, more beautiful than valuable, I think Dorothea begins her story by spurning the greatest prize the secular world of Middle-march holds: the treasure of fellowship. Family jewels are a clasp from the past; they are far from Heaven, but through them, we touch the flesh and spirit of lost ancestors. Dorothea is less attuned to the spirit of her own mother than she is to Casaubon's Aunt Julia, whose miniature morphs romantically into the enticing face of Will Ladislaw, Aunt Julia's grandson who will become Dorothea's second husband (ch. 9, 70; ch 28, 258). Dorothea's ancestral bond is capricious and impersonal, not intimate or tactile.

As for the Maltese, poor Dorothea is rejecting an enchantingly sympathetic friend, one unavailable among Middlemarch humans; even mercurial Will is too self-absorbed to emulate this responsive dog. A Maltese is uncommonly agile and preternaturally attuned to human steps and sounds. No healthy Maltese would let Dorothea, or anyone, tread on it; before the foot reached it, it would bark or skitter out of the way. Dorothea's condescension toward a clever little dog teaches her nothing about the fellowship of marriage. She will continually tread on her less clever and more fragile husband Casaubon, until he wilts. A Maltese sensing her steps and missteps might have helped her self-consciousness evolve into self-awareness.

Of course, according to the rules of courtship, Dorothea has to reject the Maltese: for Sir James, the dog portends a marriage proposal, as does the horse he offers, which she also rejects; in the still-rural world of Middlemarch, animals, not money, are the visible counters of courtship. Still, Dorothea is too myopic to know that Sir James is courting her, and even if she has inklings, she never plays by the rules; mightn't she keep the animals and forfeit the husband? Rejecting the horse seems to me a loss; not only does Dorothea love riding so intensely that she "always looked forward to renouncing it" (10) but a good rider is in perpetual communion with her horse. Riding is not only erotic excitement, though it is that; it throws a skilled rider into constant contact with the body of another, faster and stronger, creature.

Horses, though, can be perilous in George Eliot's novels, as Fred Vincy's disastrous venture into horse-trading shows. Mr. Tulliver in *The Mill on the Floss* and Dunstan Cass in *Silas Marner* gallop off on horses to their doom; in *Daniel Deronda*, Gwendolen Harleth's acceptance of a horse from the sinister Grandcourt is her first step into an evil abyss. It might be prudent to turn down Sir James's horse, but rejecting the dog seems to me a tragic error. For hundreds of pages, I wondered what happened to the Maltese, waiting until page 515 to learn that, as Dorothea had scornfully suggested at the beginning, it has gone to Dorothea's literal-minded sister Celia, now Sir James's wife. Celia is too absorbed in her baby Arthur to notice the dog, but I can only hope that pampered little Arthur will play with it when he is old enough, if Middlemarch characters ever play, and the neglected Maltese will have a friend at last.

Lovers of George Eliot are quick to exonerate Dorothea from dog-hating. Felicia Bonaparte's excellent introduction to the 1997 Oxford World's Classics edition assures us that "Eliot was very fond" of dogs, and so, finally, is Dorothea, for she "owns a St. Bernard named Monk" (xxvi). But Monk is actually, of course, her uncle Mr. Brooke's dog, part of the slovenly milieu of his estate Tipton Grange; when she marries, Dorothea fortunately makes no attempt to bring Monk to Casaubon's gloomy home at Lowick. When she returns to Tipton, she is too busy suffering to pay attention to Monk: "She leaned her back against the window-frame, and laid her hand on the dog's head; for though, as we know, she was not fond of pets that must be held in the hands or trodden on, she was always attentive to the feelings of dogs, and very polite if she had to decline their advances" (ch. 39, 366). Compare Dorothea's distant noblesse oblige to Mary Garth's easy interchange with her "small black-and-tan terrier," who may be no bigger than the Maltese:

> She took his fore-paws in one hand, and lifted up the forefinger of the other, while the dog wrinkled his brows and looked embarrassed. "Fly, Fly, I am ashamed of you. . . . This is not becom-

ing in a sensible dog; anybody would think you were a silly young gentleman." (ch. 52, 483)

Mary Garth is no model for Dorothea in great things, for she clings rigidly to the status quo; but her freedom to hold her terrier and share her wit with him exemplifies the fellowship Dorothea longs for. Her rejection of animals is not only a denial of physicality and the body, though it is that; it also withholds the sympathy so needed in Middlemarch, yet so generally absent from it.

No doubt my irritation at Dorothea is subjective, at least as far as jewels and dogs are concerned, but it pervades my reading of the novel and deepens my appreciation of its sometimes duplicitous subtlety. Though *Middlemarch* claims to be spinning an encompassing web in which egoism and secrecy implicate us all, it also seduces us into exonerating Dorothea from selfish humanity by making her as much a monument as the icon of Saint Theresa who presides over the novel's prelude. Both Ladislaw and Lydgate enthrone Dorothea in reverential imagery, enticing the reader to do the same. For most of the novel, Will wants less love from her than benediction:

> The remote worship of a woman throned out of their reach plays a great part in men's lives, but in most cases the worshipper longs for some queenly recognition, some approving sign by which his soul's sovereign may cheer him without descending from her high place. That was precisely what Will wanted. (ch. 22, 204)

In almost the same imagery, though he claims "a man can make a friend of her," Lydgate disregards friendship for a dream of a woman fixed safely in a high place. After Dorothea has subsidized his hospital and covered his debts, Lydgate rhapsodizes her in a strangely antimaterial hymn:

> "This young creature has a heart large enough for the Virgin Mary. She evidently thinks nothing of her own future, and would pledge away half her income at once, as if she wanted nothing for herself but a chair to sit in from which she can look down with those clear eyes at the poor mortals who pray to her." (ch. 76, 723)

Verbal pictures of Dorothea enthroned are strewn throughout *Middlemarch*, so that the reader, like the worshipful men around her, perceives less an active character than a charismatic icon. Slyly, George Eliot lures us into reading *Middlemarch* as a Dickens novel, with Dorothea a generic figure of salvation like Florence Dombey, swooping from a self-generated Heaven to redeem weary men. But George Eliot is smarter about people, both sanctified women and sanctifying men, than Dickens is.

For Rosamond Vincy also becomes a picture to Lydgate and Ladislaw. True, she is only a domestic miniature, a nymph tinkling decoratively at her piano, framed, not enthroned, a drawing-room respite from men's important affairs, not a beacon of inspiration. Rosamond, the novel's selfish and trivial apparent antiheroine, who aims to ensnare all men while blessing none, becomes the conduit of male delusion, by implication allowing sanctified Dorothea's overflowing spirituality to appear authentic: Rosamond's steely blond blandness makes her look like the Satanic opposite of good Dorothea. In fact, though, they are similarly locked into the poses that loving men compose, and their wifely performances are similarly, softly, murderous.

"But why all this Dorothea-bashing?" the reader may ask. Surely Dorothea is noble, if thwarted by "the meanness of opportunity" (prelude, 3), with Rosamond, her worldly foil, exemplifying that very meanness. In the tapestry of *Middlemarch*, though, I think Dorothea and Rosamond are more alike than different.[1] My suspicion of Dorothea as heroine is only tangentially related to the familiar feminist complaint against George Eliot, who allegedly blocks Dorothea from doing anything commensurate with her potential grandeur.[2] Rather, I think wily George Eliot created a character who by nature would do nothing but batten, with the best intentions, on those who try to achieve, erecting a lovely idol for deluded readers just as Rosamond is a lovely idol for sentimental men.

My evidence concerns not dogs this time but Dorothea's vulnerable first husband Mr. Casaubon, who pours his diminishing energy into a book that is probably unwritable. Dorothea marries him to exalt herself into becoming his student and research assistant, but almost instantly, she falls into disenchantment with his great work.

Because reading and writing are the heart of my life, as they were of George Eliot's, I have always identified with Casaubon. Personal disclosure: I hate people asking dulcetly when my book will be finished, as Dorothea does incessantly. I find Dorothea's well-intentioned probing particularly grating because she, quite picturesquely, never reads. Pictures of Dorothea dreaming over a book are almost as recurrent, and iconic, as those of Dorothea enthroned: "Celia observed that Dorothea, instead of settling down with her usual diligent interest to some occupation, leaned her elbow on an open book and looked out of the window at the great cedar silvered with the damp" (ch. 5, 44). To Mr. Brooke's patronizing caution "We must not have you getting too learned for a woman, you know," she can honestly reassure him: "There is no fear of that, uncle.... When I want to be busy with books, I am often playing truant among my thoughts. I find it is not so easy to be learned as to plan cottages" (ch. 39, 364). In *The Mill on the Floss*, George Eliot's earlier, less well-bred Maggie Tulliver read ferociously, often dangerously, and panted to be learned, but Dorothea, who is closer to Jane Austen's imperious dilettante Emma Woodhouse than she is to Maggie, is wealthy enough to covet the trappings of learning without actually studying—and, like Emma, Dorothea is sufficiently immune from poverty to seek out the poor for the good of her own soul, rather than enduring poverty as Maggie does.

From the beginning to the end of *Middlemarch*, Dorothea expresses her sensibility by not reading:

> Here was a weighty subject which, if she could but lay hold of it, would certainly keep her mind steady. Unhappily her mind slipped off it for a whole hour; and at the end she found herself reading sentences twice over with an intense consciousness of many things, but not of any one thing contained in the text. This was hopeless. (ch. 83, 756)

It is left to us to decide whether these pictures illustrate her great soul or her Rosamond-like veneer of pseudoculture. Marriage to a scholar, even an amateur one, teaches her only to disdain scholarship as lightly as Rosamond disdains Lydgate's puttering around with corpses. I see no great distance between Rosamond's ignorant dismissal of medicine—"I do not think it is a nice profession, dear" (ch. 45, 430)—and Dorothea's disingenuous dismissal of scholarship: "But it is very difficult to be learned; it seems as if people were worn out on the way to great thoughts, and can never enjoy them because they are too tired" (ch. 37, 341).

George Eliot of all people knew that it is indeed difficult to be learned, and so, I assume, do most readers of this essay. Is it adorable of Dorothea to dream over books instead of reading them, to sigh that great thoughts are tiring, to denigrate Casaubon's life's work primarily on the authority of jealous Will Ladislaw? We all know that Rosamond, like Laure, the homicidal actress who was Lydgate's first love, obliquely murders her husband. If we need proof, we have Lydgate's own despairing diagnosis of his wife as a "basil plant," which he glosses by explaining to her that basil "had flourished wonderfully on a murdered man's brains" (finale, 782). Rosamond is an easy target of satiric censure, but Dorothea may also have a touch of basil. Her offers of help to Casaubon are, as he senses, implicit criticisms, especially once she decides his book is worthless; her later hounding of the dying man to change his will in favor of Ladislaw is as abrasive as the more voracious relatives hounding dying Peter Featherstone about his will. Most devastatingly, her refusal even to try to work on Casaubon's Key to All Mythologies after his death is as consummate a posthumous murder as a spouse can commit, sealing her husband alone forever in the tomb he designed for her in life.

Just as I wish Dorothea had kept the little Maltese, I wish she had done something with the Synoptical Tabulation Casaubon left for her. Instead of reading it, she writes a plaintive justification to the dead: "I could not use it. Do you not see now that I could not submit my soul to yours, by working hopelessly at what I have no belief in?" (ch. 54, 506–7) I would not expect Dorothea to write the entire Key, hard on her though I may seem, but surely, had she studied her husband's notes, she would have found something of some value to extract, if only as a memorial. One thinks prophetically of George Eliot, shattered by the death of George Henry Lewes, diligently preparing for publication the final two volumes of his posthumous *Problems of Life and Mind*, an enterprise as monumental as Casaubon's. True, unlike George Eliot, Dorothea neither loves, trusts, nor depends on Casaubon, but then Dorothea has nothing else to do. One may argue that Lewes was a proven talent, while Casaubon is a deluded pedant, but whose business is it to draw that distinction? Dorothea has no more authority than Rosamond to say her husband's work is valueless; the girl who began by wanting to be learned soon sighs at the very thought of great thoughts. Though she talks a lot about work and vocation, she herself has not worked hard enough to say her husband's work is insufficiently great, or not great at all, or not even good.

DOROTHEA AND ROSAMOND ARE YOKED together less by inherent egotism or the human condition than by the conditions of wifehood—an antechamber of the "dim lights and tangled circumstances" *Middlemarch* invokes but never names. Both Dorothea and Rosamond aim to elevate themselves by marrying exceptional men, but as wives, by definition, they are shut out from the sanctuary of male achievement. Casaubon anticipates an ardent acolyte:

> He had formerly observed with approbation her capacity for worshipping the right objects; he now foresaw with sudden terror that this capacity might be replaced by presumption, this worship by the most exasperating of all criticism,—that which sees vaguely a great many fine ends, and has not the least notion of what it costs to reach them. (ch. 20, 188)

Lydgate cherishes similar self-deifying assumptions—"he held it one of the prettiest attitudes of the feminine mind to adore a man's pre-eminence without too precise a knowledge of what it consisted in" (ch. 27, 251)—and he falls into the same lacerating abandonment. But when the great man flounders, what happens to the life of his wife?

Caleb Garth, that model of rectitude and traditionalism, puts it with his usual pithiness: "a woman, let her be as good as she may, has got to put up with the life her husband makes for her" (ch. 25, 242). Caleb makes usable household objects, but if a man is entombed with ancient gods or entangled in medical disputes, he is unlikely to be equipped, emotionally or materially, to make a life for a wife. Since her husband's putative great work is her only liferaft (at the end of the novel, Dorothea and Rosamond cling to each other "as if they had been in a shipwreck" [ch. 81, 749]), a wife must attempt to control that sanctified work in order to have a life at all. Such thralldom does not make for greatness of soul.

The oppressive medium of *Middlemarch*, with its dim lights and tangled circumstances, thwarts men and women alike, but George Eliot is sometimes so scathing about wifehood that she seems to anticipate explicitly feminist imagery like that of John Stuart Mill in *The Subjection of Women*, whose suffocating medium is not, like that of *Middlemarch*, an unchanging cosmic deposit but an artificial environment constructed solely to stunt women:

> What is now called the nature of women is an eminently artificial thing—the result of forced repression in some directions, unnatural stimulation in others. . . . a hot-house and stove cultivation has always been carried on of some of the capabilities of their nature, for the benefit of their masters. Then, because certain products of the general vital force sprout luxuriantly and reach a great development in this heated atmosphere and under this active nurture and watering, while other shoots from the same root, which are left outside in the wintery air, with ice purposely heaped all round them, have a stunted growth, and some are burnt off with fire and disappear; men . . . indolently believe that the tree grows of itself in the way they have made it grow, and that it would die if one half of it were not kept in a vapour bath and the other half in snow. (Mill, 22–3)

In Mill's *Subjection,* as in *Middlemarch*, wives are the victims and the culprits of unnatural cultivation, not of the thwarted human condition. The end of the *Subjection* is an indictment of wives more explicit, if not more devastating, than anything in *Middlemarch:*

> The wife is the auxiliary of the common public opinion. A man who is married to a woman his inferior in intelligence, finds her a perpetual dead weight, a drag, upon every aspiration of his to be better than public opinion requires him to be. It is hardly possible for one who is in these bonds, to attain exalted virtue. (Mill, 80)

Such partisan language would have been anathema to George Eliot, who aims to draw her characters together, but significantly, her narrator does reserve the word "tragedy" for self-immolated men, especially Casaubon. Dorothea and Rosamond are relegated to postures of melodrama, with the nobility of one balancing the pettiness of the other, though like most melodramatic personifications they are really two facets of a single character, one alarmingly close to Mill's "dead weight."

There is much striving in *Middlemarch*, but little protest: both Dorothea and Rosamond turn against their husbands' work, but neither questions the conditions that stunt her own life. Though most readers remember the women's stories, for me at least, the book lives through its excruciating accounts of Casaubon and Lydgate, the two exemplary husbands who, once they marry, are strangled by their own aspirations. Without commenting on its denunciations, as Dickens would have done, *Middlemarch* seems to provide a scathing account of marriage as an institution. Of course the novel includes salutary exceptions, notably the durable marriage of Mary Garth and Fred Vincy, whose union, the finale implies, is so firmly rooted that it survives like a tree to this day. Mary, of course, has no exalted reforming ambitions; she keeps loving Fred because they were engaged as children with an umbrella-ring, and she fears change (sensibly, perhaps, in this milieu). Moreover, Mary has a constructive father who remakes floundering Fred as a farmer, thus putting him in a position to give Mary a life much like her mother's. Caleb is the only successful patron in *Middlemarch*, no doubt because he represents an older rural England; as in so much British fiction, the land, or what is left of it, saves and preserves.

Obliquely, the novel assures us that marriage does not always lacerate; even Dorothea and Rosamond, rootless compared to Mary Garth, thrive, apparently, in second marriages, though these unions that flourish beyond the ending are as cloudy as David Copperfield's culminating marriage to perfect Agnes after he has exorcised the wrong impulses that were the heart of his story. Most of *Middlemarch* concerns married erosion.

This is not to revive the old dull debate about whether George Eliot was, covertly or inadvertently, a feminist. All nonrural institutions in *Middlemarch*, from the ballot to medicine to the church to Parliament, seem as pointlessly ensnaring as marriage. Moreover, marriage scarcely discriminates against women. As I find myself repeating endlessly, entangled husbands suffer far more memorably than trapped wives do: we watch Dorothea and Rosamond pose, but, at least if we have tried to achieve anything ourselves, we live with Lydgate and Casaubon. Moreover, *Middlemarch* contains a chorus of wifely voices beyond the trio of Dorothea, Rosamond, and Mary Garth. On the left, there is the radical—and of course, French—motto of the actress Laure, who kills her husband during a performance: "I do not like husbands. I will never have another" (ch. 15, 144). It is tempting, for those of us with a Gothic sensibility, to see Laure as the primitive tissue underlying wifehood in *Middlemarch*. After all, Dorothea and Rosamond also learn to perform wifehood, and as we have seen, they too kill their husbands "accidentally on purpose," as children used to say. But choosing Laure as a paradigm ignores the wife at the other end of the spectrum, Harriet Bulstrode, who, silly in the background throughout most of the story, inspires perhaps the most beautiful passage in the entire Victorian novel.

Harriet Bulstrode's husband Nicholas is not merely a failure but a liar, a criminal, probably—in the oblique manner of *Middlemarch* homicide—a murderer. A wealthy banker and sanctimonious evangelical, he is not a simple Dickensian hypocrite; he believes in his own religiosity, making his exposure late in the novel all the more devastating. Harriet learns his story only as he is about to be forced out of Middlemarch. Though this innocent jolly woman has every justification for leaving him, in an inspired performance of wifehood, she changes her costume as a

> way of expressing to all spectators visible or invisible that she had begun a new life in which she embraced humiliation. She took off all her ornaments and put on a plain black gown, and instead of wearing her much-adorned cap and large bows of hair, she brushed her hair down and put on a plain bonnet-cap, which made her look suddenly like an early Methodist. (ch. 74, 707)

The truest marriage we see is a marriage of guilt:

He burst out crying and they cried together, she sitting at his side. They could not yet speak to each other of the shame which she was bearing with him, or of the acts which had brought it down upon them. His confession was silent, and her promise of faithfulness was silent. Open-minded as she was, she nevertheless shrank from the words which would have expressed their mutual consciousness, as she would have shrunk from flakes of fire. She could not say, "How much is only slander and false suspicion?" and he did not say, "I am innocent." (ch. 74, 707–8)

The novel's only saintly self-renunciation is performed by one of its worldliest characters. To accompany it, George Eliot plays her sublimely simple prose like an organ, for George Eliot, like Dorothea, "likes giving up," reserving her most resonant commentary for moments of penance or loss. Surely, at least at the moment of our reading, Harriet Bulstrode is the paradigm of wifehood, an implicit reproach to her niece Rosamond: as Mrs. Bulstrode is embracing her husband's disgrace, in which Lydgate, along with his many other troubles, is more or less unfairly implicated, Rosamond is withdrawing into self-pitying fantasies about an affair with Will Ladislaw. Harriet Bulstrode even seems a retrospective reproach to Dorothea, who, though penitential garb suits her beauty more than it does blooming Mrs. Bulstrode's, has refused to embrace her husband's Key in the spirit that impels Harriet to embrace her husband's crimes. Surely the old woman exemplifies ideal self-sacrifice to these two young wives.

When we last see her, though, her role as exemplary wife is not so clear. Like the other wives, she has remained ignorant of her husband's actual deeds—here, his crimes—though she suffers for them: Bulstrode shrinks from any confession that might evoke the word "murder." Her renunciation brings neither communion nor solace, simply erosion:

Set free by [her daughters'] absence from the intolerable necessity of accounting for her grief or of beholding their frightened wonder, she could live unconstrainedly with the sorrow that was every day streaking her hair with whiteness and making her eyelids languid. . . . Bulstrode, sitting opposite to her, ached at the sight of that grief-worn face, which two months before had been bright and blooming. It had aged to keep sad company with his own withered features. (ch. 85, 773–4)

No one is healed or redeemed. Harriet Bulstrode's glorious gesture of fidelity leads only to a shared decay. No doubt she has given a more sublime performance than that of her actress antitype Laure, with her laconic "I do not like husbands. I will never have another," but is she really an exemplar for the younger wives? Is this withering, blind grief what we want for our blooming Dorothea and Rosamond? Surely it seems a more natural ending to have them thriving in second marriages, even, in Rosamond's case, a worldly one or, in Dorothea's, an obscuring one.

THIS PERPLEXITY IS THE WEB of *Middlemarch*. Rhetorically, this web draws the characters together. The famous experiment with the pier-glass and the candle that opens chapter 27, whereby random scratches on the glass seem to orbit purposefully around the light, illuminates the egoism of all the characters, not just Rosamond's (ch. 27, 248); it may also illuminate the reader's need to make the novel more coherent than it is. The more stirring, because deceptively commonplace, passage about the ordinariness of tragedy: "If we had a keen vision and feeling for all ordinary human life, it would be like hearing the grass grow and the squirrel's heart beat, and we should die of that roar which lies on the other side of silence" (ch. 20, 182) glosses the Casaubons' honeymoon, but ostensibly—while we read at least—it articulates all of our heartbeats, all of our silent roars. The narrator of *Middlemarch* uses the material world, animal and inorganic, to draw us together in a comprehensive lament, but the stories she tells alienate while they implicate us.

The symphony of wives that composes much of *Middlemarch* scarcely allows us to extract an essence of wifeliness; rather, it confuses noble with mean, renunciation with murder. With the exception of wholesome Mary Garth, whose father remakes her suitor to her specifications, all the wives live more or less the same story, but instead of falling into order on the moral scale, they subvert each other. Dorothea's high-mindedness throws Rosamond's selfishness into relief, but once we see, or sense, that they are judging their husbands in the same way, Dorothea feels less noble and Rosamond's withdrawal becomes comprehensible, though we have been trained not to like her. And what is their precise relation to the distasteful alternatives of Laure's murder or Harriet Bulstrode's self-immolation? We want someone to believe in, even though we are no longer Victorians, but we end up with a snarl of motives and lives.

The characters who enmesh our heroes, most notably seemingly immune Dorothea, are not only wives or even women: toward the end of the novel, Dorothea enters into a tacit competition with the villainous Nicholas Bulstrode as to who can best support needy men. When Raffles the blackmailer arrives to expose Bulstrode, one of whose sins was defrauding Will Ladislaw's mother, Bulstrode offers Will a grand sum as recompense. Will, despite his poverty, grandly rejects the banker's hush money. In the high romance at the end of the novel, wealthy Dorothea promises to marry Will, and to subsidize him as well, even though she must give up Casaubon's fortune and fall back on her own: "We could live quite well on my own fortune—it is too much—seven hundred a-year—I want so little—no new clothes—and I will learn what everything costs" (ch. 83, 762). Will might presumably want new clothes for his career in Parliament, but his participation in any financial transaction is cleansed, even made idealistic and childlike, by the sweetness with which Dorothea holds out her money, apparently redeeming the desperately self-interested calculations of Bulstrode.

In the same manner, Dorothea replaces Bulstrode as Lydgate's patron, rescuing both the New Hospital and the doctor himself, who, though he is drowning in debts, is fatally compromised when he accepts money from Bulstrode. When Dorothea grandly writes Lydgate a sanctified check, Lydgate, cleansed, can save himself by returning Bulstrode's corrupt gift. Twice, Dorothea consecrates Bulstrode's wicked money, blessing rather than contaminating the men who need it. It may be, though, that Bulstrode's troubling amalgam of religiosity, philanthropy, and wealth rubs off on Dorothea after all. Both try to purify their fortune by giving it away; both involve themselves in Will Ladislaw's ancestry; and most important, they are the only praying (and paying) characters in the novel. Their flaunted piety functions as spiritual distraction from their wealth. Dorothea is certainly an antidote to Bulstrode, in that she defrauds no one but herself; but if we read irreverently, the secretive old man sheds a changed light on the pure young woman because they are doing the same thing: both engage in pious philanthropy. Both pray and pay.

Throughout *Middlemarch*, low characters like Bulstrode illuminate exemplars like Dorothea. At several points, the narrator apologizes, with awkward jocularity, for the inclusion of "low people" in her epic:

> whatever has been or is to be narrated by me about low people, may be ennobled by being considered a parable; so that if any bad habits and ugly consequences are brought into view, the reader may have the relief of regarding them as not more than figuratively ungenteel, and may feel himself virtually in company with persons of some style. Thus while I tell the truth about loobies, my reader's imagination need not be entirely excluded from an occupation with lords; and the petty sums which any bankrupt of high standing would be sorry to retire upon, may be lifted to the level of high commercial transactions by the inexpensive addition of proportional ciphers. (ch. 35, 320)

In theory lowness is a matter of class and money; ironically, the narrator assures us that the low exist only as parables for the high. This apology sits oddly on an author whose reputation was founded on the glorification of the supposedly low Adam Bede and Maggie Tulliver, but in the better-bred *Middlemarch*, low characters are deprived of moral elevation; they are vulgar opportunists like frog-faced Rigg Featherstone and his still coarser stepfather Raffles. These people are so low that they are exiled from the human condition, for they cannot suffer richly. Neither Rigg Featherstone nor Raffles is included in the narrator's definition of "universal" tragedy; they are too coarse to join the roar that lies on the other side of silence; so, for that matter, are Featherstone himself and his greedy relatives. These last would be more at home in Dickens's *Great Expectations*, whose only authentic sufferer is the charmed sinner who tells the story, than they are in the supposedly comprehensive web of *Middlemarch*. In George Eliot's novel, the low characters lack the entitlement of inner lives, but within its restricted social parameters, "low" and "high" are resonant words, keys to a complex moral interdependence whereby the low enacts what the high withholds.

On a moral scale, Rosamond and Bulstrode are lower than Dorothea, but as the novel unfolds they also become Dorothea; Rosamond lethally repudiates her husband's mission as Dorothea does, while the murdering Laure and the suicidally self-immolating Harriet Bulstrode oscillate for possession of her struggle to be a perfect wife. Bulstrode himself casts a sickly air of falsity over her piety about her wealth. Will Ladislaw too, another character who seems immune from the dim lights and tangled circumstances that hamstring Middlemarch citizens, has a cluster of low characters who dim his luminosity. Like Will, but more selfishly, Fred Vincy flounders about in search of a vocation, but Fred has the sturdy Garths to pound him into shape, while Will has only his erratic employer, Mr. Brooke, as amorphous a dilettante as he is, and his dream of Dorothea, who is herself, perhaps, a dream. Will's charming incoherence becomes, in Fred, diseased: for a Middlemarch man, a vocation may be doom, but the absence of vocation sows sorrow and disorder. As a directionless outsider, Will is echoed by the novel's most disreputable characters: Rigg Featherstone, another illegitimate son inserted like a walking dissonance into the community, and Raffles, an uncontrolled itinerant like Will and a carrier of secrets—the same secrets Will's ancestry incarnates. Like Will, Raffles refuses to leave Middlemarch, and both topple households—the Bulstrodes, the Casaubons, the Lydgates—by their persistent presence. Will wants to believe that his love story removes him to "a world apart, where the sunshine fell on tall white lilies, where no evil lurked, and no other soul entered" (ch. 82, 755), but if we are reading attentively we know that *Middlemarch* has no such set-off world. Instead of white lilies, there are obnoxious growths that taint the purest lovers. No character is free from contamination by low recapitulations of his disinterested purity.

The characters in *Middlemarch* infect each other so easily, at least as I read the novel, because, like Dickens's characters, they are unamenable to change. The narrator is so famously wise, so penetrating and embracing, that we tend to attribute her versatility to her people. After all, in the words of Mr. Farebrother, the town's natural historian manqué, and of the many appreciative critics who have quoted him since the novel was written: "character is not cut in marble—it is not something solid and unalterable. It is something living and changing, and may become diseased as our bodies do" (ch. 72, 692). This is a wonderful gloss on the novel we think we are reading, but actually, the characters in *Middlemarch* change very little; they simply reveal facets of themselves, in large part through the echoing characters who affect our attitudes almost subliminally. Dorothea ends as she began, with her ardor intact to simultaneously possess and renounce—at the beginning she spurns, then keeps, her mother's jewels; at the end she rejects and retains her fortune. Less radiant characters are more obviously static: Casaubon or Rosamond bruised are Casaubon and Rosamond still.

Lydgate, who receives the most detailed case history in *Middlemarch*, also finds his end in his beginning: his visionary voyages of discovery, his "spots of commonness" (an inherent, not an acquired, disease) that translate into sexist snobbery, his early obsession with an unregenerate husband-murderer, all recapitulate themselves in excruciating detail as his life develops, but he writes no new stories for himself. At the end, as with Casaubon, Lydgate broken is Lydgate still. Fred and Mary pride themselves on their fidelity to what they were, but in fact all the characters end up encased in their beginnings. It is their resistance to change that makes them vulnerable to infection by each other.

The titles of the different books yoke the characters together still more inextricably. The first book, "Miss Brooke," deludes us into thinking Dorothea is an autonomous, free-standing character, but parallel destinies quickly crowd around her. "Old and Young," like the last book, "Sunset and Sunrise," presents a deceptive contrast, for the young characters—Lydgate, Dorothea, Fred, Mary Garth— are in increasing subjection to the old ones, Bulstrode, Casaubon, Featherstone, who drink their youth in "a sort of vampire's feast in the sense of mastery" (ch. 16, 146), as the Middlemarch chorus says of Bulstrode. As the novel continues, the young characters age irreparably, the elegiac tone of the finale making "sunrises and sunsets" indistinguishable. Other books ("Waiting for Death," "The Dead Hand," "The Widow and the Wife") exist less to highlight individual stories than to cast a pall over all stories: through much of "Waiting for Death," young Fred seems closer to death than the desiccated characters who will actually die, while the other young characters live mournful lives; "The Dead Hand" is more potently inhibiting in the living—Bulstrode, Raffles, Mr. Brooke, the deadening medium of Middlemarch itself—than in Featherstone's or Casaubon's ineffectual wills; by the time of "The Widow and the Wife," Lydgate is so financially and morally paralyzed that it is hard to distinguish Rosamond from the literally widowed Dorothea. Death, not any one narrative, is the star of all these books, blanketing all stories not as life's end but as its primary condition. Low or high, the characters are inhibited not only by Middlemarch but by each other's plots.

"Everything is so sad," says callow Rosamond at the end (ch. 81, 750). I think, as she is so often, she is right. Many of us have been assured that, properly understood, at least for the mature reader, *Middlemarch* is not a sad book,[3] but for me at the age of sixty, it seems as sad as it did when I was nineteen. It is a novel about inhibition and entrapment, whose grand heroine Dorothea is bound to the pettiest and most degraded of her fellow-citizens. She scarcely knows these low people, for she lives in a solitary daydream of herself, but they cling to her throughout her story. For me, no "mature" reading could mitigate the diminution that is *Middlemarch*, but its sadness might have been alleviated had a little Maltese puppy been allowed in to clear its heavy air.

Notes

1. My association of Dorothea with Rosamond is not at all original; their kinship was one of the most startling insights of early feminist criticism; see for instance Beer, 188–9, and Gilbert and Gubar, 502–21. For the

most part, though, feminists legitimized Rosamond's angry intransigence by endowing it with Dorothea's grandeur. I hope to dim Dorothea's unearned aura of magnificence by exposing the Rosamond within her.

2. Lee R. Edwards has written what still seems to me the most appealing indictment of *Middlemarch*, especially of smug teachers who use Dorothea's destiny to reproach restless female students.

3. Many contributors to Kathleen Blake's revealing collection of essays about the difficulties of teaching *Middlemarch* strain to assure chafing undergraduates that the novel is not depressing but wise and true; see especially Jeanie Thomas, "Middlemarch in the Undergraduate Classroom," which concludes with the tactful hope that students who resent the novel—like Lee R. Edwards, cited above—will "return to Middlemarch later in their lives, when they may be ready to experience it differently" (170). See also Karen Chase's insistence that the ending is not after all sad: "The note of tragic compulsion fades into a note of romantic liberation, the large symphonic amplitude preventing any one tone from becoming final" (88). To me, though, the integrity of *Middlemarch* is its unrepentant sadness.

References

Beer, Patricia. *Reader, I Married Him: A Study of the Women Characters of Jane Austen, Charlotte Brontë, Elizabeth Gaskell and George Eliot.* New York: Barnes and Noble, 1974.

Blake, Kathleen, ed. *Approaches to Teaching Eliot's "Middlemarch."* New York: Modern Language Association, 1990.

Bonaparte, Felicia. Introduction to *Middlemarch,* by George Eliot. Oxford World's Classics. Oxford: Oxford University Press, 1997.

Chase, Karen. *George Eliot: "Middlemarch."* Landmarks of World Literature. Cambridge: Cambridge University Press, 1991.

Edwards, Lee R. "Women, Energy, and *Middlemarch*." *Massachusetts Review* 13 (1972), 223–38.

Gilbert, Sandra M., and Susan Gubar. *The Madwoman in the Attic: The Woman Writer and the Nineteenth-Century Literary Imagination* (1979). 2nd ed. New Haven: Yale University Press, 2000.

Mill, John Stuart. *The Subjection of Women.* 1869; reprint, Cambridge, Mass: MIT Press, 1970.

6

Negotiating *Middlemarch*

ELIZABETH DEEDS ERMARTH

◆ ◆ ◆

> The world is neither significant nor absurd. It is,
> quite simply. . . . Around us, defying the noisy
> pack of our animistic desires or protective adjec-
> tives, things *are there*.
>
> —Alain Robbe-Grillet

> To be right: who still wants to be? A few fools.
>
> —André Gide

THE BROAD POINT of this essay is to bring back into focus how original and innovative George Eliot's work was in *Middlemarch*, how forward looking philosophically and practically. Before she attempted fiction she thought through problems that have yet to dawn on some of her interpreters and that inform not just the local concerns of Middlemarchers but the strategies of the novel. The medium is the message in *Middlemarch*, as in all George Eliot's works; she is an artist first, and art is a matter of the "how," not the "what."

How the text unfolds is far more important a key to understanding it than any statements from this or any text, however explicit, because the method reveals the philosophical biases and assumptions of the text, whether they are explicitly acknowledged or not. This is true of every writer; what may be unique to George Eliot is her philosophical adequacy and the degree to which that adequacy has been thoroughly translated into art. The strategies of *Middlemarch* are based in specific philosophical traditions that reach from Spinoza almost to Lyotard and that are dedicated to circumventing the habitual dualism of the

Cartesian tradition. Where Descartes splits mind and body in order to elevate the former and depreciate the latter, the strategies of *Middlemarch* work in the opposite direction, with significant social and personal implications. For example, the novel entirely deconstructs the "metaphysical system of history" that it has so often been said to represent, as J. Hillis Miller noted long ago (470). Of course, philosophical adequacy is not a prerequisite for reading or enjoying *Middlemarch*; generations of readers have read and appreciated the novel without knowing a thing about George Eliot's essays and translations. However, knowing those texts *does* seem necessary for critics whose aim is to do justice to her achievement and to avoid misrepresenting it.

In making her commitment to art, George Eliot explicitly rejects the kind of dualistic distinction between form and content that has been the curse of art in modernity. She declares in her sketchy "Notes On Form In Art" that art is a condition, not a container. "Poetic Form was not begotten by thinking it out or framing it as a shell which should hold emotional expression, any more than the shell of an animal arises before the living creature." Instead, "emotion, by its tendency to repetition, i.e., rhythmic persistence," creates form with varying degrees of "diversifying thought." Art is experimental in the way a bivalve shell is experimental: the rhythmic response of its "unstable inhabitant" to the conditions of growth (*Essays*, 432–5). I like to think that her sketchy statement in this short essay, written well after she started writing fiction, could easily be amplified by this one, written a century later by a very different novelist:

> Political life ceaselessly obliges us to assume certain known significations: social, historical, moral. Art is more modest—or more ambitious: in art, nothing is ever known in advance.
>
> Before the work of art there is nothing—no certainty, no thesis, no message. To believe that the novelist has "something to say" and that he then looks for a way to say it represents the gravest of misconceptions. For it is precisely this 'way,' this manner of speaking, which constitutes his enterprise as a writer, an enterprise more obscure than any other, and which will later be the uncertain content of his book. Ultimately it is perhaps this uncertain content of an obscure enterprise of form which will

best serve the cause of freedom. But who knows how long that will take? (Robbe-Grillet, 141–2)

George Eliot would have agreed. Her terms anticipate other discussions of a century later, even when she explicitly defines form as "difference": "fundamentally, form is unlikeness. . . . & in consistency with this fundamental meaning, every difference is form" (*Essays*, 432–3). The linguistic and philosophical implications of such ideas, still reverberating a century and a half later, were not marginal or exotic to George Eliot but central to her commitments and achievement.

Beginning with its form, then, I want to consider one way in which *Middlemarch* engages its readers in an experimental enterprise with fairly radical outcomes. This novel accepts quietly many of the ideas about identity and about language that were already stirring in the nineteenth century and that later became focal in twentieth–century interpretation, first in phenomenology and existentialism and later in poststructuralism. Merleau-Ponty's phrase "the only pre-existent Logos is the world itself" would not be a bad motto for her work; in Eliot's translation, Feuerbach already says in so many words and long before Sartre that existence precedes essence; and Lyotard's "differend" would be entirely intelligible to George Eliot, even though she would differ from his relatively radical conclusion: at least, radical relative to Cartesian epistemology. The difference I want to concentrate on is a particular narrative quality in *Middlemarch*, present at all levels of magnitude: the frustrating reversibility of almost every generalization it sponsors.

This reversibility is part of the pleasure, but also part of the problem of reading *Middlemarch*. The pleasures of reading this novel derive from the wider narrative horizon in which we can enjoy (by differing from) the foibles and limitations of the characters, can recognize some in-jokes, and can even feel some quiet admiration for particularly apt formulations well beyond any characters' ability. Her narrator says complex things with such wit and generosity that I feel delighted, and compelled to assent. "We are all of us born in moral stupidity, taking the world as an udder to feed our supreme selves" (ch. 21, 198); or, "There are characters which are continually

creating collisions and nodes for themselves in dramas which nobody is prepared to act with them" (*Middlemarch*, ch. 19, 179–80; all
further citations are to this edition). There is always an extra margin
for amusement in the narrative language, a kind of chronic risibility
in the text. "I was not speaking in a religious sense, Harriet. I spoke
as a mother" (ch. 31, 276); or "one's self-satisfaction is an untaxed
kind of property which it is very unpleasant to find depreciated" (ch.
16, 147); or "Solomon's Proverbs, I think, have omitted to say that as
the sore palate findeth grit, so an uneasy consciousness heareth in-
nuendoes" (ch. 31, 280). *Middlemarch* is full of small turns of vocabulary that open new vistas, such as the description "in poor Rosamond's mind there was not enough room for luxuries to look small
in" (ch. 69, 659); or the references to "Christian Carnivora" (ch. 35,
242) or to Casaubon's "small hungry shivering self" (ch. 29, 263); or
the characterization of Lydgate's situation in terms of "the hamper-
ing threadlike pressure of small social conditions" (ch. 18, 169)—a
quiet, literary joke for those in the know, linking Middlemarchers
with Lilliputians. There are the little dramas of indirection, like the
immortal breakfast conversation between Rosamond and Fred
Vincy on various matters of accompaniment: her piano to his flute,
in return for his accompaniment to her expedition in search of a potential husband (ch. 11). Sometimes a casual conversation carries an
implicit commentary, as with this self-revealing commentary by
people at a party on French influence and English tradition:

> "Lydgate has lots of ideas, quite new, about ventilation and diet,
> that sort of thing," resumed Mr. Brooke, after he had handed out
> Lady Chettam, and had returned to be civil to a group of Middle-
> marchers.
>   "Hang it, do you think that is quite sound?—upsetting the old
> treatment, which has made Englishmen what they are?" said Mr.
> Standish. (ch. 10, 85)

The fun here lies in the way perspectives multiply and balance.
Lydgate's ideas receive a certain transfiguration in Mr. Brooke's way
of putting things. Thus transfigured, these ideas receive decided
opposition from Mr. Standish, whose own reliance on tradition itself

requires some deconstruction. The little dramas and new vistas sometimes even include me, the reader: for example, when her narrator speaks of "the grins of suppressed bitterness or other conversational flavours which make half of us an affliction to our friends" (ch. 18, 166); or when the narrator characterizes Mr. Bulstrode's righteous public behavior and uneasy private mind with this metaphor: "If you are not proud of your cellar, there is no thrill of satisfaction in seeing your guest hold up his wine-glass to the light and look judicial. Such joys are reserved for conscious merit" (ch. 13, 115). Such marginal commentary, explicit and implicit, runs almost continuously through this novel, and the pleasure of the text consists precisely in the recognition of the extra edge that belongs to the narrative voice, that margin of wider perspective that implicates what is not explicit and is even largely unsuspected by characters. The pleasure has to do with the complexity of viewpoint and the clarity concerning differences between one point of view and another, even as they are held together in their comic contradictoriness by the distance the Nobody narrator maintains.

Such moments as this are continuous and constitute George Eliot's narrative sequence. Around one center of interest and attention, and then the next, and the next, shifting constellations of viewpoint gather, and dissolve. This complex treatment of perspective is a mystery of realist narration that even today remains only partially recognized. In these constellations are embodied the collective awareness of a culture, perhaps even the self-consciousness of the species, but in any case an invisible community of awareness in this novel that transcends the particular moment at the same time as it finds expression there.

George Eliot has few equals—perhaps no equals—when it comes to presenting this complex of awareness. Elsewhere I have called this representation the "Nobody" narrator in order to distinguish it from anything so limited as a particular individual viewpoint. This blend of consciousness, time, and language does not belong exclusively to any character or even to the historical George Eliot; the entire range of narrative awareness constitutes it; its narrative expression is precisely Nobody (Ermarth, 1998). George Eliot's management of this complex perspectival system constitutes one of her great achievements and accounts for much of the fun of reading her. That narrative slide from one view to another engages readers in a kind of suspense that has little to do with plot, and it reminds us continually that, while nothing is final, there may be a point of rest in the middle distance.

Unfortunately, as soon as one attempts to make a generalization stick to anything in her text, there is trouble. This is a difficulty in reading *Middlemarch*. All but the most carefully formulated conclusions about George Eliot seem reversible. No sooner do you say something definitive about her novels than you confront a counterbalancing consideration, a qualifying remark, that inevitable "on the other hand." Perhaps the archetype of such moments is the one in chapter 29 when the narrator says "One morning, some weeks after her arrival at Lowick, Dorothea—but why always Dorothea? Was her point of view the only possible one with regard to this marriage?" (261). The narrative then gives us the counterbalancing viewpoint. There is never a single way of looking at things in George Eliot. There is always that "on the other hand" that makes conclusions difficult.

Consider the matter of egoism (bad) and altruism (good), both commonplaces of George Eliot criticism. There are many examples in *Middlemarch* of egoism working its destructiveness, and these might seem rather unproblematically to recommend altruism. If thinking of oneself is worst, then thinking of others must be best. It seems an obvious conclusion, and it is one that has often been stated in George Eliot criticism and attributed to the author, sometimes as a symptom of her "inability" (think of it!) to deal with her abandonment of Christianity (often characterized as a "loss" by those following unquestioned conventional assumptions of what was going on in the nineteenth century). Consider one of George Eliot's best known comments on egoism, the pier-glass metaphor, which has itself become a critical commonplace.

> Your pier-glass or extensive surface of polished steel made to be rubbed by a housemaid, will be minutely and multitudinously scratched in all directions; but place now against it a lighted candle as a centre of illumination, and lo! the scratches will seem to

arrange themselves in a fine series of concentric circles round that little sun. It is demonstrable that the scratches are going everywhere impartially, and it is only your candle which produces the flattering illusion of concentric arrangement, its light falling with an exclusive optical selection. These things are a parable. The scratches are events, and the candle is the egoism of any person now absent—of Miss Vincy, for example. (ch. 27, 248)

No sooner does one recognize a critique of egoism in this passage than something whispers, "on the other hand." That little reduction at the end—the remark about someone who is absent—might sound the warning that all is not quite as it seems here. The curious thing about this pier-glass metaphor is its double message about egoism. On the one hand I can think of several examples of egoism in *Middlemarch* to which this passage might apply—Casaubon, Raffles, Bulstrode, and of course poor Miss Vincy. Clearly egoism can't be a good thing. "On the other hand," I recognize in Dorothea Brooke an important exception. She is always thinking of others; she considers Sir James from Celia's point of view. She *likes* giving up things, as her carnally minded sister complains. In fact Dorothea is far too good at the selflessness business and it gets her into trouble. She is so badly inexperienced at acting on, or even knowing her own personal feelings that she very nearly leaves her chance for happiness pointlessly in the dust. She is the altruist whose example recommends egoism.

George Eliot explicitly says as much in an essay entitled "We Should Distrust a Man Who Sets up Shop Purely for the Good of the Community" (*Essays*, 156). Altruism in George Eliot has little to do with selflessness or lack of ego; instead, it has to do with balancing the conflicting claims of ego and community. Pure egoism may be destructive on the one hand; but (here it is again) "on the other hand," a developed ego is necessary to independent and adult life. Dorothea's example simply stands in the way of what might otherwise have been an easy generalization about the pier-glass and about egoism. The metaphor asserts the powerfully narcissistic potential of ego, but it also asserts the *importance* of ego as a condition of light and order.

This reversibility keys into a strategy of the text that occurs in several different but related ways in *Middlemarch*: a strategy that engages readers in a process that turns toward, and then away from, every formulation. Furthermore, this "on the other hand" suggests coexistence, not cancellation. There is this view, belief, thought, or feeling; on the other hand, there is also that view, belief, thought, or feeling. The only cancellation that occurs in George Eliot's work is the cancellation of absolute truth claims, in other words, claims that do not allow for alternative claims. Claims of being "right" as opposed to everyone else's "wrong" are something that George Eliot considers key to the extinction of morality. In her essay on Goethe, she writes that "the line between the virtuous and the vicious, so far from being a necessary safeguard to morality, is itself an immoral fiction," and she praises Goethe's "large tolerance" (*Essays*, 147). Where Right and Wrong begin, morality and ethics are no more. Consider "Evangelical Teaching" in these terms, as George Eliot does in her article with that title: an essay still current in the early twenty-first century as the hilarious last word on religious intolerance masquerading as virtue. Her "on the other hand" simply provides the available alternative claims that cancel any likelihood that any one of them qualifies as universally valid truth. As I will show in a moment, this has nothing to do with her supposedly having been crippled by her loss of Christian faith, and everything to do with her positive admiration for alternative philosophies that she considered more adequate to the preservation of value than the narrow confidence that one's way is the "right" way because one knows no other.

BEFORE CONTINUING WITH THE BODY LANGUAGE of *Middlemarch*, a pause is in order to consider one of the most positive influences on George Eliot's ideas about morality: Spinoza's *Ethics*. Spinoza ranks right up there with Feuerbach at the top of key influences on George Eliot's thinking. Her translation of Ludwig Andreas Feuerbach's *The Essence of Christianity* (Das Wesen des Christentums, 1847) was published in 1854, just as she and Lewes took off for the Continent and a new life. For the next two years (1854–56) she translated Baruch Spinoza's *Ethics* (published in *Opera Posthuma*, 1677), although her translation remained unpublished until the late twentieth century, thanks first to local mismanagement by a harried and distracted Lewes, her consort, friend, and agent; and thereafter by the protracted dismissiveness of critics apparently unable to get over the fact that she was as intelligent and accomplished as she was. Her translation of the *Ethics* finally was published in Austria in 1981 but it remains widely unavailable, to the detriment of her reputation, the interpretation of her work, and probably even the development of so-called ethics programs in certain quarters of American business and government. Spinoza would do more than Aristotle can to mend the ways of economic man.

Elsewhere I have written more at length on her translation of Feuerbach and how that influenced her work (see especially Ermarth, 1975); here I emphasize Spinoza. It is striking that George Eliot chose to translate the two philosophers who lost market share to empiricists and dualists, specifically to Descartes and Marx. Just as Feuerbach was alternative to Marx in the nineteenth century, Spinoza was alternative to Descartes in the seventeenth century. George Eliot chose to translate into English two philosophers who celebrate the indissoluble unity of mind and body, idea and thing, thought and materiality. They deny the dualism essential to Cartesian philosophy and deny what Feuerbach (in her translation) calls "vulgar empiricism." From the Greeks to the Enlightenment, George Eliot writes in an essay, the prolonged error of philosophy has been the separation of ideas from things.

> Severing ideas from things is the fundamental error of philosophy, and, from Parmenides downwards, has issued in nothing but the bewilderment of the human intellect. Kant's classification of Infinity and Universality as ideas à priori, and of Space and time as purely subjective forms of the intelligence, is a further elaboration of this fundamental error. These abstract terms on which speculation has built its huge fabrics are simply the x and y by which we mark the boundary of our knowledge; they have no value except in connexion with the concrete. The abstract is derived from the concrete: what, then, can we expect from a philosophy the essence of which is the derivation of the concrete from the abstract? (*Essays*, 150–3)

The antidote to this kind of inept derivation is Spinoza and Feuerbach after him. George Eliot began translating Spinoza's *Tractatus
Theologico-politicus* in 1849, when she was thirty, as a calming exercise
during her beloved father's last illness; she never completed it. Five
years later, when she and Lewes embarked on their unconventional
life together, she began translating the *Ethics*, a text also known and
admired by the German Romantics. Far too much has been made of
the difficulty of reading Spinoza; he is much easier to read than
Kant. But initially his ideas may seem somewhat counter-intuitive
because Descartes won the toss for primacy in the seventeenth century and since then Western culture has been using tools of thought
forged by Cartesians. It is telling that George Eliot turned away from
this tradition in her two most important and formative translations.

Spinoza describes a cosmos that is complete, replete, perfect in itself without need and therefore without purpose. It is going
nowhere; it is sitting At Home. In George Eliot's translation, Spinoza
calls this cosmic completeness "Substance" (other translators, perhaps more influenced than George Eliot by Descartes, call it God or
Nature). There is no dualism in Substance; there are no Manichean
separations. Substance simply is, and is without deficiency or purpose. By definition, the human share of that cosmos, however, is
anything but complete and replete. Spinoza calls it Modality. Modal
existence is finite and deficient and incapable of being Substance: at
its worst purposive, and at its best approximating (though by definition never reaching) Substance. No worldly authority is exempt
from the laws limiting human understanding; any authority is relevant only to a locality, a time, a place, that is, to a mode of existence.

It is not difficult to see what George Eliot saw in Spinoza. If any
human "universal" is just a form of modal deficiency then there can
be no valid human claim to knowledge of universal truth. The
truth claim itself is a symptom of modal deficiency. Spinoza considers factionalism the greatest malignancy in the human condition, a
disturbance to tolerance and freedom, an expression of confusion, a
mistaking of modal experience for Substance. The spirit of tolerance
breathes through Spinoza's work, springing no doubt from Spinoza's experience of persecution, not from Protestants or the Inquisi-
tion from which his ancestors fled, but from orthodox Jews who re-

garded Spinoza as insufficiently orthodox. Spinoza's tolerance, like Goethe's, must have appealed to Mary Ann/Marian Evans soon to be Lewes, soon to be George Eliot, who was not only well on her way to philosophical adequacy, but had endured her own versions of persecution at the hands of the "righteous" in various drawing rooms and pulpits.

When George Eliot writes the essays that preceded her novels she returns frequently to ideas consistent with this nondualist vision she found in Feuerbach as well as Spinoza. She was very engaged politically, and knew many of the political radicals of her time. So it is with full knowledge of what she is saying when, eight years after the *Communist Manifesto* (1848) she wrote, in an 1856 review of Riehl, that "a universal social policy has no validity except on paper" (italics George Eliot's; *Essays*, 289). She chose Feuerbach over Marx, just as she chose Spinoza over Descartes, for reasons of philosophical adequacy to the conditions of life.

Those conditions as she sees them, and as Spinoza and Feuerbach describe them, are constituted by overlapping entangled systems of meaning and value, all of which are finite and none of which justify absolute truth claims. George Eliot set out to demonstrate the often unacknowledged role of such belief systems in practice. Mr. Bulstrode's desires are stronger than his theories, and his will is too weakly developed to admit it. The evangelical Mr. Bulstrode, who could have linked his wife-to-be with her lost daughter and who kept silent in order to marry the money for himself, is an immortal portrait of someone who uses supposedly "religious" (read factional) faith to rationalize crimes. "There is no general doctrine which is not capable of eating out our morality if unchecked by the deep seated habit of direct fellow-feeling with individual fellow men" (ch. 61, 582). Such ideas are in the lineage of Spinoza and Feuerbach. To know the difference between one system and another is to grasp, however dimly, the modal deficiency of each.

The future George Eliot chose Spinoza in keeping with her expanding interests; he provided her with one particularly important confirmation of a vision she had already developed through her many studies, most especially through her study of languages. Mary Ann Evans began learning languages other than English when she was thirteen; by the time she was twenty-five, she had studied six languages (not including mathematics); and by the time she began writing fiction at age thirty-seven, she had mastered and used French, Italian, German, Latin (including medieval Latin), Greek, and Hebrew, and she continued to use them to the end of her career; later in her career she added Spanish. For my purposes here this achievement has interest, beyond the sheer ability it reflects, because it suggests the thoroughness of her knowledge of linguistic relativity, and that in turn bears on her narrative strategy of "on the other hand."

With each shift of viewpoint George Eliot invokes a difference, and a difference that depends upon deep structures, not superficial accidents, in much the same way as languages operate according to differential systems that govern but are never explicit in continuing acts of speech. In her novels a "valid claim" is never *solely* an individual matter; it is always cultural and systemic as well. Rosamond Vincy is, after all, the flower of Mrs. Lemon's school, and Lydgate chooses her for that reason; it is no good then complaining of narcissistic performances that are put on in the first place at the request of the community and with their entire approval. Where was Rosamond to learn otherwise? She meets *her* first "on the other hand" from Will Ladislaw, a man who is not interested in female flowers. And her husband Lydgate also depends on systems much larger than he is, both for his strengths and also for his weaknesses; his intellectual independence has been fostered by science; his carelessness is gender-specific and perhaps class-specific.

Just as Antigone's claims rest on a religion and Creon's on a political system, so do the conflicting claims of Rosamond and Lydgate, and every other George Eliot character, rest on something larger and more grammatical in the sense already hinted at. She often uses linguistic metaphors in her fiction and translations, as for example when her Feuerbach refers to each new individual as "a new predicate" of a humanity grounded in consciousness and language (19–23). In *Middlemarch* Lydgate is "known merely as a cluster of signs for his neighbours' false suppositions" (ch. 15, 133). Dorothea confesses that art is "a language I do not understand" (ch. 9, 73): a disability probably implicated in her subsequent failure to read a crucial scene in Lydgate's drawing room many chapters later.

It seems obvious that knowledge of languages teaches the limits of all systems as nothing else can do. To learn a second language is to discover a second system for formulating everything. The gain in perspective is powerful. A second or third language, even if one rarely uses it, always presents a limit to any way of formulating or perceiving. One's native language is no longer *the* language but instead only *a* language among others: one way, and only one way, of mapping the world and managing practical affairs. As a thoroughly modern philologist, George Eliot knew that language determines possible perception; that to inhabit a language is to inhabit a world. She would agree with Saussure that language is not a collection of tags but a system of relationship and value that makes sense internally, in other words, differentially. She would even agree that everything operates like language. But while the speech act, which includes even the unspoken gesture, is tangible, a linguistic system *itself* never appears explicitly, except in grammar books or other secondary derivations from usage. We do not go about actually saying "subject, verb, object." We speak, using the implicit structure, the common langue that supports the parole invisibly.

Various such systems of value and expression—"languages" in the large sense—overlap in *Middlemarch*, constituting a complexity that both supports and (on the other hand) hampers individuals. Rosamond, for example, functions within systems that are not unique to her and that she yet can specify with unique emphasis. Rosamond's practiced manners are the means by which not only she but an entire social group marks the boundaries of its knowledge. Learning otherwise, as Rosy heroically does for at least a moment, involves nothing less than changing one's language and the boundaries it provides and imposes. George Eliot's "on the other hand" characteristically takes an absolute and relativizes it. The Other is never singular, never oppositional, but instead, as Ladislaw is to Rosy, or Caleb Garth is to Bulstrode, just another alternative among the many that extend to infinity or at least as far as the eye can see.

It is precisely because of what we can call their grammatical properties that actions and events are intelligible or even possible at all. George Eliot's genius appears in the way she makes visible the difficult, complex fact that each individual act specifies anew some traditional arrangement, some systemic order, modifying in some minuscule way a broadly interconnected balance of things. It is precisely thus that unheroic acts become powerful: in their specification and possible modification of a grammar of belief and value.

Such grammars become evident at crucial moments in *Middlemarch*; Mary Garth's refusal to burn Featherstone's will is such a moment; so is Bulstrode's failed attempt to bribe Ladislaw, or Dorothea's misprision of the scene in Mrs. Lydgate's parlor, or Rosamond's heroic achievement of speaking to Dorothea for the first time in a new way about herself and her interests. These moments have to do with more than an individual or a single event; they carry the traces of systemic organization evident from usages in Middlemarch society and its world.

So the conflict of valid claims is never just an individual matter only but always a discursive one having to do with a cultural grammar. Because this is true, the conflict can *not* be settled easily if at all. The conflicts between systems, between languages, between discursive formations in George Eliot admit of no absolute distinction between right and wrong. What solution is easy or "right" to the conflict between rural Middlemarch and encroaching industrialism, or the conflict between social hierarchy and parliamentary representation, or between even two parts of a single person, each pulling in different directions? All George Eliot's novels feature these large conflicts of valid cultural claims: between feudal and modern society in her first novel, between national and ethnic cultures in her last. What is right for one is wrong for another, what invigorates a strong mind may derange a weak one. There is always that dratted "on the other hand." Even Rosamond Vincy has her excellent reasons. Even Rosamond Vincy has her chance to differ from herself.

Very few English novelists, for that matter very few novelists, have had anything like this grasp of the fundamental differences between languages. More than anything else, George Eliot's knowledge of language accounts for her happy grasp of systemic limitation. Her chronic "on the other hand" belongs to this deep knowledge. Her narratives engage us in a problematic where the important questions are matters of scope and emphasis, and not at all of deciding which side wins. When we come across that inevitable "on the other hand," hang it, (as Mr. Standish would say) we are probably being required to deconstruct a dual opposition. This commitment in George Eliot's *Middlemarch* is one reason why she favors metaphors of webs or networks: because they are headless and footless systems of relationship without a common center; because there are many centers in *Middlemarch*, not one. In any case, the dual experience of interpretive enjoyment and frustration amounts to a reader's version of that "antagonism of valid claims" that is a familiar moral problem to most of the characters in her novels. George Eliot did not come to this deconstructive outlook accidentally but through a disciplined search beyond dogma.

Now to return to the strategies of the text in *Middlemarch*: its perpetual "on the other hand" is only one of the more conspicuous ways in which the novel shifts attention, almost rhythmically, from one system to another. On the grand scale this novel employs the kind of transitional devices familiar from most lengthy realist novels; but in the case of *Middlemarch* the transitions can be considerably more unsettling because they do not work single-mindedly toward reunion as they so often do in other novels of the time. Take for example the seismic shifts in book 2, "Old and Young" (chs. 13–22). For two-thirds of book 2, attention remains with the relationships among various Middlemarchers, particularly the Vincys, the Bulstrodes, and the new doctor, Tertius Lydgate, who is both eligible, that is to say, comprehensible in Middlemarch terms, and professional, that is to say, incomprehensible in Middlemarch terms and, to that extent, "known merely as a cluster of signs for his neighbours' false suppositions" (ch. 15, 133). There are various lines of interest with regard to marriage and money, and we get particularly interested in Lydgate, the new man in the scene, and in the variety of intentions toward him, including his own. Being simultaneously dedicated to science and ready to throw everything at the feet of his latest romantic obsession, Lydgate is famously a man who has "two selves within him apparently": a sort of personal "on the other hand." His laissez-faire attitude toward this internal threshold proves to have dangerous implications, but initially it seems only troublesome, as in this quick retrospective loop in a central chapter.

> He knew that this [sudden determination to propose to Mme Laure] was like the sudden impulse of a madman—incongruous even with his habitual foibles. No matter!
>
> It was the one thing which he was resolved to do. He had two selves within him apparently, and they must learn to accommodate each other and bear reciprocal impediments. Strange, that some of us, even with quick alternate vision, see beyond our infatuations, and even while we rave on the heights, behold the wide plain where our persistent self pauses and awaits us. (ch. 15, 143)

We are deep in the details of Lydgate's "on the other hand" when the narrative voice suddenly reappears and moves to a generalization quite far in tone and style from the locale: a sort of ripple in the surface of what otherwise seems like solid Middlemarcher "reality." Attention shifts in chapter 19, the Duke of Wellington is invoked, some half-idle conversation is reported between two artists in Rome, about the qualities of female perfection in general and of Mrs. Casaubon in particular. By chapter 20 attention has a new and very specific focus: "Two hours later, Dorothea was seated in an inner room or boudoir of a handsome apartment in the Via Sistina. I am sorry to add that she was sobbing bitterly." (180). In this almost casual way, these two chapters deflect attention away from the prevailing interests of book 2. With artists and scholars and "the quality" in Rome we are into new territory in almost every way. The lingering assertion of identity maintained by the title "Old and Young" seems almost unrealistic.

This kind of textual transaction happens in every book of *Middlemarch*, and each book has its own internal pattern of mnemonic loops whereby shifts in time and space correspond to shifts from one center of interest, one plot, to another (see for example my discussion of book 7 in *Realism and Consensus*). These kinds of shifts are large-scale versions of that "on the other hand" that takes place in smaller ways within chapters and shifts attention not just from one point of view to another or from one clearly defined line of motivation to another but instead from one constellation to another, from what almost seems one settlement, or one grammatically separate system to another. Some of the shifts involved are alarmingly profound, like seismic shifts of the ground under our feet.

Another more limited example is what happens to the Lydgate–and–Rosy plot of book 2 within the larger architecture of *Middlemarch*. What seems a casual shift of attention turns out to be mountainous travel to an entirely different corner of the cosmos. When Casaubon falls ill in book 3, Sir James sends a messenger who finds Mr. Lydgate "leading his horse along the Lowick road and giving his arm to Miss Vincy" (ch. 29, 267). The relationship between Rosamond and Lydgate, and all the conflicting interests they represent, have at one time been so central that it comes as a slight shock to realize that Rosamond and Lydgate have been offstage and out of focus for many chapters. Even here they figure only in passing, as a relay into the next plot development of book 3, to do with conflicts at Casaubons' and drama concerning Featherstone's will. Even when Lydgate finally decides the long-pending question, will he marry Rosamond, it is almost accidentally (ch. 31) and in a way that is incidental to the plot interests of book 3. The swing of attention that backgrounds what had been so immediate, and that does so, as it were, unbeknownst to us, is a dizzying experience: one consistent with George Eliot's intention to ensure that we experience what actually happens in the translation from one system to another.

In other, more fleeting ways George Eliot shifts attention from one disposition to another, but the effects are the same. Bulstrode experiences an unwelcome internal shift of emphasis, from one hand to the other hand, when he meets Raffles in the lane near Stone Court. "Five minutes before, the expanse of his life had been submerged in its evening sunshine.... And now, as if by some hideous magic, this loud red figure had risen before him in unmanageable solidity—an incorporate past which had not entered into his imagination" (ch. 53, 491–2). In this case, the shock is confined to Mr. Bulstrode, and readers discover its precedents only gradually. But the gesture is the familiar one of fairly dramatic course correction, even though it is invisible to the eye, as a pebble under the wheel revolutionizes the course not of just an individual life or two but eventually of a larger system of social perception and understanding erected around Mr. Bulstrode's fraud.

Chance encounters frequently create a similar destabilizing effect. After he meets Bulstrode and Caleb in the lane, Raffles just happens to remember the forgotten name—"Ladislaw!" (ch. 53, 498). On the day he had intended to stay home Lydgate just happens by the Vincy's and ends up engaged. Apparently extraneous metaphors to do with electric batteries or foreign wars get mixed into the language, always requiring a step back from the moment; and occasionally a completely foreign system of intelligibility, such as Railroad workers laying track (ch. 56), intrudes even into Middlemarchers' awareness. In this continuous compounding of apparently extraneous matter we begin to hear the roar that lies on the other side of silence—the "noise" factored out by any system in order to remain intelligible.

Finally, readers experience a shift of attention whenever the narrative slips into the present tense, which it does almost rhythmically throughout the text. I have discussed this at length elsewhere, so I will only mention for example the passage just cited, where Lydgate's self–reflection gives way to a narrative reflection, and ends with this present-tense comment by the narrative voice: "Strange that some of us, even with quick alternate vision, see beyond our infatuations, and even while we rave on the heights, behold the wide plain where our persistent self pauses and awaits us." Such moments, called by some "intrusions," do not so much indicate what to think (few generalizations stand in George Eliot) as they shift the context—widening it, and creating instability in the narrative perspective.

The points of encounter between one system and another—large ones and small ones—are the cruxes of George Eliot's novel. They tend to take place at public gatherings or in public places such as a road, or a gambling den—as if to invoke the chorus for a momentous step or seminal crossing: when Dorothea visits Rosamond, twice; when Fred encounters Lydgate at the gambling table; when Farebrother confesses his competitive interests to Fred; when Raffles reappears to Bulstrode the Virtuous, bringing with him knowledge of the other Bulstrode, the criminal; when Ladislaw confronts Rosamond in her drawing room; when Dorothea confronts Dorothea and decides not to honor her dead husband's will; when Mary Garth refuses Featherstone's dying request to change his will. Such occasions bring two or more grammatical systems into mutual influence or conflict, and such confrontations are the growing points of the novel.

At all levels, then, this narrative tactic of shifting attention—this changing the subject—creates chronic instability in *Middlemarch* with regard to interpretive product. When a particular line of thought, or plot development receives a check—from something Other, extraneous, fortuitous—and gets deflected in favor of a different course of action and attention, all kinds of issues are left hanging, and the new focus does not turn out, as so often in Dickens, to be a fortunate coincidence leading to a reunion. This constant relay, constant hand-off in new and unexpected directions operates from the sentence to the macro structure, and keeps readers off balance with regard to settled conclusions. Shifts from one set or one system to another, from Dorothea to Rosamond for instance, do sponsor comparison. *They do not sponsor choice.* It is never this *or* that; never Dorothea (good), Rosy (bad). It is always this *and* that. In fact, and because form is difference, even their differences are constitutive. This agenda appears in all George Eliot's novels, but in *Middlemarch* it may reach its apogee of subtlety and thoroughness.

The moments of opportunity for individuals, as for readers, are almost always such moments of encounter between one system of intelligibility and another. Generally there is very little direct exchange between such systems; they can be said to be "foreign" to each other because most characters are like Fred, who "knew little and cared less about Ladislaw and the Casaubons" (ch. 59, 562). Any mutual relationship between things normally separated by class or geography or occupation remains a potential—a feature of the book titles in *Middlemarch*—"The Dead Hand," "Three Love Problems," "Two Temptations," "Sunset and Sunrise"—until a surprise encounter works its alchemy. But the message of those potential symmetries is not so much that people should take an interest in what doesn't currently concern them. The message is more reserved but at the same time more potentially disturbing to settled views: the message that (to recoin a phrase) those other interests and systems *are there*. They *are*, quite simply.

For interpreters approaching the novel with empirical assumptions ("vulgar empiricism" as George Eliot's Feuerbach has it), this amount of reserve will not do. Empiricism requires Socrates to take a position. But *Middlemarch* makes that difficult. It is not unusual to end up with more questions than answers. Book 6, for example, "The Widow and the Wife" has a most intriguing format. It begins and it also ends with two separate occasions on which Will Ladislaw comes to say a final goodbye to Dorothea. But the book deals mainly with other plots. What do Fred's romantic interests, the Lydgates' domestic unhappiness, and Bulstrode's fear of discovery have to do with the fact that Dorothea considers herself prevented from accepting Ladislaw by her dead husband's will? What does any of this have to do with the encroachment of the Railway system into the countryside of Middlemarch or the behavior of electric batteries? And why do we have those interestingly, conspicuously repetitive farewells between Ladislaw and Dorothea?

In interpreting such a text we come round again to the problem of language. My discussion has contained echoes of contemporary theoretical debate about language as a model of systemic order. Since Saussure, it has become increasingly useful for those interested in language to consider the extent to which everything operates like language: politics, marriage, music, fashion—all systems that operate just as English or Chinese or Portuguese do, that is, according to differential functions governed by invisible grammars or discursive rules. These systems of meaning and value—"languages" in the large sense—govern what it is possible to do, and not do, who can speak, what can be heard. Awareness of this power of discourse to form and limit perception comes directly from the nineteenth century. With poststructuralist theory we are still working on this problem of plural systems, and the difficult problem of negotiating between them where there seem to be no common denominators, no possibility of a common world. Awareness of this problem is everywhere in Middlemarch. Even though temporal and spatial horizons may seem to be continuous in the novel, even those potential common denominators can seem threatened by opacity or intractability in one or another system.

Poststructuralist theory has developed the radical implications of this problem. It is precisely the intractable, perhaps absolute differences between one language, one discourse, and another that Jean-Francois Lyotard christened "the differend": "a case of conflict, between (at least) two parties, that cannot be equitably resolved for lack of a rule of judgment applicable to both arguments. One side's legitimacy does not imply the other's lack of legitimacy"; and "applying a single rule of judgment to both in order to settle their differend as though it were merely a litigation would wrong (at least) one of them (and both of them if neither side admits this rule)" (Lyotard, xi). This is not all that far from what George Eliot claims: that what is right for one is wrong for another; that what stimulates a strong mind only deranges a weak one; that what applies in the one system simply does not apply in another.

Lyotard addresses a twentieth–century version of the pluralism problem, but it is an old problem. The problem of the plurality of worlds was well known to seventeenth-century cosmologists, and it has been present in English traditions since the Reformation. Certainly it was the cosmological dimension of the problem that most exercised George Eliot and her contemporaries. George Eliot shows in so many ways that no "faith" can claim absolute truth because every system is finite. All faith can claim is faith in a particular way of doing things, a particular system of belief and value distinct from other, perhaps equally valid ones.

So the question arises, if you change your faith once, why not a hundred times? In the nineteenth century, the question was urgent in terms of religious faith but was often raised, as it often is in George Eliot's novels, in philosophical and secular terms. In *Middlemarch,* a cantankerous Old Mrs. Farebrother takes up this contention with Lydgate of an evening, and in terms that seem to echo the debates of the Oxford movement. She certainly regards changing one's viewpoint as something little short of disease: "I shall never show that disrespect to my parents, to give up what they taught me. Any one may see what comes of turning. If you change once, why not twenty times?" Lydgate suggests that "a man might see good arguments for changing once, and not see them for changing again." To which the old lady retorts that such shifting only leaves you liable to argument. "If you go upon arguments, they are never wanting, when a man has no constancy of mind. My father never changed, and he preached plain moral sermons without arguments, and was a good man—few better." "My mother is like Old George the Third," says the Vicar, "she objects to metaphysics" (ch. 17, 159). Fortunately, and like many another in George Eliot, Mrs. Farebrother is better than her opinions. Meanwhile, around her rock wash the heavy tides of *Middlemarch*, entirely bracketing the possibility of such protected constancy.

The differences that create form in George Eliot could be and were sorted much differently in other narrative universes. The plurality of worlds is not a value in Jane Austen, at least not until *Persuasion*. The differences between persons, couples, groups—between the Bennetts the Bingleys and the Darcys, for example—are hierarchical differences, not systemic ones, and that is how they are sorted. Each "kind" has its place in a single and "natural" social hierarchy. When a heroine like Elizabeth Bennett or Emma has her moment of staggering recognition—"till this moment I never knew myself"—that in no way amounts to a recognition of worlds within worlds revolving onward in which one's own tiny portion vanishes to a speck. No success to be found here "on the other hand." Instead, these are moments when the character breaks out of a fantasmal condition into a single world of social truth and reality. Natural hierarchy resolves conflict through an accommodation that stratifies the world and resists the open horizons that had been building in European institutions and art for several hundred years. Any individuals who do not fit that accommodation—Jane Austen's Crawfords, for instance—are dangerous outliers.

In *Middlemarch*, the problem of language almost reaches a point of crisis, as it did in some fields (for example, physics, visual arts, linguistics) half a century later: the point of distinguishing between recoverable relativism on the one hand and unrecoverable relativity on the other. What is at stake in this distinction is whether the constructed world is one or many: whether the grammatical differences between systems can be mediated according to some common denominator, perhaps even a common grammar of some kind, or whether their differences are absolute and unmediateable. If the latter, the problem of relationship must be deeply reconceived without reference to any mediating conditions, and in that case, the problem of translation—the problem of mediation between systems—becomes acute, perhaps insoluble. What do we do when there seems to be no way to establish unanimity or even privilege between systems, even moral systems: when there seems to be no common denominator but only, as Lyotard later calls it, perpetual "phrases in dispute"?

George Eliot fully understands the problem in these terms, but she makes her choice in favor of mediation and linkage. In *Middlemarch* the very form—by virtue of its constant shifting from this to ("on the other hand") that, asserts the possibility of translation between languages, discursive sets, grammars of perception; even though those shifts are sometimes difficult (Farebrother giving up Mary), sometimes well-nigh impossible (Lydgate controlling expenses). Partial recovery is at least possible. Although *Middlemarch* cruises precariously the boundaries between different systems of intelligibility, and although the recovery George Eliot envisions is more difficult and provisional than what is imagined by most of her contemporaries, in the end George Eliot's narrative style always maintains a common horizon. Even Rosy and Dodo can communicate. It is the same world for everyone. The recovery of a potentially common–denominator world appears in the narrative voice and the language in ways thoroughly discussed elsewhere. In contradistinction with Mr. Dagley's darkness—or for that matter the relative darkness of almost any character—*Middlemarch* presents us with a ripple and amplification of language, and with a narrative perspective system that deflects attention and returns it within a horizon as wide as it is possible to imagine.

Wide, but not infinite. In keeping with her acknowledgment that every language has its limit, George Eliot also gives color and even some individuation to her narrative voice, so that even the common world it supports can seem bounded by potential difference. Within that common world of *Middlemarch* and its horizon, communication may be hampered by tradition and prejudice but it remains possible. Across the gaps produced by physical and moral location, minds may get nearer. Presiding over that possibility is the Nobody narrator, maintaining its hovering promise of relationship between systems. But though relativism does not tip over into relativity in *Middlemarch*, it still leaves us with much the same practical consequences as would the more radical move. Even the stress and stretch of mediation in *Middlemarch* claims to sustain only a view of "this particular web," not the entire range of relevancies. The only possible unities are local unities. Bridging the differences between them is an effort always tentative, provisional, fraught, delightful.

Note

Portions of this essay were first published in my "George Eliot and the World as Language," in John Rignall, ed., *George Eliot and Europe* (Aldershot, England: Scolar Press, 1997), 33–44.

References

Eliot, George. *Essays of George Eliot*. Ed. Thomas Pinney. New York: Columbia University Press, 1963.

Ermarth, Elizabeth Deeds. *The English Novel in History, 1840–1895*. London: Routledge. 1996.

———. *George Eliot.* Boston: G. K. Hall, 1985.

———. "Incarnations: George Eliot's Conception of 'Undeviating Law.'" *Nineteenth-Century Fiction* 29, 3 (1975), 273–86. Reprinted in Stuart Hutchinson, ed., *George Eliot: Critical Assessments*, vol. 4, *Twentieth-Century Perspectives from 1970.* New York: Routledge, 1996.

———. *Realism and Consensus in the English Novel: Time, Space and Narrative* (1983). 2nd ed. Edinburgh: Edinburgh University Press, 1998.

Feuerbach, Ludwig Andreas. *The Essence of Christianity* (Das Wesen des Christentums). Trans. George Eliot. With an introduction by Karl Barth and forward by H. Richard Niebuhr. New York: Harper and Row, 1957.

Haight, Gordon S. *George Eliot, A Biography*. Oxford: Oxford University Press, 1968.

Lyotard, Jean-François. *The Differend: Phrases in Dispute* (Le différend [1983]). Trans. George Van den Abbeele. Minneapolis: University of Minnesota Press, 1988.

Miller, J. Hills. "Narrative and History," *ELH* 41 (fall 1974), 455–73.

Robbe-Grillet, Alain. *For a New Novel: Essays on Fiction* (*Pour un nouveau roman* [Paris: Editions de Minuits, 1963]). Trans. Richard Howard. 1965; reprint, Evanston, Ill.: Northwestern University Press, 1989.

Spinoza, Benedict de. *Ethics.* Trans. George Eliot. Ed. Thomas Deegan. Salzburg Studies in English Literature no. 102. Salzburg: Institute für Anglistik und Amerikanistik, Universität Salzburg, 1981.

7

A Conclusion in Which Almost Nothing Is Concluded

Middlemarch's *"Finale"*

J. HILLIS MILLER

❖   ❖   ❖

THE "FINALE," IT WOULD SEEM LIKELY, is the place to look for an "ending" to *Middlemarch*, drawing all its threads tight.[1] The finale, however, it turns out, ends the novel only by presenting generalizations about openness. The first sentence of the finale says this clearly enough: "Every limit is a beginning as well as an ending." The novel's eighth book, of which the finale is a part, is entitled "Sunset and Sunrise." What this might mean is indicated by what is said proleptically in the finale about the future lives of Dorothea and the other characters. The marriages of Dorothea and Will, Fred Vincy and Mary Garth, end the narrative conventionally enough. The narrator reminds the reader, however, that marriage, too, is a beginning as well as an ending, in real life and in realistic fiction, as well as in epics and in the Bible: "Marriage, which has been the bourne of so many narratives, is still a great beginning, as it was to Adam and Eve, who kept their honeymoon in Eden but had their first little one among the thorns and thistles of the wilderness. It is still the beginning of the home epic" (finale, 779). George Eliot here calls attention to a relation of similarity and difference between epics and realistic fiction. She invites the reader to think of *Paradise Lost* as though it were a bourgeois novel. All marriages are "home epics." We all in our marriages repeat Adam and Eve. This both domesticates the epic and raises what Northrop Frye called "low mimetic" realism, while at the same time universalizing the latter. *Paradise Lost* already does this by inviting all Protestant readers to think that each moment of their lives repeats the momentous alternatives open in the instant before Eve ate the apple. No final end comes to human history, until the last end. The meaning of each human life, moreover, remains open as long as the person is alive. That meaning remains open even after the person's death, insofar as the meaning of each life is his or her effect on others, down through the generations.

The openness of *Middlemarch* is also demonstrated in the way the finale modulates for the last time, though not in any "definitive" way, the key metaphors of the novel: the tropes of history, of the web, of flowing water, of seeing, and of interpretation.[2] These figures appear for the last time in a dissonant mode, not as a harmonious assemblage in a grand concluding chord. One by one, the power of each figure adequately to image human life is dismantled. Speaking of the newlyweds' futures, the narrator says there is no way to be sure that their after-lives will be continuous with the fabric which has been woven up to the "now" that ends the novel:

> Who can quit young lives after being long in company with them, and not desire to know what befell them in their after—years? For the fragment of life, however typical, is not the sample of an even web: promises may not be kept, and an ardent outset may be followed by declension; a past error may urge a grand retrieval. (finale, 779)

If what Nietzsche called "monumentalische" (monumental) history, that is, the history of great men, is, for George Eliot, not a straightforward sequence governed by cause and effect, neither is a given human life.[3] A speech act such as a promise does not guarantee the future. The promise may not be kept. Emotion as motive does not necessarily continue through time with the same force. It may "decline." An error, such as Dorothea's or Bulstrode's, does not necessarily lead to permanent disaster. It may, paradoxically, be the cause of a turn for the better, as in the touching solidarity in catastrophe of Bulstrode and his wife. Eliot's figure of the uneven web rejects both the method of synecdoche so basic to narration in *Middlemarch* and the assumption that the totality of Middlemarch society, or of human life generally, is a web of regular pattern permitting universal judgments. The validity of synecdoche has been presupposed in all those places in which the narrator moves from particular examples to absolute generalizations, for example when, apropos of "poor Mr. Casaubon," the narrator says, "we all of us, grave or light, get our thoughts entangled in metaphors, and act fatally on the strength of them" (ch. 10, 79). The social fragment, the finale now says, cannot be counted on to stand for the whole. If human life, in its minute particulars and in its total configuration, is a web, it is that particular form of web that is "uneven." It does not form a unified design that can be seen at a glance. It may shift unpredictably from one pattern to another, for example when a promise made in good faith is not kept. As a result, no safe generalizations about the texture of human life may be made, though the narrator makes yet another in saying that the fragment of a life is not the sample of an even web.

A similar doubt is cast on the figures of "interpretation" and of "vision." The determining acts of Dorothea's life, says the narrator,

> were the mixed result of young and noble impulse struggling amidst the conditions of an imperfect social state, in which great feelings will often take the aspect of error, and great faith the aspect of illusion. For there is no creature whose inward being is so strong that it is not greatly determined by what lies outside it. A new Theresa will hardly have the opportunity of reforming a conventual life, any more than a new Antigone will spend her heroic piety in daring all for the sake of a brother's burial: the medium in which their ardent deeds took shape is for ever gone. (finale, 784–5)

The word "error" used here is part of the vocabulary in *Middlemarch* that describes the act of reading. Interpretation is often, George Eliot asserts, a misreading of signs motivated by "great feelings" that are in themselves good, like Dorothea's infatuation with Casaubon. Her "great faith" in him produces a mistake in seeing, an optical illusion. She sees concentric circles where there are only random scratches, to borrow a celebrated trope from the novel (ch. 27, 248). Dorothea's "affectionate ardour" and her "Quixotic enthusiasm" (ch. 42, 394), to use Casaubon's words for her most salient qualities, are the motivating energy that drives her to read badly and to see wrongly. Eliot places the blame partly on outward conditions, for example the genteel sexism that contributes to Dorothea's misery. When she returns from her wedding journey she finds that no one expects her to do anything in particular. "What shall I do?" she asks, and is answered "Whatever you please, my dear" (ch. 28, 257). Dorothea's ardor and her theoretical bent need some male person who can match her idealism. In her society no such men exist (did they ever?), and so she misreads Casaubon as like Pascal or Milton or John Frédérick Oberlin (ch. 3, 27, 22, 29). Even these patriarchal worthies, seen in close domestic surroundings, the final twist of George Eliot's irony implies, might not have matched Dorothea's ideal image of the man she would like to marry. In any case, Saint Theresa and Antigone were lucky enough to have a surrounding social "medium" equal to their heroic ardor, and lucky enough never to marry, while poor Dorothea has no such medium and no luck in her first marriage choice. The reference to Saint Theresa in the finale echoes of course the description in the prelude of Dorothea as a "Saint Theresa, foundress of nothing" (4) and as one of those "later-born Theresas" who "were helped by no coherent social faith and order which could perform the function of knowledge for the ardently willing soul" (3). The reference to Antigone in the finale is also not fortuitous, since she has been mentioned once before in the novel. Antigone as the heroine of Sophocles' tragedy was a key figure in German Romantic speculation about the conflict between individual ethics and the state, for example in Hölderlin, Hegel, and August Böckh. George Eliot herself published in 1856, long before she wrote *Middlemarch*, a little essay on Antigone that mentions Böckh. Böckh was perhaps one source of George Eliot's rhetorical and tropological sophistication in *Middlemarch*, for example in the reflection on metaphors cited earlier.[4]

The last paragraph of *Middlemarch* ends the novel on a note of eloquent openness to an unpredictable future. It also gathers up one last time the image of human life as flowing water. That image has been present in the novel since the prelude. In the prelude, Dorothea is a cygnet reared among ducklings in a brown pond and deprived of fellowship with its own kind in the "living stream" (4). That stream in the finale is modulated into a river that disperses itself in the sand. The last paragraph also makes one last reference to the stream of history that has provided a (false) model throughout for the writing of narrative. If the reference to Cyrus, taken from Herodotus, draws a last parallel between *Middlemarch* characters and grand personages on the stage of world history, the passage goes on to say that Dorothea's life was "unhistoric." Her effect on those around her exceeded the public power of naming that makes the writing of grand histories possible. The result is that her influence cannot be measured except hypothetically. What cannot be named exactly cannot enter into that precise calculation of cause and effect that historians pretend to make. It is impossible to understand Dorothea's life according to the gross model of visible historical causality. The parallel between writing history and writing fiction about ordinary middle–class people, important earlier in the novel, here breaks down. People like Dorothea are not historic:

> Her finely-touched spirit had still its fine issues, though they were not widely visible. Her full nature, like that river of which Cyrus broke the strength, spent itself in channels which had no great name on the earth. But the effect of her being on those around her was incalculably diffusive: for the growing good of the world is partly dependent on unhistoric acts; and that things are not so ill with you and me as they might have been, is half owing to the number who lived faithfully a hidden life, and rest in unvisited tombs. (finale, 785)

The somber echoes of Gray's "Elegy Written in a Country Churchyard" at the end of this passage may remind the reader that George Eliot's tomb in Highgate Cemetery outside London is not visited all that often and was in a rather shabby state when I last saw it. Karl Marx's elaborate gravestone with an elegant bust, however, just a few feet away, was, when I saw it on the same pious visit, in highly polished splendor. It was adorned with fresh flowers just being put there by a Soviet delegation. This was before the disintegration of the Soviet Union, the vanishing of communism, and Fukuyama's end of history in the worldwide triumph of capitalism. I wonder how Marx's grave is managing today.

Middlemarch, in deconstructing the characters' possibilities of verifiable knowledge, implicitly deconstructs also both its own power to make an orderly narrative and the reader's power to comprehend the novel integrally. *Middlemarch* may therefore be called a "parable of unreadability." The word *parable* is taken here in George Eliot's own sense, as she uses it in chapter 27 (248). The characters' stories parabolically dramatize the narrator's problems and those of the reader. If this is the case, the novel is, paradoxically, readable. It invites the reader to master it as the story of the impossibility of cognitive mastery, though the invitation takes away with one hand what it offers with the other. Insofar as the reader understands what the text is saying, masters it, he or she understands any reader's powerlessness to understand either this particular text or his or her own actions on the stage of history. The reader is overmastered or deprived of mastery.

A stage beyond this cognitive impasse is, however, dramatized in the novel. This stage is expressed in parable, too, though in a different mode of saying one thing and meaning another. The emblem of this further stage is Dorothea's commitment to Will, her marriage to him, and her after-life "only known in a certain circle as a wife and mother" (finale, 783). The ending presents in Dorothea's marriage an exemplary emblem of what might be called an ethical or ethico-performative evaluation of human life. Such an evaluation involves a return to the "real world" of the reader, as when the narrator says, in a direct appeal to you or me: "that things are not so ill with you and me as they might have been. . . ." The ending therefore involves a form of reference, though not a straightforwardly mimetic one. The reference takes place rather by way of a performative appeal to the reader to recognize and accept a debt. Beyond the dismantling of the characters' efforts to comprehend totally, beyond the turning-back of that on similar efforts by narrator and reader, beyond the ruination of any cognitive enterprise of totalization, the novel proposes the positive affirmation of a performative power, possibly for good, possibly for evil, in actions and in words. These words and actions are necessarily blind to their full meaning and effect. They are, in George Eliot's precise formulation, "incalculably diffusive." They have power to make something happen, but exactly what that is, to what degree it will be for good or for ill, may not be calculated or known, neither before nor after the fact.

The move from cognitive to performative language occurs when Dorothea, in a scene shortly before the finale, throws herself in Will's arms in a "flood" of "passion" that matches the storm outside the window before which she and Will stand: "Oh, I cannot bear it—my heart will break, . . . I don't mind about poverty—I hate my wealth" (ch. 83, 762). This episode is parabolic in the sense that Christ's inscrutable stories in the Gospels are exhortations to certain kinds of ethical action that are enjoined by his parables, though the cognitive justification for those actions can never be clearly given. Even exactly what kind of action should be performed in a given situation remains not wholly clear. How would I ever know that I was correctly imitating Dorothea? Just what sort of action does Jesus's parable of the sower enjoin? Such a performative parable as Dorothea's commitment of herself to Will lacks the more or less unambiguous cognitive meaning of George Eliot's parable of the pier-glass, enunciated in a celebrated passage earlier in the novel (ch. 27, 248).

Dorothea's spontaneous and unpremeditated commitment of herself to Will is the last of the important decisions she makes in the novel. Each is ratified in one way or another by an explicit speech act or writing act. Each in one way or another has to do with a commitment to marriage. In Dorothea's social milieu, the acceptance or refusal of a marriage proposal was the chief place where a gentlewoman had the opportunity to make a free decision. Dorothea refuses Sir James Chettam's marriage proposal. She accepts Casaubon's marriage proposal. In various scenes of solitary meditation after her marriage, scenes that deeply influenced Henry James's novel *The Portrait of a Lady*, Dorothea recognizes that she has misinterpreted Casaubon. She has misread him. She comes to recognize that "he had an equivalent centre of self, whence the lights and shadows must always fall with a certain difference" (ch. 21, 198). She resolves nevertheless to do the best she can with the marriage state she has erroneously chosen. Ultimately, after Casaubon's lucky death, lucky for Dorothea that is, since it occurs just before she might have committed herself to lifelong futility by promising to finish Casaubon's "Key to All Mythologies," Dorothea entrusts herself to Will Ladislaw by throwing herself in his arms and uttering the words just quoted. Her decision is a felicitous speech act, even in the legal sense. It activates the clause in Causabon's will disinheriting her if she marries Ladislaw after Casaubon's death. Dorothea says: "We could live quite well on my own fortune—it is too much—seven hundred a year—I want so little—no new clothes—and I will learn what everything costs" (ch. 83, 762).

Though Dorothea's decision to marry Will may be unpremeditated, she ratifies that decision in a later deliberate speech act uttered to her sister Celia. Celia asks her why in the world she has given up all that money to marry Will Ladislaw. "I have promised to marry Mr. Ladislaw; and I am going to marry him" (ch. 84, 771), says Dorothea. She will marry Will even though it activates a will that disinherits her. The implicit play on the word "will" indicates that Ladislaw's given name is not unmotivated. Will Ladislaw is willful, impulsive, motivated by emotion. That is part of his attraction for Dorothea. That Dorothea's commitment to Will is a true decision and not the preprogrammed following of a moral rule is indicated by what Dorothea says to her sister Celia when she asks Dorothea just how it came about that she decided to marry Will Ladislaw. Dorothea says this is something that is impossible for Celia to "know." "Can't you tell me?" asks Celia. "No, dear," answers Dorothea, "you would have to feel with me, else you would never know" (ch. 84, 771). A true decision is a matter of feeling, of unpredictable and inexplicable "ardor," never of rational choice based on balancing pros and cons, or on following a moral law, or on obedience to what family and friends tell you you should do. Dorothea defies her whole community in choosing to marry Ladislaw. Because it is based on ardor, not prudence, her decision constitutes a true historical event. It is a break in the predetermined sequence of happenings. Isabel Archer, in James's *Portrait of a Lady*, says much the same thing as Dorothea says to Celia. When Isabel's rejected lover, Caspar Goodwood, her aunt, Mrs. Touchett, and her cousin, Ralph Touchett, in succession, ask her to explain why she has decided to marry Gilbert Osmond, she answers each in the same evasive way. To Caspar: "Do you think I could explain if I would?"[5] To Mrs. Touchett: "I don't think it's my duty to explain to you. Even if it were I shouldn't be able. So please don't remonstrate; in talking about it you have me at a disadvantage. I can't talk about it" (4:55). To Ralph: "I can't explain to you what I feel, what I believe, and I wouldn't if I could" (4:72).

The commitment to family life and political action by Will and Dorothea after their marriage confirms the rechanneling of Dorothea's ardor when she throws herself in Will's arms. Dorothea, the novel makes clear, does not move from blindness to full insight, from illusory misinterpretation to clear seeing of the way things are. She comes, it is true, according to the narrator, to see that Casaubon has "an equivalent center of self, whence the lights and shadows must always fall with a certain difference," different, that is, from those that fall from her own center or from anyone else's (ch. 21, 198). Dorothea is never, however, shown as able to articulate her understanding as clearly as the narrator does. The narrator must speak for her more or less inarticulate intuitions and feelings.

In another celebrated scene, Dorothea looks from her window in the early morning, after her night of sorrow over Will's supposed betrayal of her. She sees a man and a woman moving across the landscape. The woman is carrying a baby. This scene repeats in the modern world that moment when Adam and Eve, who celebrated their honeymoon in paradise, had to nurture their first child in the thorny wilderness outside Eden. Seeing this emblem of our fallen state leads Dorothea to feel her kinship with "the manifold wakings of men to labor and endurance" (ch. 80, 741). In this moment her insight most clearly coincides with that of the narrator. The narrator must still, however, give words to what Dorothea sees and feels. Her spirit from the beginning has been both ardent and "theoretic" (ch. 1, 8), but her hunger for theoretical certainty, if one may use that phrase, can never be satisfied, any more than can ours. Dorothea's falling in love with Will and her decision to give her life to him are based on ardor, feeling, and "will" (in the sense of spontaneous life force) rather than on clear-seeing theory.

The final determining act of Dorothea's life is, like her other decisions, performative rather than cognitive. Her love for Will is as much an "error," in the sense of overvaluing and in the sense of blind submission to the guidance of another, as is her love for Casaubon. She is never shown as making out her own way clearly. The lesson Dorothea's life teaches is that such clear seeing is impossible: "She had now a life filled also with a beneficent activity which she had not the doubtful pains of discovering and marking out for herself" (finale, 782). Such irresponsibility was just what she wanted to get by marrying Casaubon. The difference is that she actually gets what she wants by marrying Will Ladislaw.

The difference, the reader will say, is that Dorothea's choice of Will is good. It has good effects, both for her and for others, whereas her choice of Casaubon was mistaken and had bad effects. Is that so certain? By what right, on what grounds, does Dorothea, or the narrator, or the reader, make this judgment? The last paragraph of the novel forbids the possibility of making a final evaluation, in spite of the apparent confidence expressed in a beneficent teleological orientation of history in the phrase, "the growing good of the world." The world's good will grow only if we are lucky enough to have a sufficient number of Dorotheas. Dorothea's life is said to be "incalculably diffusive." The world "incalculably" forbids definitive cognitive judgment. It deprives the narrator of its authority of understanding. It deprives the reader too of the power to make an authoritative judgment, to render full justice to Dorothea's choice. Another way to put this is to say that any judgment the narrator or the reader makes is itself performative rather than cognitive. It is another act of will following Dorothea's impulsive choice and repeating it.

Middlemarch puts all these ardent acts under the aegis of Ariadne. Dorothea's decision to marry Will may be called Ariadne's choice. Many hints scattered here and there throughout the novel invite the reader to think of Dorothea's story as a repetition with difference of the myth of Ariadne. The difference lies not only in the change from archaic Greek times to nineteenth-century England, but also in the way Dorothea is Antigone and the Virgin as well as Ariadne. The narrator presents her as an uneasy incarnation of several conflicting mythological archetypes. Within the reenactment of the myth of Ariadne, Casaubon is both a grotesque parody of Theseus and at the same time the devouring Minotaur at the center of the labyrinth. It might be better to say that Dorothea's masochistic notions of self-sacrifice in the name of an imaginary absolute end make Casaubon into her Theseus and her Minotaur. Dorothea's misreadings of Casaubon transform him, but the danger is real enough. "You have been brought up," says Will impetuously to her, "in some of those horrible notions that choose the sweetest women to devour—like Minotaurs. And now you will go and be shut up in that stone prison at Lowick: you will be buried alive. It makes me savage to think of it!" (ch. 12, 206). If Casaubon is Dorothea's Minotaur, he is also, in a conflation of two myths characteristic of George Eliot's use of mythology, the Creon who buries her alive as another Antigone. Like Theseus, Casaubon is self-righteous and cold, a prig. Like Theseus, he marries his Ariadne and then abandons her, though, unlike Theseus, he has not even accepted her proffered help in escaping that self-made labyrinth of moldy notes and outmoded theories in which he dwells. Dorothea, however, is also buried alive by Casaubon, as Creon buried Antigone for defying his edict.

Dorothea is made into a Christian and modern repetition of Ariadne in the scene in which Will Ladislaw and his German painter friend Naumann find her in the Vatican beside the statue of "the Reclining Ariadne, then called the Cleopatra" (ch. 19, 177). Naumann calls her the "antithesis" of Ariadne, as well as her modern replica. The parallel with Ariadne, moreover, is complicated by accompanying references to Cleopatra, to Antigone, and, a little later, to Santa Clara. In the prelude she is likened to Saint Theresa, and late in the novel to the Madonna. "This young creature has a heart large enough for the Virgin Mary" (ch. 76, 723), says Lydgate, in grateful praise of her decisive intervention in his life. What a bewildering set of comparisons! If Dorothea is Saint Theresa, Cleopatra, Antigone, Santa Clara, and Mary, as well as Ariadne, there is much doubt implicitly cast on solemn Hegelian theories of repetition to which the novel makes oblique reference. Both Will Ladislaw and the narrator make fun of such theories. Casaubon's futile search for a key to all mythologies hardly inspires confidence in the reader that he or she might find a key to the mythological references in *Middlemarch*. Nevertheless, the reader is invited, with whatever ironic qualifications, to think of Dorothea as in some way like Ariadne. "What do you think of that as a fine bit of antithesis?" asks Naumann, as he and Will watch Dorothea beside the statue of Ariadne/Cleopatra in the Vatican. "There lies antique beauty, not corpse-like even in death, but arrested in the complete contentment of its sensuous perfection: and there stands beauty in its breathing life, with the consciousness of Christian centuries in its bosom" (ch. 19, 177). A moment later Naumann describes Dorothea as "antique form animated by Christian sentiment—a sort of Christian Antigone—sensuous force controlled by spiritual passion" (ch. 19, 178). Will, to be sure, pours scorn on this and on the corresponding aesthetic notion of "the divinity passing into higher completeness and all but exhausted in the act of covering your bit of canvas" (178). If metaphysical notions of repetition are firmly rejected in *Middlemarch*, it may be that the reader is left to devise, on the basis of the text, an alternative notion of repetition, one not controlled by any divinity or by any fixed mythological archetypes. The final paragraph of the novel, cited earlier, gives the rationale for such an alternative notion.

Felicia Bonaparte, to my knowledge, was the first critic to argue cogently that the mode of George Eliot's novels is not straightforward realism but allegory. George Eliot, Bonaparte argues, habitually manipulates parallels between her mimetic narratives of everyday life and various mythological prototypes.[6] The realistic story reenacts these in complex interfering patterns and with various degrees of ironic dissonance. My reading of George Eliot differs from Bonaparte's, at least in what I find in *Middlemarch*, in seeing more irony and more dissonance than she does. Her reading of *Romola* sees a dialectic movement in the title character from Ariadne to Antigone to the Madonna. This, Bonaparte argues, involves a rejection of the pagan affirmation of selfish sensuous feeling for the Christian values of sorrow, renunciation, and service. Bonaparte's interpretation of the ethical meaning of George Eliot's novels reaffirms what has often been said of them. I find, on the contrary, in *Middlemarch* at least, that Ariadne wins out over Antigone and over the Virgin, or that the three remain in uneasy and unreconciled tension as models for the understanding of Dorothea's marriage to Will. The marriage of Dionysus and Ariadne remains the dominant prototype, even though Dorothea may be an Ariadne with centuries of Christian understanding of sorrow to modify her apotheosis.

It might be possible to say that Dorothea's repetition of Ariadne in her marriage to Will indicates her regression to inferiority to Romola, the modern Mary. The tonality of *Middlemarch*, however, invites the reader to see Dorothea positively. We are asked to see her as having, somewhat blindly, made the right choice at last. She has done the best that can be done with her life within the lamentable circumstances of nineteenth-century England. The novel powerfully dramatizes a rejection of any large destiny that would make Dorothea a repetition of Saint Theresa or the Virgin, a savior of her people or someone able to perform epic actions on the broad stage of history. In place of those impossibilities for the modern world are put the obscure affirmations of a Christian Ariadne. Those affirmations have a power to do a hidden incalculable good in a narrow circle. Dorothea, the reader is encouraged to believe, made the only possible good choice, given her historical placement.

If Dorothea is a modern Ariadne, Will is her Dionysus. He is Dionysus-like in his association with art and light, in his irresponsibility, in his willingness to be guided by impulse and strong emotion. He is also Dionysus-like in having an obscure association with animals. That association is affirmed by the connection between the miniature of Will's grandmother and the tapestry of a stag. Both hang on the walls of Dorothea's boudoir at Lowick. Will is like Dionysus in the slight effeminacy that has troubled some critics. Like Dionysus, he is given to metamorphosis. In the admirably somber chapter describing the newly married Dorothea at Lowick, the portrait miniature of Will's grandmother, "who had made the unfortunate marriage," turns into Will himself as Dorothea looks at it:

Nay, the colors deepened, the lips and chin seemed to get larger, the hair and eyes seemed to be sending out light, the face was masculine and beamed on her with that full gaze which tells her on whom it falls that she is too interesting for the slightest movement of her eyelid to pass unnoticed and uninterpreted. The vivid presentation came like a pleasant glow to Dorothea. (ch. 22, 258)

Various anomalies stand out in the presentation of Will throughout the novel. These are odd features that seem in excess of the requirements of realistic portraiture. They even seem in excess of the need to present Will as sexually attractive to Dorothea, as Rosamond is attractive to Lydgate, or as Fred Vincy is attractive to Mary Garth. The somewhat covert mythological parallel with Dionysus best explains these oddnesses. The hidden connection surfaces perhaps most openly in a passage in chapter 21, though still without explicit reference to Dionysus. Without the support of all the references to the myth of Ariadne to characterize Dorothea, one might have thought Will is as much Apollo as Dionysus, though the emphasis throughout on Will's power of shape–changing suggests more Dionysus than Apollo. As Felicia Bonaparte has seen, for George Eliot, as for Nietzsche, there is a secret kinship as well as an antithesis between Apollo and Dionysus:

> The first impression on seeing Will was one of sunny brightness, which added to the uncertainty of his changing expression. Surely, his very features changed their form; his jaw looked sometimes large and sometimes small; and the little ripple in his nose was a preparation for metamorphosis. When he turned his head quickly his hair seemed to shake out light, and some persons thought they saw decided genius in this coruscation. (ch. 21, 196)

Dorothea's marriage to Will, I am arguing, repeats that marriage of Ariadne to Dionysus on Naxos that changed Ariadne's situation from that of forlorn betrayal to semidivine status. In her researches for *Romola*, George Eliot had encountered many versions of the myths of Bacchus and Ariadne. She knew Ovid well. She knew many of the antique Greek statues of Bacchus, as well as that Ariadne in the Vatican mentioned in the novel. She knew the painting by Piero di Cosimo in the Vespucci Palace in Florence, *The Discovery of*

Honey. This includes the figures of Bacchus and Ariadne in triumph. This was a favorite subject in Renaissance Florence, both for literary and for pictorial representation. The marriage of Bacchus and Ariadne was also an important Renaissance and post–Renaissance theme. George Eliot may have known, for example, two admirable paintings of the marriage of Bacchus and Ariadne, one by Titian, one by Tintoretto. The theme of the marriage of Bacchus and Ariadne was treated often in opera by composers from Monteverdi on through Jiri Benda in the eighteenth century (Benda composed a monodrama, *Ariadne auf Naxos*, in 1774), and of course down to Richard Strauss's *Ariadne auf Naxos* in our own century.[7] Alongside all these many presentations of the theme, George Eliot's *Middlemarch* may claim an honorable place.

Dorothea's choice of Will is her spontaneous affirmation of the unpredictable and contradictory energy of the life force. Almost against her will, she has embodied this force from the beginning, in her beauty and in her "ardor." This life energy is dangerous, disruptive. Just as Clara Middleton in George Meredith's novel *The Egoist* causes much trouble to all those around her, so Dorothea in *Middlemarch* in both her marriages upsets the conventional economy of marriage and the distribution of property in Middlemarch. Mrs. Cadwallader speaks for those conventions and proprieties. Dorothea's energy is the order-destroying, order-creating vitality of her emotions. This vitality is the fuel that feeds her illusions. It also, however, gives her such power to do good as she has. Her marriage is her choice for the expression of her ardor over her need for theoretic justification. If Dorothea is both ardent and theoretic, the lesson of *Middlemarch* is that the two needs cannot both be satisfied, or rather that her theoretical need cannot be satisfied, even if she were willing to abandon her ardor. Dorothea's failure implies that the narrator's wished-for theoretical clear seeing is also impossible, as is the reader's. Dorothea's marriage is a spontaneous saying yes, like Ariadne's acceptance of Dionysus when he appears to her in her state of forlorn betrayal. Jacques Derrida calls such an acceptance "l'ouverture affirmative pour la venue de l'autre" (the affirmative openness for the coming of the other).[8] Dorothea's "Oh, I cannot bear it—my heart will break" (ch. 83, 762), the opening of the floodgates of her tears, is the moment, in Nietzsche's phrase, of her "ungeheure unbegrenzte Ja," her immense limitless yes.[10] This yes breaks the bind in which Casaubon's will has placed her.

Middlemarch ends with the narrator's analysis of the meaning of Dorothea's life. No evidence is given that Dorothea herself understands her life even so well as the narrator does. Her consciousness disappears from direct representation in the finale. The "openness" of the ending of *Middlemarch* lies partly in the still remaining gap between what the narrator and reader know and what Dorothea is shown as knowing. Neither narrator nor reader can calculate precisely the meaning of Dorothea's life. Nevertheless, they have more insight than she is shown as having. Dorothea's choice of Will imposes a pattern on that roar on the other side of silence that the narrator names in another celebrated passage earlier in the novel (ch. 20, 182).[10] That pattern, however, like the parables in the narrator's discourse, is not an accurate picture of the roar, nor is it justified by or grounded in the roar. No literal representation of the roar is possible. Any coherent pattern given a life by ethical choices lacks depth, in that it is without solid ground in any archetype that it repeats. Nor is it founded on any metaphysical *logos*, even one apprehended as a "roar" to which it can be shown to correspond.

Dorothea's commitment of herself to Will is a performative catachresis. It is a figure projected on the unknown and unknowable X. This figure covers the unknown X over rather than bringing it into the open. It cannot be brought into the open. Dorothea's choice repeats Ariadne's choice, not in the sense of being grounded in it as avatar is grounded in archetype but in the sense of performing once more the blind affirmation figured in Ariadne's acceptance of Dionysus. The marriage of Ariadne and Dionysus, moreover, like the marriage of Dorothea and Will, exists in the artistic representations of it, not as some celestial archetype. It, too, is a human creation. Each marriage helps to understand the other, but neither is the ground of the other, nor are they both versions of some more ancient model, some key to all mythologies. Dorothea's marriage to Will in *Middlemarch* is George Eliot's interpretation of the myth of Ariadne and Bacchus. The novel functions as a commentary on the myth that changes it, as all interpretation does. Each marriage, whether we think of it as an imagined actual event or as an artistic representation, is no more than what is made of it. It is something incalculably diffusive, to be measured by the effects it has.

This alternative mode of repetition, in its opposition to the traditional metaphysical one, is repeated in five different ways in George Eliot's life and in her work. No one of these has priority over the others, as its "source" or "key." All five are related as Dorothea's marriage is related to Ariadne's. Each is a different manifestation of the same inaugural performative. One way is Marian Evans's own life in her relations with her father and the various men with whom she was associated. Another way is in her writing of her novels. Another way is in the interpretation of the characters' lives by her novels' narrators and in the tropological modes of narration used. The latter might be called George Eliot's rhetoric of narration. Another is in the lives of the characters themselves. The fifth is in the interpretation of all these proposed by readers and critics.

In her own life Marian Evans repeatedly enacted an odd female version of the Oedipal triangle. This version has father, mother, daughter, rather than father, mother, son. The myths of Ariadne, of Antigone, and of the Virgin Mary, each in its own way, are modes of this. In this story the daughter seeks to replace the mother in the father's affections. That would make possible a position of willing submission to the father's authority. The daughter hopes thereby to give her life an absolute justification. The father is then recognized to have no valid authority. The daughter, discovering this, replaces the father in one way or another as the authority figure. Even the Virgin, in her submission to the divine mandate, takes on within the Catholic tradition a more or less independent power as mediator. The authority of these various figures has what might be called a peculiarly feminine nuance. In one way or another it challenges or displaces the divine fathering energy. This pattern was repeated at least five times, with variations, in Marian Evans's own life: with her father, with Dr. Brabant, with John Chapman, with G. H. Lewes, and a final time with J. W. Cross, whom she married a few months before her death.[11]

One salient way in which Marian Evans became an authority figure was in the assumption of a masculine persona as the narrator of her novels. Within the novels she plays the role of an omniscient paternal deity, all-knowing, all-wise, all-powerful. In *Adam Bede*, for example, she changes her real father into the fictive Adam and becomes, so to speak, the father of her father. In speaking as a putatively masculine narrator this "she" becomes a fictive "he." This imaginary he makes universal generalizations on the basis of the particular persons and events Marian Evans has invented. The narrator is like a God in judgment dividing the sheep from the goats. Marian Evans's decision to become George Eliot was an imperious assertion of masculine authority and power, even if that assertion remained in the mode of a fictive "as if." This was especially the case when, after everyone came to know the actual identity of "George Eliot," Marian Evans chose not to drop the pseudonym. She never published fiction in her own name. The masculinity of the implied author and narrator of "George Eliot's" novels remains to the end a fundamental part of their mode of existence.

The narrators of Eliot's novels, however, deconstruct masculine authority, even though they employ it. Those narrators show that conventions of realist fiction, in which a fictively "omniscient" narrator plays God, producing and judging an authoritative replica of things and people as they are, only exists in the mode of "as if." Moreover, that kind of authority is systematically dismantled in the discourse of the narrator himself. A feminine narrative authority that has no transcendent base replaces it. This authority takes responsibility for its own creative power. "George Eliot" becomes once again "feminine," within the pattern of sex differentiation the novel has set up, for example in the opposition between the deluded search for an originating "key" by Casaubon or for a "primitive tissue" by Lydgate on the one hand, and on the other hand, Dorothea's abandonment of that kind of search. An expression of that feminine insight is Mary Garth's somewhat detached, thoroughly demystified, ironic wisdom. Mary is perhaps of all the characters in *Middlemarch* closest to Marian Evans herself. In the shift in the narrator back from masculine arrogation of justified cognitive power to feminine performative power, realism as referential mimesis becomes realism as a function of language's autonomous authority. It is narration under the aegis of Ariadne.

Some of the claims made for George Eliot as a feminist writer seem to me unpersuasive. She remained, in her novels at least, conservative on the issue of a woman's place. Dorothea fulfills herself by becoming a wife and mother. This destiny is hardly an argument for women's liberation. Nevertheless, in the subtle and pervasive dismantling of male claims to a divinely grounded authority in storytelling as well as in the conduct of life, and in the replacement of this by what might be called a feminine mode of narration, George Eliot, in spite of her masculine pseudonym, or rather because of what she does with it, is one of the most powerful of feminist writers.

If a female version of the Oedipal drama is enacted and reenacted in Marian Evans's own life, and in what happens to the narrator's claims to authority, the same drama is in another way the figure in the carpet in the stories told in the novels. It is repeated in permutations and combinations in *Adam Bede* and *Silas Marner*, in *The Mill on the Floss*, and in *Daniel Deronda*. Dorothea's story in *Middlemarch* is perhaps the most powerful example. All George Eliot's stories dramatize in one way or another the failure of the search for a legitimate masculine authority to which to submit. Such authority in each case ultimately is replaced in one way or another by what might be called Ariadne's authority, which has the authority of performative ethics. The latter generates its own authority by way of unauthorized speech acts, such as Dorothea's "Oh, I cannot bear it—my heart will break."

The reader in turn repeats the story once more by experiencing the bafflement of his or her search for a definitive interpretation of *Middlemarch*. The concept of organic form inviting cognitive mastery, often invoked in praise of *Middlemarch*, is deconstituted. It is replaced by the experience of a failure to make a definitive reading and in a recognition of the heterogeneity of this text. This failure may be defined by saying that the reader cannot know whether or not a definite reading is possible. It may be possible, and the reader may have it in hand, but he or she can never know for sure. All reading and all criticism, this uncertainty would imply, are performative, productive. They are not a form of certain knowledge but a form of construction. The constructive net of the critic's work of interpretation is subject to all the interpretative acts already performed by narrator and characters within the novel, but it adds its own interpretation to those already made. A reading, such as the one you are now reading, must, like the novel itself, or like the determining acts of Dorothea's life, or like Ariadne's marriage to Dionysus, take responsibility for effects that are unpredictable and "incalculably diffusive."

The reader or critic is no more able to get outside the human situation than is the narrator, the author, or the characters. All are inside the system of signs the novel proffers as a replica of ordinary human life. Like Dorothea, the reader, the narrator, and the author are "part of that involuntary, palpitating life, and [can] neither look out on it from [their] luxurious shelter as . . . mere spectator[s], nor hide [their] eyes in selfish complaining (873). The ending of *Middlemarch*, in what it says of the effects of Dorothea's life, provides an emblem of the novel's uncertainty of meaning and effect. If her effect is incalculably diffusive, so also is the effect of the novel on its readers. One effect of *Middlemarch* is the critical essays it generates. These tend to cover it over, to repress and limit its power in one way or another, but they also receive that power and pass it on.

The novel, something Marian Evans has made out of words, is not the reflection or discovery of some preexisting nonverbal truth, neither the truth about human nature in general nor an historical truth about England at a certain time and place within a certain social class. The novel is rather a web woven of language that produced then, and produces now, unpredictable effects on its readers. It cannot be justified by an idealist theory of art, or by the symmetrical converse of that theory, the notion of an objective mirroring realism. The novel imitates neither things as they are nor the "being" at the origin, end, or base of those things. *Middlemarch*, like Dorothea herself, is unpredictably diffusive. Though the text when read works as a performative or imperative imposing of meaning on its readers, this meaning can never be calculated in advance. It depends on an activity of interpretation that is always to some degree spontaneous, revealing some things in the text, occluding others by silence or evasion. The reading of any sign, in spite of the power of the sign over its reader, is always to some degree fortuitous.

This does not mean that the reader can make *Middlemarch* mean whatever he or she wants it to mean. The openness of *Middlemarch* is an intrinsic feature of the novel, part of its nature as a complex system of signs. The novel itself programs all the diversity of its interpretations. Any interpretation in one way or another repeats the indeterminacies of a text. This is true even of those readings that most try to reduce a given text to a single determinate meaning. The novel is not like the random scratches on the pier-glass. It is, rather, like those scratches already organized into signs. Like the ruins of Rome with the living city atop, in another celebrated passage in *Middlemarch* (ch. 20, 181–2), these signs have a layered incoherence that forbids exhaustive coherent interpretation. The reader too is inhabited by a system of signs. This gives him or her a certain power of interpreting other signs. The reader is open to certain possibilities of meaning in *Middlemarch*, blind to others, though what the reader is blind to will also reappear, in spite of that blindness, in the reading. The reader's own sign-system, too, has its incompleteness, its too little or too much. The ruins of Rome exert power over Dorothea, but she can nevertheless reappropriate them as an emblem of her own life. She can read the ruins as a parable of her state. *Middlemarch*, like the ruins of Rome for Dorothea, is of no use now unless we take possession of it for some present purpose, repeat its performatives with a performative of our own. That taking–possession, however, is always a dispossession, a being–possessed by the power of the text. The language of the novel takes possession of the reader and speaks again through him or her, as those people Dorothea influences, Lydgate and Rosamond, for example, act in ways they would not have not acted but for her. The reader of *Middlemarch* too is in the situation of Ariadne confronted by Dionysus and must make, in one way or another, Ariadne's choice, with its resonances all down through history.

The ultimate paradox or contradiction in the finale is the double meaning it gives to the word and concept of "history." On the one hand, Dorothea's life is not historic. It could not find a place in any old-fashioned "monumental" history, with its tales of world leaders, kings, emperors, popes, battles, and wars. Herodotus can write about Cyrus but not about ordinary women of his time. On the other hand, real history is made by innumerable almost invisible acts such as Dorothea's "Oh, I cannot bear it. My heart will break."

Such events are truly inaugural speech acts. They interrupt the course of history, as Antigone's defiance did. The effects of such events are incalculably diffusive in the sense that they deflect the course of human history, in however minuscule a way.

People like Dorothea make things better for all of us, but they do this often against the understanding of the communities in which they live. One recurrent theme of the finale is the general misinterpretation of the characters by collective community judgment. People erroneously think that Mary Vincy must have written Fred Vincy's agricultural work on "Cultivation of Green Crops and the Economy of Cattle-Feeding," while, equally erroneously, they think Fred must have written the children's book Mary has written. "In this way," says the narrator somewhat acidly, "it was made clear that Middlemarch had never been deceived, and that there was no need to praise anybody for writing a book, since it was always done by somebody else" (finale, 779). The reader may remember that a certain male imposter came forward and claimed to have written *Adam Bede*, no doubt to Marian Evans's chagrin. The Middlemarch community is wrong about Dorothea too. According to Middlemarch tradition, both her marriages were big mistakes: "Those who had not seen anything of Dorothea usually observed that she could not have been 'a nice woman,' else she would not have married either the one or the other" (finale, 784). Even local history gets Dorothea wrong and does not recognize the incalculably diffusive good effects of her goodness. George Eliot's writing of *Middlemarch* is another on the whole beneficent historical event, like Dorothea's second marriage, as is, in its more infinitesimal way, each reading of the novel, such as this one, however good or bad. That is still the case even if the reading never gets spoken publicly or written down. From this it may be concluded that the (im)possibility of reading should not be taken too lightly.

Notes

1. I have discussed the finale briefly in "The Roar on the Other Side of Silence: Otherness in *Middlemarch*," in Shlomith Rimmon-Kenan, Leona

Toker, and Shuli Barzilai, eds., *Rereading Texts/Rethinking Critical Presuppositions* (Frankfurt: Peter Lang, 1997), 137–48; see pp. 144–6.

2. I have discussed these metaphors, in their contradictory interaction, in "Narrative and History," *ELH* 41, 3 (fall 1974), 455–73, and in "Optic and Semiotic in *Middlemarch,"* in *The Worlds of Victorian Fiction*, ed. Jerome H. Buckley, Harvard English Studies 6 (Cambridge, Mass.: Harvard University Press, 1975), 125–45.

3. Friedrich Nietzsche, "Vom Nutzen und Nachtheil der Historie für das Leben," in *Sämtliche Werke*, Kritische Studienausgabe, ed. Giorgio Colli and Mazzino Montinari, 15 vols. Berlin: de Gruyter, 1988),1:258; "On the Utility and Liability of History for Life," in *Unfashionable Observations*, trans. Richard T. Gray, in *Complete Works*, ed. Ernst Behler, 20 vols. (Stanford: Stanford University Press, 1995), 2:96.

4. "The Antigone and Its Moral," in *Essays of George Eliot*, ed. Thomas Pinney (New York: Columbia University Press, 1963), 261–5. Eliot concludes that "Whenever the strength of a man's [*sic!*] intellect, or moral sense, or affection brings him into opposition with the rules which society has sanctioned, *there* is renewed the conflict between Antigone and Creon" (265).

5. Henry James, *The Portrait of a Lady,* in *The Novels and Tales*, reprint of the New York edition (Fairfield, N.J.: Augustus M. Kelley, 1977), 4:51. Further references are to this edition.

6. See Felicia Bonaparte, *Romola: The Tryptych and the Cross: The Central Myths of George Eliot's Poetic Imagination* (New York: New York University Press, 1979). Especially relevant to my discussion here is the chapter that focuses on the function of the myth of Ariadne in *Romola*: "Bacchus and Ariadne Betrothed," 86–109.

7. See Bonaparte, "Bacchus and Ariadne Betrothed," 86–93, for a discussion of some of these sources in relation to the use of the myth of Bacchus and Ariadne in Romola. See also Gordon Haight, *George Eliot: A Biography* (Oxford: Oxford University Press, 1968), 152, for George Eliot's response to Johann Heinrich von Dannecker's painting *Ariadne Seated on a Panther*, which she saw in a private house in Germany: "I never saw any sculpture equal to this—the feeling it excites is the essence of true worship—a bowing of the soul before power creating beauty."

8. Jacques Derrida and Bernard Stiegler, *Échographies* (Paris: Galillée, 1996), 19, my trans.

9. Friedrich Nietzsche, *Also Sprach Zarathustra,* in *Sämtliche Werke*, 4:208; *Thus Spoke Zarathustra*, trans. Walter Kaufmann, in *The Portable Nietzsche* (New York: Viking Press, 1954), 277. Kaufmann translates the phrase as "the uncanny,

unbounded Yes." Nietzsche's Zarathustra asserts that he shares this yes-saying power with the empty sky before sunrise.

10. See my "Roar on the Other Side of Silence."

11. See Haight, *George Eliot,* for the most authoritative account of these relationships, and see also his useful sketches of each of these persons and of their roles in Marian Evans's life in *The George Eliot Letters*, ed. Gordon S. Haight (New Haven: Yale University Press, 1954), 1:lv–lxi, lxii–1xvii, lxviii–lxx.

8

Losing for Profit

DANIEL SIEGEL

◆   ◆   ◆

IN THE CLIMATE of surrender that hangs over George Eliot's novels, there is no shelter for those who clutch. Hetty Sorrel with her dreams of being a lady, Silas Marner with his golden coins, Tito Melema with his burgeoning reputation—all of these characters find that they must painfully and inevitably lose hold of the things they value most. Many of Eliot's readers have commented on the drama of release that plays itself out over and over again in her fiction. One traditional form of moral release lies in the movement from egotism to altruism, a movement frequently identified by critics as the key to Eliot's social vision. In exceptional moments of sympathy, moments often arising from sorrow and humiliation (like the kind that besets Silas Marner when he loses his gold), characters shake off the chains of self-absorption and enter the wider world of fellow feeling. Having lost the objects they are most attached to, these people look for new resources in the community they had shunned. The movement toward altruism has been criticized over the years by readers who object to the great renunciations demanded of Dorothea Brooke and Gwendolyn Harleth. Recent critics have traced the pattern of release to more material realms. Alexander Welsh, for instance, sees the novels as narratives of public exposure, while Jeff Nunokawa describes the market logic by which Eliot's characters are necessarily separated from their property. Studies of Eliot's fables of release differ in their emphasis on the material or the ethical, as well as in their opinions as to whether loss is ultimately punishing or redemptive. But critics are united in seeing loss as the inevitable outcome of clutching too tightly; while it is hopelessly difficult to hold on to a thing, losing it is effortless, a remedy or punishment that is delivered free of charge.

It is curious, therefore, that the characters of *Middlemarch* seem to work as hard to relinquish what they have as they do to get or keep it. In fact, many of the novel's failed efforts are efforts not to hold on but to let go. Such is Featherstone's final act of "generosity," in which he relents his hardheartedness and tries to burn the more vindictive of his wills, but to no avail. Dorothea's attempts at charity are famously frustrated, including even her hope to keep Lydgate at the Fever Hospital in Middlemarch. And Bulstrode's confession to Will, along with his attempts at restitution, are flatly rejected. What are we to make of these stillborn legacies? They seem to call the simplicity of release into question, suggesting that altruistic designs and desperate concessions are as uncertain to succeed as egotistical ambition.

The struggle to let go gripped Eliot's own society, in which charity-minded liberals and conservatives alike endeavored to prove that they could give as good as they could get.[1] Parting with one's money, setting aside one's airs of respectability, even befriending the "wrong" kind of people—these were all the philanthropic achievements of an enlightened and prosperous middle class, exactly the crowd who, in their regular lives, knew how to *make* money and meet all the *right* people. In other words, the competitive spirit that drove professional enterprise also drove the charity business, and in the 1850s and 1860s it was firmly established that charity, like profit, required a certain genius. In a more traditional society, charity was the province of anyone with the means to contribute, the intention to help, and the sympathy to feel. But the Victorians knew better: real charity was a question of outcomes, not intentions. Philanthropists and parliamentarians were preoccupied with the idea that charity could *fail*—that offers of help could be superfluous or even pernicious. The image of failure most often took the familiar shape of the Lady Bountiful, the complacent philanthropist who, as she dispensed money and advice, would be rewarded with a "glow of benevolent patronage," as Helen Bosanquet put it.[2] This was the bad philanthropist, the one who made a show of sacrifice while barely suppressing a self-satisfied smile. But the problem of satisfaction was easier to deplore than to avoid, and everyone interested—from the Poor Law commissioners, to the visiting associations, to the evangelical missions, to the Charity Organisation Society, to the socialists— agreed that a great proportion of public benevolence was misguided, disingenuous, and self-serving.

How could this crisis be met? From one point of view, the answer was to remove the focus entirely from the giver, and to evaluate acts of charity solely on the basis of their efficacy in the lives of the poor. But another response, the one typically associated with liberal guilt, kept the feelings of the giver very much in the equation: charity needed to involve some kind of palpable sacrifice or compromise on the part of the one who gave. The benefactor had to give up not only her time and money but also her complacency, and suffer (if only symbolically) a loss that transcended the loss of the gift itself. It was not enough to relinquish a thing; instead one must relinquish authority, compromise the self. In a sense, then, every true act of charity was double: the benefactor both offered a gift and suffered a loss. These two ideas, both folded into the act of giving, represent two distinct rationales for what might appear a simple, familiar transaction. As Marshall Sahlins explains, the very act that is called "giving" in a culture based on voluntary exchange is cast as "losing" in a culture based on advantage.[3] In the milieu of Victorian charity, the traditional gesture of the gift is enacted only to be supplanted by loss, since in a competitive society, a person can only be said to have gained if someone else has diminished.

The benefactor, then, needed to bear the mark of loss and to hide the traces of satisfaction, perhaps even from herself. We can only imagine with what consternation the Lady Bountiful faced these facts, as she read about them in the Proceedings of the National Association for the Promotion of the Social Sciences. How, after all, was a person to know when she had given enough? If losses there must be, how best to control them, to afford them? And if one gave enough to satisfy even the social scientists, then who would ever need to know that a spark of complacency remained—that, in fact, far from compromising herself, the giver had managed to secure that very complacency?[4] Despite the hardening philosophical distinction between them, giving and losing could easily be mistaken for one another, and someone who had mastered the art of losing might give up a fortune and still come out very well.[5]

Eliot was very conscious of the "problem" of bad giving, of styles of renunciation that tried to evade or transcend real loss. That is why, in *Middlemarch*, there is nothing ethically clear or automatic about the process of release. To the contrary, losing is just as deliberate and complicated a moral act as gaining and keeping are. And just as the ideology of profit unites the beggar and the man of business, so does the compulsion to lose range beyond charity itself, exerting its logic not only between but also within classes, even within households. The economics of renunciation matter not only to the social worker or missionary prowling the slums or the colonies but also to the childless widower who must choose an heir, or the dutiful daughter who surrenders her salary to her parents. If, as critics argue, the inevitable loss of one's possessions and interests is a specter that haunts the world of *Middlemarch*, the inhabitants of that world know that loss is in the air, and their question is less often how to hold on to what they have than how to let go of it advantageously.

Middlemarch is a novel of strategic abdication, in which, by making various concessions and sacrifices, characters attempt to establish an authentic way to survive in a landscape of loss. The novel doesn't choose either for or against renunciation; rather, it explores the ethical contours of the renunciations whereby characters try to secure their lives. With a continuous stream of abdications—of power, authority, property, potential, plans, ambitions, fantasies, and opinions—*Middlemarch* considers the difficulty of release, a difficulty that is epitomized by the many characters who steep themselves in expense in order to ward off their ruin.

Legacy: Securing Your Property

One of the great strategic abdicators is Peter Featherstone, who cannot bear the idea that his death will allow his estate to pass beyond his control. Featherstone relinquishes his wealth in a way calculated to produce the sharpest disappointment among the family members who have attended him in his final years; that is, he leaves everything to an illegitimate son who is a stranger to Stone Court and the Middlemarch community. It is clear that, by bequeathing his estate to Joshua Rigg, Featherstone is thinking less of establishing an heir than of disappointing the other suitors:

> In writing the programme for his burial he certainly did not make clear to himself that his pleasure in the little drama of which it formed a part was confined to anticipation. In chuckling over the vexations he could inflict by the rigid clutch of his dead hand, he inevitably mingled his consciousness with that livid stagnant presence, and so far as he was preoccupied with a future life, it was one of gratification inside his coffin. (ch. 34, 304)

Featherstone's legacy is an abdication designed to clutch, to withhold his wealth for his own posthumous gratification. Even if he cannot possess his estate after he dies, Featherstone has "Rigged" his will, losing all without giving a thing to those who clamor outside his room. It is a legacy that amounts to no legacy at all. The narrator herself calls Rigg a "superfluity" (ch. 41, 386) and so he is—not so much an inheritor as a personification of Featherstone's will to frustrate. Of course, Featherstone's grasping legacy ultimately fails him; he can no more hold on to his fortune by throwing it away than he could bring it into his coffin with him. In an earlier chapter Featherstone has contrasted the importance of himself and his land with "Bulstrode and speckilation" (ch. 12, 103) but it turns out that Rigg is speckilation incarnate—a man whose fondest wish is to become a money-changer—and that he is more than ready to sell to Bulstrode. If Featherstone has limited his loss in one way, keeping it from enriching the people nearest him, he ends up losing Stone Court more completely than he could have imagined.[6]

The real loss to Featherstone is not Stone Court but that which goes along with it: his power of denial. The two go together, in that Featherstone's refusal to pass his property on to his suitors is the next best thing to keeping it himself. Simply leaving the estate to Rigg, unchallenged, would bring no satisfaction, since the power of Featherstone's grasp is exactly as great as the sum of the petitions, hopes, and expectations he is denying. He attempts to create desires and expectations among his prospective heirs so that he can baffle them; and yet these suitors, or at least the flesh-and-blood relatives, are on to his game, aware that he will never leave an inheritance where it is expected. So just as Featherstone lets his fortune slip through his fingers so that nobody else can take it from him, his suitors anticipate their disappointment by neurotically abandoning their expectations at every moment. Of course they do have expectations: the penultimate chapter of "Waiting for Death" explains the sound reasoning by which Jane, Solomon, Jonah, Martha, and the others decide independently that Peter will favor them in the will, to the exclusion of rival contenders. But at the same time that the Waules and Featherstones are asserting their right to the property, they repeat their suspicions that the estate will go to the Garths and Vincys, refusing their relative the satisfaction of denying them. They are aware, both during his life and after his death, that they have been contending with him as if in battle (or in a game), and when Rigg eventually sells Stone Court to Bulstrode, they can claim to have taken the upper hand:

> what Peter would say "if he were worthy to know," had become an inexhaustible and consolatory subject of conversation to his disappointed relatives. The tables were now turned on that dear brother departed, and to contemplate the frustration of his cunning by the superior cunning of things in general was a cud of delight to Solomon. Mrs Waule had a melancholy triumph in the proof that it did not answer to make false Featherstones and cut off the genuine; and sister Martha receiving the news in the Chalky Flats said, "Dear, dear! then the Almighty could have been none so pleased with the almshouses after all." (ch. 53, 489)

So Featherstone's affront was "cunning" all along—not ingratitude, or malice, or even insanity. In other words, it's not the wrongness of Featherstone's will that his brother and sisters rebel against, but its effectiveness, since they feel that by leaving it to Rigg he actually has in some sense kept hold of it. Thus when it goes to Bulstrode, the survivors can rejoice that the dead man has finally lost. Featherstone's grasping gift to Rigg has been abandoned—has, in fact, entered the market—losing Featherstone whatever feeble kind of "possession" might derive from the disappointment of his would-be heirs.

When Rigg sells Stone Court, Featherstone is effectively punished for his attempts to bequeath his property in a way that would withhold it. But as we are absorbed in this family struggle, we forget that even before Bulstrode takes possession—even when the whole estate is still securely in Rigg's hands—Featherstone has lost, since this was not, indeed, his final intention. At the eleventh hour, the dying man does *not* clutch, or not entirely; he tries to pass a substantial sum on to Fred. His legacy to Fred is presumably not one merely designed to frustrate the other suitors, but one that bespeaks genuine affection, even a kind of recuperation from Featherstone's many years of selfishness. Considering the well-meaningness of this attempt—the destruction of the second, more grasping will—it seems hard that Featherstone should be so firmly denied. In fact, his turn to Fred almost redeems the earlier scenes of manipulation, suggesting that perhaps Featherstone has all along intended to leave a legacy to Fred, preparing the second will simply as a way of delaying his actual, more generous intention.[7] Featherstone's culpability, then, must rest somehow in this postponement. He may very well know how he wants to commit his money, but he still tries to prepare the gift, to give it value, by continually denying it, holding it back, veiling his intentions. Without any kind of malice, Featherstone genuinely believes that his legacy to Fred derives value from his own insistence that he does not *have* to give it; he therefore takes constant pains to invoke the possibilities of other fates for the estate, even to the extent of writing a second will. Only by establishing an Esau, an older son with a truer claim, can Featherstone make his gift to Fred exceptional or valuable. And yet the novel seems to suggest that by withholding the thing so often with such imaginative resolve, Featherstone has tainted it, made it ungiveable; the postponement may lend the gift significance as a gesture, but it gradually siphons *out* any significance it might have had as a willing and full release. By the time Featherstone makes his decision, it is just another in a series of alternations back and forth; Featherstone has allowed his whole volitional life to become a group of contradictory movements, inadvertently ensuring that even a final resolve will be taken for a momentary impulse.

So Featherstone fails not once but twice with respect to his legacy; in the battle he wages against his siblings, he tries to give-in-order-to-withhold, and in his postponement of his legacy to Fred, he tries to withhold-in-order-to-give. Neither strategy works—and yet it's strange that Eliot mingles these very different failures. The first by itself would be sufficient: Featherstone could leave everything to Joshua Rigg, who would then sell it to Bulstrode, showing that there is no way, even through a rigged legacy, to keep a thing from being passed on to others against one's will. Or alternately, Eliot need never have introduced Bulstrode to this story at all, allowing Featherstone's tragedy to culminate simply in his final scene with Mary, as he finds himself unable to do the generous thing at last, after a lifetime of postponing and withholding his generosity. These are hardly the same story: wanting to give generously at a time of one's choosing is a different fault from wanting to hold on to one's property forever, and yet by allowing Featherstone to sin in both ways, Eliot seems to be drawing a connection between them.

We see a similar duplication in Casaubon, who also fails twice in the legacy department. The first failure relates to his work, which he attempts to release posthumously, through Dorothea, after years of delay. He has apparently thought better of his fairly recent decision to withhold it, against Dorothea's advice: "My love . . . you may rely upon me for knowing the times and the seasons, adapted to the different stages of a work which is not to be measured by the facile conjectures of ignorant onlookers" (ch. 20, 188). Casaubon's delay is, like Featherstone's promises, an attempt to maintain the value of his work by allowing it to be manifested only in expectation. As he persists in his research and postulates ever more on the significance of his project, Casaubon is living on credit; to finish the book during his lifetime would be to gamble against the possibility that the book might strike somewhere below the mark—that it might be worth rather less than his aspirational investments.[8] When Casaubon becomes apprised of his heart condition, his strategic delays lose their attraction; the term of his life has been fixed, and postponement forfeits all of its value.[9] He rushes toward completion with an avidity of which Dorothea had thought him incapable: "Dorothea was amazed to think of the bird-like speed with which his mind was surveying the ground where it had been creeping for years" (ch. 48, 448). But Casaubon's strategic postponement—his conscious abandonment of the work itself in favor of the fantasy—comes at a cost after his death. His scholarship has been so fully associated with fruitlessness and incompletion that Dorothea's unwillingness to continue it comes not from any particular revulsion to the work itself but from a sense that it must never be completed, never fulfilled, always a matter of working "as in a treadmill fruitlessly" (ch. 48, 450). Dorothea, like Mary in Featherstone's room, faces a legacy that she has seen recede from her time and time again; even had she not replaced the "Synoptical Tabulation" in the locked drawer, one imagines it must have found its way there of its own will.

This injunction of Casaubon—the injunction that Dorothea should continue his work after he has died—is referred to as "that promise by which he sought to keep his cold grasp on Dorothea's life" (ch. 50, 463), but the dead hand also clutches elsewhere and otherwise. Casaubon's other failure comes not through a deferral of his legacy but in his attempt to control it, to haunt it. With the condition he places on Dorothea's inheritance, he ensures that he, his intentions for the property and his intentions for Dorothea, will maintain their hold. But this isn't exactly true, for if Dorothea were not to marry, or were to marry a stranger—were, in fact, to do anything other than the thing Casaubon most dreads—then Casaubon's hold would vanish, and his relationship to the property would become irrelevant. Thus Casaubon creates a condition by which he only survives if Dorothea betrays him, or at any rate if she would like to; his legacy lies in the denial of the disloyal Dorothea, just as Featherstone's lay in the denial of his family. Casaubon cannot bring himself to release his property and influence, just as Featherstone couldn't; instead, he gives it in a way that withholds it. In Casaubon's scheme, the "loyal Dorothea," like Joshua Rigg, inherits solely in order to exclude another—the "disloyal Dorothea."

The double problem of the novel's two principal legators, then, is that they manage their legacies in a way that holds on as tightly as possible, and that, when they do look to the possibility of a more genuine release, they try to capitalize on this through anticipation and deferral. The problems are separate but related. In neither scenario does the owner resist the loss of his possessions; rather, he attempts to delay or qualify the loss so that it cannot be transformed into another's gain. If the inheritor's gain is deferred or erased, than the loss is only partial, and its very incompleteness stands in for actual possession. The novel's third and final delayed inheritance—Will's inheritance from his mother—suffers the same fate: because it has been withheld, it can never be fully given. In this case, Will doesn't want the gift, and Bulstrode's equivocation has purchased Will the power of refusal: "What I have to thank you for is that you kept the money till now, when I can refuse it" (ch. 61, 586). Bulstrode's postponement, like the postponements of Casaubon and Featherstone, has branded this legacy ungiveable. When he wants to give up his plunder, Bulstrode finds that every avenue of release has closed to him; his problem is not that he can't keep what he has but that he can't relax his grip.

Charity: Securing Your Prerogative

If it is so hard to give authentically even through the "natural" process of inheritance, it is almost impossible for the characters of *Middlemarch* to give anything away outside the bounds of ordinary expectation. As I have noted, Eliot's emphasis on the problem of release relates to a midcentury crisis of philanthropy, a crisis that was crystallized with the foundation of the Charity Organisation Society (COS) in 1869, the year Eliot began her composition of *Middlemarch*. One of the primary objects of the COS was to quell impulsive benevolence and bring charity under a more reliable, system-atic, and scientific administration. According to the COS, the mis-guided feelings of the public led the middle classes to give more than was necessary or helpful; the administration of charity, they argued, should depend on its particular effects on the poor, and not on the moral gratifications of the rich. As the century wore on, the conservative arguments of the COS dovetailed with the claims of socialists, who saw middle-class philanthropy as a guilt-offering to ease the conscience of the wealthy. Something of this logic haunts Casaubon's gifts to Will, gifts taken from a fortune that, Dorothea decides, should have belonged to Will in the first place. Casaubon's generosity allows him to avert greater losses, and indeed the charity we see throughout the novel is often no more than a way of justify-ing and securing possession. The novel draws a sharp distinction between the intentional abdications that aim to justify the giver and the compulsory abdications that help the receiver.

At Dorothea's engagement party, Mrs Cadwallader remarks that Lydgate "is a sort of philanthropist, so Brooke is sure to take him up" (ch. 10, 85). To be a philanthropist, from the Tory point of view, is no virtue; it is to concern oneself with desultory public objects rather than one's proper responsibilities (to family, tenants, church, etc.). The Freshitt crowd has contempt for Brooke's interest in con-demned criminals and Fever Hospitals, advocating instead the ordi-nary functions of the landlord, which range from managing the es-tate to haggling with the tenants. Paradoxically, to spend time and money *beyond* one's own sphere of obligation—to spend it in an ex-ceptional way—does not, in Brooke's case, equate to altruism or self-transcendence. Instead it is a way of making the self conspicu-ous, consequential. Brooke has his eyes fixed on his own image; in this his leniency resembles the more severe charity of Bulstrode and the apostolic Tyke, whose "doctrine," Lydgate explains, "is a sort of pinching hard to make people uncomfortably aware of him" (ch. 50, 465).[10] The reason that Brooke is able to sustain a style of philan-thropy that does so little good is that for him, charity is a matter of politics and principles rather than outcomes. And the more ab-stract, the better: abstract charity purchases a kind of moral security that more personal exchanges cannot, because as long as the benefactor has no natural relationship to the person he or she helps, his or her charity cannot be mistaken for an obligatory act but must be recognized as exceptional, noteworthy. Eliot's famous statement about doing wrong could apply here, equally, to doing good. She says that "we are most of us brought up in the notion that the highest motive for not doing a wrong is something irrespective of the beings who would suffer the wrong" (ch. 24, 234); the same egotism could be said to motivate philanthropists who have no clear sense of who the needy are, or what their claims might be.

Ultimately, the only kind of charity that helps is that which is compulsory rather than voluntary, that which acknowledges its motive to be obligation rather than munificence. Dorothea recognizes this and, throughout the novel, struggles to involve herself in ties of obligation.[11] She is quick to decide that Casaubon is in Will's debt, a construction that even Will hasn't put on the situation. She recognizes that Lydgate will not accept her money as a gift but might take it as a loan: "He might call her a creditor or by any other name if it did but imply that he granted her request" (ch. 76, 724). After her husband's death, Dorothea becomes progressively more preoccupied with the "duties attached to ownership" (ch. 50, 464) and, even while she looks into schemes for the broader expenditure of her wealth, invests herself in actions of local consequence. When she puts off her mourning clothes, Dorothea effectively abjures the forms of renunciation that are trained on herself; she is no longer the girl of chapter 1 who "enjoyed it [riding] in a pagan sensuous way, and always looked forward to renouncing it" (10). In fact, renunciation becomes so fully associated with selfishness by the end of the novel that, had Casaubon left no codicil at all on his will, there arguably would be no way for Dorothea to give up her wealth, no path to Ladislaw. It's only because it is compelled—because she has no choice in the matter—that Dorothea's loss can be productive.

As the fruits of obligation, Dorothea's renunciations seem to align themselves with the Tory doctrine of duty, an alternative to Whiggish cause-mongering and exceptionalist philanthropy. But even the promptings of obligation are no help when the contours of one's duty are vague, as they almost invariably are. Some species of vagueness haunts Casaubon and his duties from the very beginning, as emblematized by the fact that his parish has no poor to be attended to, no vice to be ameliorated (ch. 9, 71). As if they themselves are an emanation of their rector's incapacity to give, the Lowick farmers bear a mysterious relationship, at least according to Mrs Cadwallader, to the lord of the manor: "They are quite different from your uncle's tenants or Sir James's—monsters—farmers without landlords—one can't tell how to class them" (ch. 34, 306). The murky question of Casaubon's "duty" to his independent tenants is rather different from Brooke's much more clear-cut negligence, and indeed Eliot never implies that the rector has neglected his duty in order to chase philanthropic windmills. Brooke explains, "Casaubon and I don't talk politics much. He doesn't care much about the philanthropic side of things; punishments, and that kind of thing" (ch. 6, 49). But while Casaubon may not be an idealistic dilettante, he shares Brooke's inability to think in terms of duty, as is made most clear in his patronage of Will. Casaubon cannot allow his charity to Will to present itself as the fulfillment of an obligation; such a construction would wreck the complacency that his gifts purchase him. It's only because Casaubon believes he is being generous toward Will, rather than acquitting his duty, that he can tell himself that Will owes him something in return; his sense of self-congratulation keeps Casaubon stuck in a cycle where he tries to take back everything that he gives.[12]

Compromise: Securing Your Integrity

The characters of *Middlemarch* lose more than just their money; they also lose reputation, authority, and self-respect. And just as they compromise their economic resources in order to prevent greater losses, so do they compromise various forms of assertion in order to maintain some measure of authority or complacency. Rosamond perhaps does this most successfully; in her battles with Lydgate, she acquiesces in order to refuse. This pattern plays out in ways almost too familiar to mention in debates over her jewelry, her home, her riding, and so on. Rosamond holds her ground by giving way, precisely what her husband—particularly with respect to borrowing—

becomes eventually unwilling to do. When challenged, Rosamond quickly falls into silence, securing her opinions untrammeled, and preparing for the chance to act on them. She compromises to avoid being compromised.

Over the course of the novel, Sir James Chettam, too, learns how to silence himself, to suppress his opinions; in his case perhaps more than in any other, we see the costs of being a Company Man, the kinds of concession necessary to stay in the group. Chettam seems at first perfectly confident that his own opinions accord with those of other right-thinking people. While he is uneasy as to his ability to decide difficult questions (ch. 3, 29), he finds it absurd that he should have to justify or defend his feelings about matters of common sense. Thus when Mr Cadwallader asks him to defend his bad opinion of Casaubon, "Sir James paused. He did not usually find it easy to give his reasons: it seemed to him strange that people should not know them without being told, since he only felt what was reasonable" (ch. 8, 64). But Chettam finds increasingly that his opinions, which he had assumed were universally shared, put him at odds with the crowd. Although it is clear to Sir James that Brooke should interfere with Dorothea's marriage, interfere he will not, nor does Cadwallader think he should. Later, in light of Casaubon's will, Sir James insists that Mr Brooke send Ladislaw away, but Brooke cannot bring himself to do so—and indeed the community at large finds Ladislaw's presence fully supportable. What Chettam learns, with some pain, is that he can't afford to speak his mind about the things that touch him most deeply:

> Sir James was informed that same night that Dorothea was really quite set against marrying anybody at all, and was going to take to "all sorts of plans," just like what she used to have. Sir James made no remark. To his secret feeling, there was something repulsive in a woman's second marriage, and no match would prevent him from feeling it a sort of desecration for Dorothea. He was aware that the world would regard such a sentiment as preposterous, especially in relation to a woman of one-and-twenty; the practice of 'the world' being to treat of a young widow's second marriage as certain and probably near, and to smile with

meaning if the widow acts accordingly. But if Dorothea did choose to espouse her solitude, he felt that the resolution would well become her. (ch. 55, 517–8)

When Dorothea's second marriage is eventually announced, Chettam can't restrain himself. "It would have been better if I had called him out and shot him a year ago," he exclaims; he chokes out a litany of epithets against Will, declares "That is my opinion," and crosses his legs (ch. 84, 765–6). But Chettam's explosions catalyze an opposite response from his wife, his father-in-law, and the Cadwalladers, who combine to determine that this outcome is perfectly logical, that Dorothea deserves pity rather than blame, and that Chettam is getting his principles mixed up with his feelings. When Mr Brooke suggests that he is willing to cut off the entail—to leave his estate, in other words, to Chettam's own son rather than Dorothea's—Sir James is stung into silence. Having for once insisted on his opinions, he is cut to pieces by a chorus of his closest associates. Self-repression was the best thing after all.

Bulstrode too is a man of negotiations, but the strategic compromises that serve Rosamond so well are delivered most grudgingly by the banker, and unlike Chettam, Bulstrode never learns to concede fully or quickly enough to afford him the approval of others. Reluctant to make any concessions at all, Bulstrode finds himself required to do so whenever his own integrity is in doubt. He demonstrates this tendency during his first appearance in the novel, as Vincy pressures him to write a letter on Fred's behalf. When Bulstrode offers his principled objections, Vincy assaults the banker's business practices and sense of family loyalty. Under the pressure of accusation, Bulstrode quickly backs down, as is his habit: "This was not the first time that Mr Bulstrode had begun by admonishing Mr Vincy, and had ended by seeing a very unsatisfactory reflection of himself in the coarse unflattering mirror which that manufacturer's mind presented to the subtler lights and shadows of his fellow-men" (ch. 13, 123). Here and elsewhere, Bulstrode panics when he sees the *image* of himself as one who grasps, and, in order to mitigate that image, he is willing to incur whatever losses he thinks he can sustain. Thus, when he fears his wife will be put off by his unwillingness to help

Lydgate and Rosamond, Bulstrode offers to let Stone Court to Fred Vincy. When Raffles emerges as a kind of tangible manifestation of Bulstrode's will-to-power, the compromises come fast and furious: the banker confesses to Will, offers a bribe to Lydgate, and plans to leave Middlemarch. Bulstrode's tragedy is not that he is unable to make concessions but that he can only do so when it is too late. His piecemeal compromises are swept away in the rush of restitution.

These narratives of loss reveal an entire domain of ethical inquiry, in which release suggests a varied array of motives and consequences much in the same way that possession and control do. The idea that loss is a kind of mirror image of gain—that it is largely by giving up that individual persons construct their moral character, for better and for worse—is an idea especially resonant in the 1860s and 1870s, after the early Victorian faith in voluntary philanthropy had begun to slip, but before the socialist discourse branding charity a useless palliative had substantially taken hold. In these years, loss might redeem or condemn, fail or succeed—indeed, it might be narrated.[13] This is less true in Eliot's early works: Janet Dempster, evicted by her husband, spends ten short paragraphs on the street before her recovery begins, while the great losses sustained by Hetty Sorrel and Arthur Donnithorne are as sudden as they are absolute. But in *Middlemarch,* episodes of loss and acts of release have a shape and a duration: the decay of Dorothea's marriage and the dwindling of Bulstrode's fortune take on a narrative scope reminiscent of the death of Clarissa Harlowe a century before. Losing no longer signifies the wheels of agency grinding to a halt; rather, it is the very axle on which they spin, such that even gain can seem to be another loss. As Mary Garth admits, "Everything seems too happy for me all at once. I thought it would always be part of my life to long for home, and losing that grievance makes me feel rather empty: I suppose it served instead to fill up my mind" (ch. 40, 383).

Notes

1. Among the classic works on Victorian charity are David Owen, *English Philanthropy 1660–1960* (Cambridge, Mass.: Harvard University Press,

1964), Gareth Stedman Jones, *Outcast London* (Oxford: Clarendon, 1971), Frank Prochaska, *Women and Philanthropy in Nineteenth-Century England* (Oxford: Clarendon, 1980), and Brian Harrison, *Peaceable Kingdom* (Oxford: Clarendon, 1982). The last fifteen years have seen a number of revaluations of the material and cultural issues surrounding philanthropy, including Peter Mandler's collection *The Uses of Charity* (Philadelphia: University of Pennsylvania Press, 1990), Gertrude Himmelfarb, *Poverty and Compassion* (New York: Knopf, 1991), Audrey Jaffe, *Scenes of Sympathy* (Ithaca: Cornell University Press, 2000), and Dorice Elliott, *The Angel out of the House* (Charlottesville: University Press of Virginia, 2002).

2. Himmelfarb, *Poverty and Compassion,* 197.

3. Marshall Sahlins, *Stone Age Economics* (Chicago: Aldine, 1972), 193–5. In showing the different *qualities* that attach to structurally identical transactions, Sahlins moves beyond a "formal typology of reciprocities"—a description that looks at the "material and mechanical dimensions of exchange"—seeking a description that takes the "spirit of exchange" into account. Sahlins associates a culture's complex of attitudes toward exchange with kinship, arguing that in societies with greater kinship distance (including, of course, nineteenth-century Europe) reciprocity tends to be cast in "negative" terms related to seizure and competition (195).

4. As a drama of self-recognition, charity has much in common with the scenes of sympathy that Audrey Jaffe discusses, although for Jaffe it is not giving but looking that sets the process of recognition in motion. She argues that, as the middle-class spectator witnesses a poor person deserving of sympathy, both the witness and the witnessed are displaced by "images, or fantasies" that move the spectator both to identify with the sufferer and to reject this identification because of the attendant degradation to the spectator (*Scenes of Sympathy,* 4, 12). I would argue that in charity, too, identification can be a kind of talisman for the middle-class philanthropist, allowing her momentarily to break down the distinction between classes in order to assure herself that the distinction is really there. Of course one hesitates to assume that this was the universal or even the usual rationale for charity; and yet it would be equally naïve to assume that none of the old complacency haunted the new, "professional" charity.

5. This and many other ideas in this essay are greatly indebted to Jeffrey Nunokawa's argument about the alienation of property in Eliot; see Nunokawa, *The Afterlife of Property: Domestic Security and the Victorian Novel* (Princeton: Princeton University Press, 1994). Nunokawa cites Mill's claim that the right to alienate property—to bestow it as one chooses—is the central prerogative of ownership (82–83). This concept, I would argue, ac-

counts for both the great power of the gift, since it is at the moment when a person gives a thing that, paradoxically, she most absolutely asserts her ownership of it; and the great limitations of the gift, since giving a thing (as opposed to losing it) can always be seen as an assertion of power, an act that is trying to get something back in return. See Jacques Derrida, *Given Time. I, Counterfeit Money* (Chicago: University of Chicago Press, 1992) for a discussion of the returns necessitated by gifts.

6. Nunokawa discusses Featherstone's inability to control his property once it leaves his hands, demonstrating that the bestowal of property is both a proof and a relinquishing of ownership: "expenditure is an event rather than a condition; the alienation of property is an irreversible act, at once the realization and the termination of ownership's potence" (*Afterlife of Property*, 85).

7. To be clear: leaving the property to Fred is more generous not because Fred is needier or more deserving than Joshua Rigg but because, as we have seen, the gift to Rigg is, for Featherstone, no more than a denial of the other suitors.

8. Eliot gives an example of exactly this predicament in the case of Dr. Sprague, who has forfeited his ability to interact with the new medical men because his own "standing had been fixed thirty years before by a treatise on Meningitis, of which at least one copy marked 'own' was bound in calf" (ch. 16, 146–7). The doctor's accomplishment becomes feeble and limiting simply because it is "fixed"; he has cashed his chips, and unlike Casaubon and Lydgate, who work constantly toward a goal that eludes them, Sprague has lost the luxury of anticipation.

9. See D. A. Miller, *Narrative and Its Discontents: Problems of Closure in the Traditional Novel* (Princeton: Princeton University Press, 1981) for a discussion of the sense in which closure brings about a "surrender of desire or its reductive rescaling" (149).

10. Even though many readers of *Middlemarch* associate public charity with Dorothea and her cottages, it comes up more often with reference to Mr. Brooke's philanthropic causes and Bulstrode's charitable investments. Bulstrode has "gathered, as an industrious man always at his post, a chief share in administering the town charities, and his private charities were both minute and abundant" (ch. 63, 145). Whether Bulstrode's charities are any different in kind from Dorothea's can only be a matter of speculation, but it becomes very clear at the point that Dorothea offers to take over the Fever Hospital that for Eliot the value of charity has everything to do with its motives.

11. Her inclinations in this direction can be compared to Farebrother's:

"I don't enter into some people's dislike of being under an obligation; upon my word, I prefer being under an obligation to everybody for behaving well to me," 606).

12. Of course, the novel does not allow us to say with any certainty that Casaubon is wrong on this matter or that Dorothea is right. Casaubon's feeling that he has been generous above and beyond the call of duty accords with Will's own understanding of the situation, and the novel never decides whether Dorothea's construction is more correct, or simply the expression of a more duty-oriented imagination.

13. The type of loss discussed in this essay is in every case particular, local, interested; it should be distinguished from the broad sense of collective (national, cultural, racial) decline that preoccupied England during the latest decades of the nineteenth century, as explored by Stephen Arata, *Fictions of Loss in the Victorian Fin de Siècle* (Cambridge: Cambridge University Press, 1996). The distinction is not incidental: the midcentury demand for particular losses—the demand that informs so many of the episodes discussed in this essay—rests on the supposition that discrete, well-deserved losses can contribute to a more just society and a general prosperity.

References

Arata, Stephen. *Fictions of Loss in the Victorian Fin de Siècle*. Cambridge: Cambridge University Press, 1996.

Derrida, Jacques. *Given Time. I, Counterfeit Money*. Chicago: University of Chicago Press, 1992.

Elliott, Dorice. *The Angel out of the House: Philanthropy and Gender in Nineteenth-Century England*. Charlottesville: University Press of Virginia, 2002.

Harrison, Brian. *Peaceable Kingdom: Stability and Change in Modern Britain*. Oxford: Clarendon Press, 1982.

Himmelfarb, Gertrude. *Poverty and Compassion: The Moral Imagination of the Late Victorians*. New York: Knopf, 1991.

Jaffe, Audrey. *Scenes of Sympathy: Identity and Representation in Victorian Fiction*. Ithaca: Cornell University Press, 2000.

Jones, Gareth Stedman. *Outcast London: A Study in the Relationship between Classes in Victorian Society*. Oxford: Clarendon Press, 1971.

Mandler, Peter, ed. *The Uses of Charity*. Philadelphia: University of Pennsylvania Press, 1990.

Miller, D. A. *Narrative and Its Discontents: Problems of Closure in the Traditional Novel*. Princeton: Princeton University Press, 1981.

Nunokawa, Jeff. *The Afterlife of Property: Domestic Security and the Victorian Novel.* Princeton: Princeton University Press, 1994.

Owen, David. *English Philanthropy 1660–1960.* Cambridge, Mass.: Harvard University Press, 1964.

Prochaska, Frank. *Women and Philanthropy in Nineteenth-Century England.* Oxford: Clarendon Press, 1980.

Sahlins, Marshall. *Stone Age Economics.* Chicago: Aldine, 1972.

Welsh, Alexander. *George Eliot and Blackmail.* Cambridge, Mass.: Harvard University Press, 1985.

9

Narrative Vision in *Middlemarch*

The Novel Compared with the BBC Television Adaptation

JAKOB LOTHE

◆　　◆　　◆

WHAT EXACTLY DID Virginia Woolf have in mind when, in a deservedly famous statement, she described *Middlemarch* as "one of the few English novels written for grown-up people"?[1] We cannot know for certain, of course, but Woolf was probably thinking of not just one but several of the novel's characteristic features. She may have been reflecting on the ways in which its constituent aspects—narrative, structural, thematic, metaphorical—interact in the formation of an exceptionally complex and multifaceted narrative discourse. More specifically, she may have been thinking of the diverse functions and effects of George Eliot's third-person narrator—a narrator who, even though she is possessed of the powers and characteristics of realist narration, anticipates the narrators Woolf employs in novels such as *Mrs Dalloway* and *To the Lighthouse*.

This essay will discuss how Eliot uses the literary device of a third-person narrator in order to present, and cumulatively enrich and complicate, her narrative vision in *Middlemarch*. I will also discuss how this vision can be presented on film. The complexities of narrative associated with Eliot's third-person narrator pose a challenge to any director attempting to adapt this particular novel to the screen. Focusing on three chapters that present different facets of the visual in *Middlemarch*, I will compare these textual passages with the corresponding filmic segments in the BBC adaptation from 1994, a TV version popular in England and sold to many countries.[2] As we shall see, the passages under consideration illustrate different problems and possibilities as far as the transformation from verbal prose to film is concerned.

Although it is difficult to adequately explain what is meant by "the visual," both in fiction generally and in *Middlemarch* in particular, it does not follow that the concept is critically unproductive. I will concentrate on those elements of Eliot's discourse that perform a characteristically double function throughout the narrative: on the one hand, Eliot uses the flexible instrument of a third-person narrator to show how the characters both see and fail to see; on the other hand, she repeatedly signals that just as the characters' ability to see is limited, so is that of the narrator, the author, and the reader. Part of Eliot's achievement in *Middlemarch* is to demonstrate, in convincing detail, both the necessity of seeing and the unavoidable limitations of seeing. That even Dorothea Brooke, one of the novel's most intelligent and perceptive characters, is peculiarly shortsighted is a pertinent reminder that human understanding is, at best, partial. Investing the novel's narrative with an attractively humble quality, this kind of insight into human beings' limited capacity for understanding tends, in the textual fabric of *Middlemarch*, to generate difficult questions that are insistently explored rather than unambiguously resolved. A number of these questions are associated with the ways in which the characters' limited vision complicates the author's literary representation of their actions, thoughts, and feelings. Thus, constituent aspects of the visual are closely linked to other parts of the novel's discourse. As George Levine has observed, "the intensity and formal complexity of George Eliot's novels . . . must be credited in part to her refusal to disentangle representational precision, psychological states, formal coherence, and moral significance."[3] As far as *Middlemarch* is concerned, Eliot's "representational precision," which contributes significantly to what J. Hillis Miller has called her "enterprise of totalization,"[4] would appear to be closely affiliated with the novel's narrative vision.

In an adaptation this literary vision is transformed into a filmic one. One complicating factor here is, of course, the visual nature of the film medium: watching an adaptation, we see what is presented on the screen rather than what the literary narrator makes us visualize as we read. Thus we are engaged in what Boris Eikhenbaum, in a seminal essay from 1926, calls a "new and heretofore undeveloped kind of intellectual exercise."[5] For Eikhenbaum, seeing a film is a radically new way of reading—a reading of visual signals (as he is referring to silent films). Although the forms of vision engendered by literature and film are very different, watching a film is also an "intellectual exercise," an interpretive activity that, for the viewer, involves a processing of the wealth of visual images projected over the screen. The need for interpretation, for making meaning, is arguably stronger for the viewer than for the reader, since film is a complex system of successive, encoded signs that work on the viewer through their kinetic energy. These generalized points also apply to the BBC adaptation of *Middlemarch*.

Chapter 1 of Eliot's novel begins thus:

> Miss Brooke had that kind of beauty which seems to be thrown into relief by poor dress. Her hand and wrist were so finely formed that she could wear sleeves not less bare of style than those in which the Blessed Virgin appeared to Italian painters; and her profile as well as her stature and bearing seemed to gain the more dignity from her plain garments, which by the side of provincial fashion gave her the impressiveness of a fine quotation from the Bible,—or from one of our elder poets,—in a paragraph of to-day's newspaper. (7)

The novel's opening paragraph introduces the reader to a third-person narrator whose powers of seeing are very considerable and yet curiously restricted. The key word "seems," repeated in the past tense in the following sentence, invests the narrative with an element of uncertainty, adding a note of qualification. "Seems" suggests that although the narrator's impression of Dorothea is probably correct, her vision of this character is necessarily limited and potentially biased. This kind of limitation is elaborated on and refined as the narrative progresses. In the labyrinthine verbal complexity of *Middlemarch*, narrative vision approximates to narrative perspective, defined by Willie van Peer and Seymour Chatman as "the location from which events in a story are presented to the reader."[6] As they point out, "location" can have both a literal and a figural meaning. "Literally, 'perspective' refers to the spatiotemporal coordinates of an agent or observer; figuratively, it signifies the norms, attitudes, and values held by such an agent or observer."[7] Both these aspects of perspective are operative throughout the narrative discourse of *Middlemarch*. The opening identifies the narrator as a careful observer who reports, rather than participates in, the novel's plot. But the opening also indicates that this third-person narrator is no "neutral" and "omniscient" narrative agent. As we continue reading, we note numerous links between the narrator's observations and those made by several of the characters. Thus the norms, attitudes, and values noticeable in the opening sentences start the process of delineating the novel's original variant of third-person narrative. The result is a literary discourse in which the possibilities of realist narrative are brilliantly exploited, and yet combined with reservations about precisely this kind of narrative. As D. A. Miller puts it, *Middlemarch* "oscillates in a curious and exemplary way: between a confident re-enactment of traditional form, in the magisterial manner of a *summa*, and an uneasy subversion of its habitually assured validity, as though under the less magisterial pressure of a doubt."[8] What I want to stress is how early this narrative project commences, and how it is blended, already at the beginning of chapter 1, with the issue of seeing. Looking at Dorothea, the narrator invites the reader to share her gaze, and she also invites us to relate our gaze to those of other characters in the novel. Throughout *Middlemarch*, Eliot demonstrates that, as Jeremy Hawthorn puts it, "our looking activities are saturated with the residues of our social and cultural existence."[9] The opening of the novel's first chapter is an early indication of this insight.

How does the BBC adaptation of *Middlemarch* begin? Since the media of literature and film are vastly different, in asking this question I have perhaps embarked on a form of comparison that is critically dubious.[10] Still, a consideration of the film's beginning can tell us something important about the different ways in which these two media operate.[11] I have already indicated that this adaptation, directed by Anthony Page, became popular when it was shown in 1994—it was seen by millions of viewers and widely discussed. Thus there is a strong sense in which this BBC production is a an example of, and a contribution to, popular culture. Page chooses to serve— or perhaps rather, due to the financial demands of large-scale TV productions, *has* to serve—a wide range of viewers' expectations while at the same time considering, and at least partly complying with, a number of generic requirements pertaining to this kind of adaptation. Among these are dramatic events and action (involving not just dialogue but also conflicts between characters), considerable and relatively constant plot progression, and some form of climax or heightening of suspense at the end of each episode. Clearly, the novel's conflicts and dramatic action enable Page to easily meet these conventional expectations of a mass TV audience. However, if we ask what this kind of audience might want, or tolerate, when watching this particular film, we note a convergence of two kinds of problems: on one level, there is a limit to how much filmic experimentation the audience is likely to accept; on a different yet related level, an adequate and comprehensive filmic representation of the novel's pervasively reflective quality, noticeable above all in the narrator's commentary, would seem to invite such experimentation. Page could have chosen to respond to the first problem by suspending the second. I am going to argue, however, that although he cannot afford to overlook the expectations of his audience, he manages to present, and in some cases intensify, many of the observations and reflections that Eliot makes her narrator share with the reader.

A number of the literary narrator's functions in the novel are transformed into filmic ones in the adaptation. I am not suggesting that the latter unproblematically correspond to or replace the former. As George Bluestone puts it, "the end products of novel and film represent different aesthetic genera, as different from each other as ballet is from architecture."[12] As a sophisticated and highly effective form of narrative communication, however, a narrative fiction film such as Page's adaptation of *Middlemarch* invites, even urges, the viewer to fill in what appears to be missing—to move beyond what is visible and audible. Whereas the reader's impression and understanding of a character like Dorothea is guided by the third-person narrator's account of not only her speech and action but also her thoughts and feelings, the viewer's impression is formed by a subtle combination of visual and auditory signals. Enriching and modifying each other both structurally and thematically, these signals enable the viewer to extrapolate a meaning from, for example, Dorothea's facial expression that moves significantly beyond what is displayed on screen.

By "visual and auditory signals" I mean a combination of elements that combine to produce film narration, and that can all be subsumed under the concept of "film narrator." I am aware that this term is somewhat controversial. For David Bordwell, film has narration but no narrator: "in watching films, we are seldom aware of being told something by an entity resembling a human being. . . . [Therefore film] narration is better understood as the organization of a set of cues for the construction of the story. This presupposes a perceiver, but not any sender, of a message."[13] The emphasis Bordwell puts on the viewer's active role is critically illuminating. Yet although it is true that the viewer, on the basis of an indeterminate number of visual and auditory impressions, first constructs connected and comprehensible images and then a story, it is difficult to imagine that a film is "organized" without being "sent." If, as Seymour Chatman suggests, "narration" at least partly inhabits the film, "we can legitimately ask why it should not be granted some status as an agent," and then, for films as for novels, we can

> distinguish between a *presenter* of a story, the narrator (who is a component of the discourse), and the *inventor* of both the story and the discourse (including the narrator): that is, the implied author . . . as the principle within the text to which we assign the inventional tasks.[14]

In the case of the BBC adaptation under consideration here, it is natural to link the implied author to director Page's imprint on the film: the combined result of his choices, priorities, and decisions during the process of filmmaking. Yet since this particular film is an adaptation, Eliot is an "implied coauthor," that is, an implied author whose story, ideas, and value system Page both represents and interprets. As regards the film narrator, it is important to emphasize his, or perhaps rather its, multiplexity. As the diagram presented by Chatman indicates, the film narrator is the sum of a large number of variable elements, and the narrative functions and effects of these typically depend on the manner in which they are combined.[15] In Page's adaptation, the two elements of film that perform the most obvious, and most crucial, narrative functions are moving photographic images of acting characters and phonetic sound (voice) spoken by these characters. Operating in combination with each other and with other constituent aspects of film, these two elements form the basis for Page's film narration. The facets of this narration to be identified and discussed here can all be subsumed under the complex and fragmented concept of the film narrator—including what the camera reveals and what the film characters do and say.

Moving, as Eikhenbaum puts it, "from comparison of the moving frames [of film] to their comprehension," the viewer of *Middlemarch* who sees the film as an adaptation (because he or she has read the novel) is likely to construct an "internal speech" that approximates to that of the narrator in the literary text.[16] Such interpretive activity is an integral aspect of seeing the film version of a novel we have read. Since our construction of the film's "internal speech" will inevitably not only resemble but also differ from the literary narrator's speech, we must be wary of considering this kind of difference to be a weakness of the adaptation. There are different forms of adaptation, and the great difference between the two media complicates any evaluative comparison. That this particular adaptation begins by showing a horse carriage moving through a beautiful British landscape, and that its first close shot is of Lydgate as a passenger in that carriage, deviates sharply from the beginning of chapter 1 quoted earlier, but it does not follow that the beginning of the adaptation is "bad." Consider, for example, the first sentence spoken in the film. As one of the passengers exclaims "Look, the future!" the camera focuses on workers building a railway that runs parallel to the road. Highlighting the class aspect, this opening remark pinpoints the contrast between the tradition of rural Britain and the accelerating process of modernity, represented here both by the railway and by the character of Lydgate, who, for the viewer who has read the novel, personifies that process. The way in which the adaptation links Lydgate's vision of modern medical treatment in the new hospital to Dorothea's vision of building cottages for the poor is also thematically productive. First we see Lydgate studying the architect's drawing of the hospital; then there is a direct cut to Dorothea looking, also with keen interest, at similar drawings of cottages. In both cases, we are looking at characters who are looking at drawings of buildings not yet built. Aiming to alleviate the conditions of the sick and the poor, Lydgate and Dorothea represent forms of idealism that are laudable and yet, as the viewer is soon made to understand, somewhat naïve. When, in the adaptation, Celia urges her sister to look at the jewels and Dorothea comments "They look like fragments of heaven," a significant connection is established between Dorothea's vision of two different objects—a drawing and jewels. For Dorothea, the unifying feature of these two acts of seeing is the promise of a better future.

Seeing idealistically is also a character feature of Don Quixote, the hero of Miguel de Cervantes's novel whose importance for George Eliot, and for European nineteenth-century fiction, can hardly be exaggerated. Even though most of the novel's epigraphs are both thoughtful and thought-provoking, that to chapter 2, a quotation from the chapter in *Don Quixote* in which Don Quixote encounters somebody he thinks is a "cavalier" but whom Sancho correctly identifies as "a man on a grey ass" (15), is particularly effective. Not only does Don Quixote fail to listen to the common sense of Sancho, whose role here is comparable to that of Celia, he also proceeds to act in accordance with this wrong impression, his false vision. So does Dorothea, and the result is disastrous for both. But the similarity between these very different characters (there is an enormous difference between being mad, as Don Quixote is in part 1, and short-sighted) does not stop here. If Dorothea is deluding herself in her idealized view of Casaubon, like Don Quixote she, too, is forced, as a result of her wrong impression and misguided action, reluctantly to embark on a painful process of learning. In the narrative discourse of the novel, the stages of this long-drawn-out process of learning to see more adequately and realistically are inseparable from the third-person narrator's information and evaluative observations. Although a large portion of this discourse unavoidably disappears in the adaptation, significant aspects of it are retained, and in some cases accentuated.

In order to discuss how this is achieved I want to briefly consider the literary and filmic presentations of chapters 22 and 28. Both of these chapters further plot progression by marking significant points of transition, typically reflected in the main characters' changing relationships. Moreover, they display different yet related facets of the novel's drama of the visual. While the passage to be discussed from chapter 22 is relatively simple, perhaps even deceptively easy, to adapt, that from chapter 28 is difficult to translate into filmic discourse. Thus they illustrate different problems of narrative visualization and adaptation.

The last of the three chapters set in Rome, chapter 22 continues the line of development that commences in chapter 19 when Will Ladislaw and his friend Adolf Naumann, a young German artist, see Dorothea in the Vatican gallery. They both find her strikingly beautiful. That Casaubon, on honeymoon in Rome with his lovely young wife, should decide to bury himself for weeks in studies in the Vatican library is beyond their comprehension. While for Naumann Casaubon is pathetic and vaguely amusing, Ladislaw is provoked by his second cousin's self-centeredness and neglect of his wife. In a rhetorically effective manner, the narrator links Ladislaw's feeling of indignation to the feelings experienced by Dorothea herself. Shocked by Ladislaw's information that her husband's research methods may be outdated, Dorothea, the narrator informs us toward the end of chapter 21, "did not even speak, but sat looking at her hands" (195). This simple narrative description underlines the importance of seeing in *Middlemarch*. Although she cannot speak, she is looking, while Ladislaw is looking at her, at that part of her body that metonymically represents her skills—skills neither activated nor appreciated by her husband. There is a close link between this tableau and the more extended one in chapter 22 in which Dorothea, who is the real reason why Naumann wants to make a sketch of Casaubon's head, comments that "it would be a pity not to make the head as good as possible" (202). The combination of the narrative description of Dorothea in chapter 21 and Dorothea's remark in chapter 22 prompts dramatic irony, for Casaubon reveals no interest in making his wife's head (or hands) "as good as possible."

Consider this key passage in chapter 22:

> "My friend Ladislaw thinks you will pardon me, sir, if I say that a sketch of your head would be invaluable to me for the St Thomas Aquinas in my picture there. It is too much to ask; but I so seldom see just what I want—the idealistic in the real."
>
> "You astonish me greatly, sir," said Mr Casaubon, his looks improved with a glow of delight; "but if my poor physiognomy, which I have been accustomed to regard as of the commonest order, can be of any use to you in furnishing some traits for the angelical doctor, I shall feel honoured. That is to say, if the operation will not be a lengthy one, and if Mrs Casaubon will not object to the delay."
>
> As for Dorothea, nothing could have pleased her more. (201)

While Eliot in her presentation of Middlemarch exploits, as D. A. Miller puts it, "the potential narratability of social routine itself," she here brings together, in the contrastive setting of Rome, not just three of the main characters but also several of the problems, ideas, and desires with which they are associated.[17] The passage introduces one of the novel's most striking tableaux. Sitting still, Mr. and Mrs. Casaubon are being observed by Ladislaw and also by Naumann, who has been granted permission to make "a slight sketch" (ch. 22, 202) of Dorothea in addition to that of Casaubon. The variant of irony briefly commented on earlier is supplemented by Naumann's ironic description of a sketch of Casaubon's head as "invaluable." Verging on sarcasm, this irony is so obvious that we are mildly surprised Casaubon does not seem to detect it. Nor, apparently, does Dorothea, partly perhaps because both husband and wife are flattered by the comparison with Aquinas. This common failure to appreciate the irony in Naumann's request suggests the extent to which the diverging versions of dedication associated with

Casaubon and Dorothea can blur, and damagingly distort, their visions of "the real." If Casaubon is shortsighted in his research, responding only to the kind of material that can be included in his unpublishable notebooks, Dorothea fails to see how strongly her husband mistrusts Ladislaw. There is an important link between Naumann's remark in this passage and an observation the narrator makes a couple of pages further on in chapter 22: "Dorothea, who had not been made aware that her former reception of Will had displeased her husband, had no hesitation about seeing him" (204). In the narrative fabric of *Middlemarch*, needing to be "made aware" of something is synonymous with being dangerously unaware of something you ought to have seen.

Although Naumann links the phrase "the idealistic in the real" to Casaubon, he is clearly thinking primarily of Dorothea. And yet he may be thinking of Casaubon too, if only as a possible explanation of why Dorothea has chosen him. The productive ambiguity of this phrase is closely connected with Naumann's attempt to form an impression of the two based on his *visual* impression of them. "It is difficult for the gaze," notes Jean Starobinski in *The Living Eye*, "to limit itself to ascertaining appearances. By its very nature it must ask for more."[18] Asking for more is precisely what Naumann does when he sketches Casaubon's head in order to make "a slight sketch" of Dorothea. A sketch (from Italian *schizzo*, and Greek *skhedios*, which mean "done rapidly") indicates that crucially important early stage at which a visual impression is transformed into a representation of that impression. In the context of this particular scene, it is significant that only one of the two sketches drawn by Naumann is made into a portrait. Actually the transition from sketch to finished product can more easily be made in the case of Casaubon. When Naumann, continuing in his ironic vein, comments "*Schön!* I will talk of my Aquinas. The head is not a bad type, after all" (ch. 22, 203–4), the word "type" signals the relative simplicity, the stagnant nature of Casaubon's character. In contrast, Naumann sketches Dorothea in the pose of Santa Clara, "leaning so, with your cheek against your hand—so—looking at that stool, please, so!" (ch. 22, 202). Although this comment is another indication of Dorothea's shortsightedness, it also suggests a complexity of character far exceeding that of Casaubon.

The narrator's characterization of, and interest in, the main characters is centered on their development, a process of *Bildung* depending not least on the character's ability, and readiness, to respond to and learn from visual impressions.[19] One strength of Page's adaptation is to retain, and in one sense heighten, this tension in the filmic rendering of the honeymoon that Casaubon and Dorothea spend in Rome. Unsurprisingly but effectively, we are introduced to the location of Rome by means of a long shot of spires and domes, some of which are recognizable to the viewer who has visited the city. Broadly speaking, however, the film focuses on interiors: the art gallery where Naumann first sees Dorothea, the Vatican library, where Casaubon is hard at work, and the room in which Naumann makes the sketches of Casaubon and Dorothea. This is a good choice, since it enables Page to highlight their increasingly problematic relationship. I want to comment of two aspects of film narration in this part of the adaptation.

The first is the technique of voice-over, which some filmmakers use in order to present parts of the literary narrator's information and evaluative comments that cannot be imparted in any other way. "Voice-over" is one of the many elements that constitute the film narrator: a voice outside the film image. While *voice* determines the medium (we must hear somebody speaking), *over* applies to the relationship between the sound source and the images on the screen (the viewer cannot see the person speaking at the time of hearing his or her voice). Voice-over is thus a variant of film narration in which somebody introduces, supplements, and comments on what is shown visually.[20] Many filmmakers regard voice-over as an "unfilmic" device, and although some of the literary narrator's commentary could have been presented as voice-over, Page is probably right to use it sparingly. The variant of voice-over he does employ in the scene under consideration here, however, is thematically productive. It intensifies the visual drama by revealing how Casaubon, studying in the Vatican library, is forcibly reminded of the words Dorothea has just addressed to him: "Isn't it time to begin . . . to make your vast knowledge known to the world?" The question is embarrassing because it is perceptive and challenging: in the conversation with Dorothea it makes Casaubon angry, and in the Vatican library it keeps haunting him. The scene's suggestiveness derives from a particular combination of sight and sound: Page presents a medium shot of Casaubon bent over his books, working in the silence of the library and yet hearing Dorothea's voice, which is audible as voice-over to the viewer too. One significant aspect this particular use of voice-over is that while it illustrates all the characteristics of the device briefly mentioned earlier, it identifies the voice as Dorothea's. But because her voice is audible as voice-over only, it acquires a narrative authority comparable to that of the novel's third-person narrator. Suddenly we understand that Casaubon will never publish his "Key to all Mythologies," and we also gather that Dorothea's suspicion that he may be unable to do so is actually shared by Casaubon himself.

Second, the adaptation establishes a thematically productive link between this partial, though sadly insufficient, insight on Casaubon's part and the filmic presentation of the passage quoted earlier. As far as the possibility of adapting a literary text is concerned, the rendering, in verbal prose, of an artist sketching somebody's head would appear to be situated at the opposite extreme of a passage of narrative commentary. Yet although such a scene can effectively be transferred to the film medium, a presentation of this part of the adaptation can, of course, be more or less convincing. Page makes suggestive use of counterpoint, a variant of filmic narrative that supplements the voice-over already commented on. The camera focuses on Casaubon, who, assuming the pose of a meditating Aquinas, holds a skull in his right hand. There is a touch of the comic as well as the macabre in this image, which is kept in stable focus for as long as six seconds. Then the camera zooms in on Naumann's sketch—and the viewer is surprised, and amused, to discover it is one of Dorothea rather than of her husband. This exposure of Casaubon's ignorance is an illustrative example of film's capacity for ironic presentation: left in the dark by Naumann, whose real interest is in Dorothea, Casaubon fails to see that while being sketched he is actually being mocked. Responding to a significant feature of the literary text, the adaptation elegantly displays the contrast between seeing in a purely literal sense and seeing what is going on in a much larger sense. Casaubon fails on both counts. Unable to see the sketch of Dorothea, he also fails to appreciate both the irony of the situation and the association of his own head with the skull. The camera's narrative function is crucial in order to obtain this effect, and it depends in large part on a succession of shot and reverse shot that not only constitutes a visual tableau but also situates this tableau in a narrative development. This combination illustrates how the camera establishes varying perspectives, and thus the adaptation accentuates the characters' different ways of seeing and their limited insight. As glances are exchanged between Casaubon and Naumann, and as their remarks are accompanied by moments of silence, the camera represents both their perspectives and that of the narrator.

If this filmic segment illustrates how a scene from novel can be adapted, how about a passage in which the novel's narrative vision is closely associated with, and largely dependent on, the narrator's observations and reflections? In order to briefly consider this question I turn to chapter 28. For Dorothea, the transition back to Middlemarch after their six-week honeymoon in Rome is distinctly anticlimactic: "The duties of her married life, contemplated as so great beforehand, seemed to be shrinking with the furniture and the white vapour-walled landscape" (257), and she now inhabits "a pale fantastic world that seemed to be vanishing from the daylight" (258). The vision experienced by Dorothea here is a negative one, contrasting with her earlier "ideas and hopes" (258), which now appear disappointingly unrealistic. I want to comment on two aspects that, mutually reinforcing each other, serve to make this transition at once psychologically persuasive and rhetorically effective.

First, Dorothea's vision here is characteristic blend of on the one hand an accurate narrative presentation of what she sees and on the other hand her own interpretation of what she sees. As in James Joyce's "The Dead," the combination of January and "light snow" (256) suggests an absence not just of color but also of life. This suggestion presents itself both to the narrator and to Dorothea. The third-person narrator's account of the events, which is, of course, directed at the reader, is blended with Dorothea's interpretation of these events. "Was it only her friends who thought her marriage unfortunate?" (258). Eliot's use of free indirect discourse here resembles the manner in which modernist writers such as Kafka and Woolf employ this narrative technique. The narrator's voice and perspective approach that of one particular character, and yet the lack of complete identification with Dorothea grants the narrator the possibility of distancing herself from the character if such a maneuver is required. This is exactly what happens in the first two sentences of the following chapter: "One morning some weeks after her arrival at Lowick, Dorothea—but why always Dorothea? Was her point of view the only possible one with regard to this marriage? I protest" (ch. 29, 261).

This significant narrative variation condenses into one question Eliot's commitment to a form of narrative presentation that, although it neither can nor wishes to be "neutral," aims to understand the interests, desires, and motivating forces of all the characters, including the male ones and the less likable ones. Calling attention to Dorothea's "point of view," Eliot makes her narrator remind us that although Dorothea's perspective is not unimportant, it is neither the only possible one nor the only one represented in the plot.[21] There is a revealing link between this remark and the narrator's reflections in the second paragraph of chapter 10. How, asks the narrator on Eliot's behalf, can a character such as Casaubon be "fairly represented" (77)? Outlining different ways of knowing a character—the narrator's account, the report of other characters, or the inward reflections of a self—Eliot dismisses each of these in turn as only partial, and often misleading. Thus the problem of knowledge is closely related to the problem of knowing, and seeing, both ourselves and those around us.

Second, in chapter 28, as in the opening of chapter 1, the different dimensions of seeing, of visualizing both in a literal and metaphorical sense, are associated with narrative qualifications suggested by the verb "seem." The past tense of "seem" is used as often as seven times in this short chapter, and the verb occurs in several of its most important sentences. Let us consider one of them more closely. Turning away from the window (and thus from the wintry landscape outside), Dorothea, walking "round the room" she is in at Lowick, is overcome by "a keen remembrance":

The ideas and hopes which were living in her mind when she first saw this room nearly three months ago were present now only as memories: she judged them as we judge transient and departed things. All existence seemed to beat with a lower pulse than her own, and her religious faith was a solitary cry, the struggle out of a nightmare in which every object was withering and shrinking away from her. Each remembered thing in the room was disenchanted, was deadened as an unlit transparency, till her wandering gaze came to the group of miniatures, and there at last she saw something which had gathered new breadth and meaning: it was the miniature of Mr Casaubon's aunt Julia, who had made the unfortunate marriage—of Will Ladislaw's grandmother. (ch. 28, 258)

Dorothea is fascinated by the portrait not just because she sympathizes, and even tends to identify, with her aunt, but also because this woman was the grandmother of Will Ladislaw, who, contrasting with Casaubon's tiringly predictable routine, had awakened her emotional life. How does Eliot's narrative vision work here? On the one hand, Eliot's narrator emphasizes the importance of seeing as a physical act performed by Dorothea as character: after having looked at the snow outside, her gaze, resembling a film camera's panning movement, wanders round the room and finally comes to rest on the miniature. On the other hand, "seemed" is related to, indeed prompts, what Dorothea sees. The act of memory is strikingly visualized, and so are Dorothea's ideas, hopes, and religious faith. But rather than being near, and thus forming an integral part of Dorothea's personality, they are "withering and shrinking away from her." Seen in this light, the status of the miniature is ambiguous. It presents a strong and vivid image of aunt Julia, whose "hair and eyes seemed," to Dorothea, "to be sending out light" (ch. 28, 258). And yet its association with Ladislaw is problematic because he is connected with two of the underlying reasons for her restlessly wandering gaze: the memories of Rome that form a contrast to her present situation at Lowick, and the equally strong contrast between Ladislaw and her husband. There is a sense in which the kind of reassurance linked to, and provoked by, Dorothea's impression of the miniature exemplifies her myopia.

Although the prominence of narrative commentary makes this passage difficult to adapt, Page's film version presents several important aspects of Dorothea and Casaubon's relationship at this difficult stage of their married life. That Page deals with this particular passage in an oblique manner does not in itself make his filmic rendering inadequate. A variant of the film medium, Page's adaptation has "its own specificity deriving from its respective materials of expression."[22] To those materials already mentioned, moving photographic image and phonetic sound, we need to add, of course, the written materials of *Middlemarch*. Page's adaptation deals with various kinds of translations and transformations, including the problem of knowing ourselves and those around us as it presented in chapter 28. For Eliot, as Kay Young puts it,

> looking to "see" the consciousness of another as a means of knowing another means seeing the other through the lens of the self. Seeing involves a negotiation between image and its analysis, an analysis based on the seer's past knowledge or experiences or desires. To see the other means always to know a "negotiated" other, or reflection of the self.[23]

If we can only know others "through the lens of the self," how can we get to know them through the lens of the camera? The camera eye is mechanical, it has its own way of seeing the world, and there is something refreshingly deanthropomorphizing about it that contrasts with the way human beings see. The camera can, for instance, focus on details not noticed by the human eye. And yet we must not forget that the camera is after all steered—by a photographer, and behind him or her a director. If the camera is a mechanical instrument, it is also a device that enables Page as director to make a series of decisions, ranging from the trivial to the significant and existential. Page decides where and how to place the camera in relation to the filmed object, and this kind of relation serves to establish perspective as well as distance. The film camera can register the effect of seeing one character on another in a manner that makes visually accessible to the viewer a double image, that of the figure of "the known" along with that of the figure of "the knowing." Such an effect is achieved as Page, combining a series of medium and long shots, presents the Casaubons' arrival at Lowick in a manner that highlights the contrast between husband and wife. Characteristically untactful, Mr. Brooke comments that Casaubon looks "a little pale." This is an obvious and yet interesting variant of seeing: though superficial in his dealings with others, Mr. Brooke can still see, more clearly than Dorothea, that Casaubon is aging rapidly. Once the latter has left the group in the hall in order to rest, the atmosphere changes—toasts are proposed, and all of a sudden the mood is lighter. Not just drawing attention to Casaubon's tiredness and unwillingness to talk with those presumably close to him, this scene suggests that Dorothea is becoming estranged from her husband.

In this scene, as in many others, Page exploits film's capacity for showing faces, and facial expressions, in a way that prompts interpretive activity on the part of the viewer. In this particular scene our desire to understand a character's facial expression is strengthened by Mr. Brooke's remark: when he comments that Casaubon looks pale we suddenly see the latter's face in a new light. Peter Wollen's concept of the Index offers a possible way of theorizing this significant aspect of Page's adaptation. For Wollen—and also for James Monaco, who appropriates his theory of three kinds of cinematic signs—"the Index . . . measures a quality not because it is identical to it but because it has an inherent relationship to it."[24] Positioned between the Icon (a sign in which the signifier represents the signified mainly by its likeness) and the Symbol (an arbitrary sign in which the signifier represents the signified through convention), an Index can be thematically productive by adding a touch of the unknown or unexplained to the familiar. Neither an arbitrary sign nor one representing identity or similarity, the Index "suggests a third type of denotation that points directly toward connotation."[25] In Page's adaptation, Casaubon's paleness is an example of such an Index: although Page has never presented him as particularly healthy or physically active, suddenly the combination of camera angle, focus, and color makes us realize that while Dorothea is a young woman, Casaubon has indeed, as Sir James puts it as early as chapter 6 of the novel, "one foot in the grave" (54). But the significance of this particular Index does not stop here. Not just suggesting that Casaubon has aged, his paleness betrays his devotion to his studies (rather than his wife) during their honeymoon in Rome, and it is also linked to the skull of Aquinas he is holding in the scene discussed above. Thus the Index's narrative dimension is accentuated, and its thematic import further enhanced.

Since Page connects his portrayal of the increasingly tense relationship between Casaubon and Will Ladislaw with Dorothea's feeling of gradually becoming estranged from her husband, he heightens the film's narrative suspense. Thus he also invites the viewer to regard this stage of the plot as especially important, marking the beginning of the end of Dorothea's relationship with Casaubon and the start of a possible new one with Ladislaw. In his presentation of this transitional stage Page highlights, as a TV audience would expect him to do, what Lydgate, in conversation with a clearly upset Dorothea, refers to as Casaubon's "attack" in the library. Just before this conversation, a medium shot shows Dorothea and Lydgate positioned to the right and left of the frame. Using the technique of deep focus, Page makes the camera reveal that Casaubon, lying in bed in the center of the frame, is very pale. Blending denotation and connotation, Casaubon's paleness suggests that his studies have not only ruined his health but made him embittered and self-centered, an old man jealous of Ladislaw and insensitive to his wife's genuine wish to help her husband. As the caring Dorothea is totally without self-importance, Pages stresses the contrast between husband and wife by linking Casaubon's stubborn refusals (both before and after the attack, and directed both at Dorothea and Ladislaw) to the genuine concern and understandable frustration noticeable in Dorothea's facial expression during her conversation with Lydgate.

The Index of Casaubon's paleness takes on additional importance in the scene in which a partly recovered Casaubon is presented with the portrait of himself. Once again it is the insensitive Brooke who tells Casaubon that Dorothea has asked him to write to Ladislaw, and that this "excellent young man" has brought Naumann's portrait to Lowick. Here, as in the presentation of the scene in Rome in which Naumann draws the sketch forming the basis for the portrait, the combination of shot and reverse shot creates a distinctly ironic effect. The irony becomes all the more obvious when Brooke, just after Ladislaw has unveiled the portrait and they are all looking at it, comments that the skull in the portrait is "drawing attention to our ultimate destination." The painted face of Casaubon, positioned above the skull he is holding in his right hand, is just as pale as that of Casaubon looking at his own portrait, but Casaubon himself does not seem to notice this. Contributing to the scene's dramatic irony, the Index of paleness furthers the viewer's interpretation by drawing attention to a striking similarity that the main character fails to see.

In the paragraph of *The Living Eye* from which I have already quoted, Starobinski goes on to note that "each sense aspires to exchange its powers with the others. In a celebrated *Elegy* Goethe said: the hands want to see, the eyes want to caress. We may add: the gaze wants to speak." Starobinski specifies that "by gaze in this context I mean not so much the faculty of collecting images as that of establishing a relation."[26] This observation provides the basis for my first concluding point. Dorothea's vision is closely related to what she can and wants to do—using her intelligence to read and learn and using her hands to write. Dorothea's gaze wants to speak in the sense of forming, and gradually developing, a relation with her husband in which she could put both her head and her hands to good use. Was she naïve to believe this could happen? Probably, but Dorothea is by no means the only shortsighted character in *Middlemarch*. Moreover, certain forms of naïvety may be preferable, Eliot suggests, to variants of disillusionment that further a passive and noncaring attitude. It is to the credit of Page and his collaborators, not least his actresses and actors, that the adaptation too makes this suggestion.

Second, activating and combining a number of filmic devices and effects, Page eloquently presents a range of relationships in which, albeit in different ways and to a varying extent, the development of each character is linked to, and measured against, "the potential narratability of social routine itself." As D. A. Miller rightly observes, the literary narrator's presentation of this routine is less nuanced than that of the main characters. The visions of characters such as Dorothea, Lydgate, and Ladislaw complicate their relationships with the community. And yet, as Miller implies, this difference is not absolute. If, as he suggests, "the community substitutes a myth of eternal return for a history of its development," that development is furthered in large part by just those characters whose *personal* development Eliot presents.[27] This interplay of the community and the characters who are both part of it yet outside it is emphasized in Page's adaptation.

Finally, although Eliot's narrative vision in *Middlemarch* is inseparable from the multifaceted role of the third-person narrator, Page is able to activate and combine constituent facets of the film narrator in a manner that presents a number of the literary narrator's functions. It is, of course, impossible to incorporate all her statements, reflections, and ideas into the filmic narrative. The humanity and patience of Eliot's narrator are striking. Her attitude and concern modulate toward those of her main characters in ways that, as in Dostoevsky's *Crime and Punishment*, point toward the modernist fiction of Kafka and Woolf. In common with these three writers, Eliot, too, uses a third-person narrator who, although she can see what the characters fail to see, links her perspective to them in a sustained narrative act of human solidarity and compassion. Yet for all the differences between the literary narrator and the film narrator, Page uses the latter's multiplexity in order to make a comparable impression on the viewer. No neutral presenter of events, Page's film narrator endeavors to make us sympathize with Dorothea and Lydgate while increasingly wanting to distance ourselves from Casaubon, Rosamond, and several members of the town community. As Page's adaptation has a value of its own, and as it induces the viewer to reread Eliot's novel, it illustrates how productive and thought-provoking the relationship between the two media can be.

Notes

1. "George Eliot," in *The Essays of Virginia Woolf, 1925–1928*, vol. 4 ed. Andrew McNeille (London: Hogarth Press, 1994), 175–6.

2. *Middlemarch* (1994). Director, Anthony Page; screenplay, Andrew Davies; producer, Louis Marks. With Juliet Aubrey (Dorothea), Douglas Hodge (Lydgate), Patrick Malahide (Casaubon), Trevyn McDowell (Rosa-

mond), Rufus Sewell (Ladislaw). Running time: 356 minutes. Originally transmitted by the BBC January12–February 16, 1994; video, Universal.

3. George Levine, "Introduction: George Eliot and the Art of Realism," in George Levine, ed., *The Cambridge Companion to George Eliot* (Cambridge: Cambridge University Press, 2001), 9. See also Karen Chase, *George Eliot: "Middlemarch"* (Cambridge: Cambridge University Press, 1991).

4. J. Hillis Miller, "Optic and Semiotic in *Middlemarch*," in Jerome H. Buckley, ed., *The Worlds of Victorian Fiction* (Cambridge, Mass.: Harvard University Press, 1975), 125.

5. Boris Eikhenbaum, "Literature and Cinema" (1926), in Stephen Bann and John Bowlt, eds., *Russian Formalism: A Collection of Articles and Texts in Translation* (Edinburgh: Edinburgh University Press, 1973), 123.

6. Willie van Peer and Seymour Chatman, eds., *New Perspectives on Narrative Perspective* (Albany: State University of New York Press, 2001), 5. See my *Narrative in Fiction and Film: An Introduction* (Oxford: Oxford University Press, 2000), 38–45.

7. Van Peer and Chatman, *New Perspectives*, 5.

8. D. A. Miller, "George Eliot: 'The Wisdom of Balancing Claims,' " in John Peck, ed., *George Eliot: "Middlemarch"* (London: Macmillan, 1992), 84. See also David Lodge's contribution to this volume, "*Middlemarch* and the Idea of the Classic Realist Text," 45–64.

9. Jeremy Hawthorn, "Theories of the Gaze," in Patricia Waugh, ed., *Modern Literary Theory and Criticism: An Oxford Guide* (Oxford: Oxford University Press, forthcoming).

10. Although I do not, for the critical purposes of this essay, find it necessary to distinguish sharply between a film made for television and one made for the cinema, it does not follow that there are no differences between these two variants of adaptation. But these differences are minor ones compared to those between literature and film. A recent study of the kind of adaptation discussed here is Sarah Cardwell, *Adaptation Revisited: Television and the Classic Novel* (Manchester: Manchester University Press, 2002).

11. One of the best discussions of this issue remains Robert Scholes, "Narration and Narrativity in Film," in Gerald Mast and Marshall Cohen, eds., *Film Theory and Criticism: Introductory Readings* (Oxford: Oxford University Press, 1985), 390–403. See also Robert Stam, "Beyond Fidelity: The Dialogues of Adaptation," in James Naremore, ed., *Film Adaptation* (New Brunswick, N.J.: Rutgers University Press, 2000), 54–76.

12. George Bluestone, *Novels into Films: The Metamorphosis of Fiction into Cinema* (Baltimore: Johns Hopkins University Press, 1957), 5.

13. David Bordwell, *Narration in the Fiction Film* (Madison: University of Wisconsin Press, 1985), 62.

14. Seymour Chatman, *Coming to Terms: The Rhetoric of Narrative in Fiction and Film* (Ithaca: Cornell University Press, 1990), 126, 133, original emphasis.

15. Chatman, *Coming to Terms*, 134–5. The diagram is also presented in my *Narrative in Fiction and Film*, 31.

16. Eikhenbaum, "Literature and Cinema," 123.

17. Miller, "George Eliot," 90.

18. Jean Starobinski, *The Living Eye*, trans. Arthur Goldhammer (Cambridge, Mass.: Harvard University Press, 1989), 3.

19. As the German word *Bildung* indicates, Eliot links character development to a process of education that is far more inclusive and complex than the kind of scholarly work Casaubon is engaged in. There is an interesting connection between Eliot's understanding of character development and the German Romantics' understanding of *Bildung* as a process generating a potentially infinite series of thought acts. In *Blüthenstaub* Novalis writes: "Die höchste Aufgabe der Bildung ist, sich seines transzendentalen Selbst zu bemächtigen, das Ich seines Ichs zugleich zu sein" (The highest goal of *Bildung* is to take possession of one's transcendental Self, to be the I of one's own I simultaneously). See Novalis (Friedrich L. von Hardenberg), *Werke*, vol. 2, ed. H. J. Mähl (Munich: Carl Hanser Verlag, 1978), no. 28.

20. See Sarah Kozloff, *Invisible Storytellers: Voice-over Narration in the American Fiction Film* (Berkeley: University of California Press, 1988), 2–3.

21. The meaning Eliot attaches to "point of view" would appear to approximate to "perspective" as defined earlier.

22. Stam, "Beyond Fidelity," 59.

23. Kay Young, "*Middlemarch* and the Problem of Other Minds," *Literature Interpretation Theory* 14 (July–September 2003), 227.

24. James Monaco, *How to Read a Film: The World of Movies, Media, and Multimedia*, 3rd ed. (Oxford: Oxford University Press, 2000), 164. See also C. S. Cohen, *Signs and Meaning in the Cinema*, 2nd ed. (New York: Viking Press, 1972). Like Monaco, I capitalize "Icon," "Index," and "Symbol" in order to indicate that these terms are here used as Cohen, inspired by the philosopher C. S. Peirce, defines them.

25. Monaco, *How to Read a Film*, 165–6.

26. Starobinski, *Living Eye*, 3.

27. Miller, "George Eliot," 90.

Further Reading

Books

Auerbach, Nina. *Woman and the Demon: The Life of a Victorian Myth.* Cambridge, Mass.: Harvard University Press, 1982.

Barrett, Dorothea. *Vocation and Desire: George Eliot's Heroines.* London: Routledge and Kegan Paul, 1989.

Beatty, Jerome. *"Middlemarch": From Notebook to Novel: A Study of George Eliot's Creative Method.* Urbana: University of Illinois Press, 1960.

Beer, Gillian. *Darwin's Plots: Evolutionary Narratives in Darwin, George Eliot and Nineteenth-Century Fiction.* London: Routledge and Kegan Paul, 1983.

——. *George Eliot.* Brighton, England: Harvester Press, 1986.

Bonaparte, Felicia. *Will and Destiny: Morality and Tragedy in George Eliot's Novels.* New York: New York University Press, 1975.

Carroll, David, ed. *George Eliot: The Critical Heritage.* London: Routledge and Kegan Paul, 1971.

Chase, Karen. *Eros and Psyche: The Representation of Personality in Charlotte Bronte, Charles Dickens and George Eliot.* London: Methuen, 1984.

——. *George Eliot: "Middlemarch."* Cambridge: Cambridge University Press, 1991.

Correa, Delia da Sousa, ed. *The Nineteenth-Century Novel: Realisms.* London: Routledge and Kegan Paul, 2000.

Ermarth, Elizabeth Deeds. *George Eliot.* Boston: Twaye, 1985.

————. *Realism and Consensus in the English Novel.* Edinburgh: University of Edinburgh Press, 1998.

Gilbert, Sandra M., and Susan Gubar. *The Madwoman in the Attic.* New Haven: Yale University Press, 1979.

Graver, Suzanne. *George Eliot and Community: A Study in Social Theory and Fictional Form.* Berkeley: University of California Press, 1984.

Hardy, Barbara. *Particularities: Readings in George Eliot.* London: Peter Owen, 1982.

Miller, D. A. *Narrative and Its Discontents: Problems of Closure in the Traditional Novel.* Princeton: Princeton University Press, 1981.

Mintz, Alan. *George Eliot and the Novel of Vocation.* Cambridge, Mass.: Harvard University Press, 1978.

Paris, Bernard. *Experiments in Life: George Eliot's Quest for Values.* Detroit: Wayne State University Press, 1965.

Paxton, Nancy L. *George Eliot and Herbert Spencer; Feminism, Evolutionism and the Reconstruction of Gender.* Princeton: Princeton University Press, 1991.

Pinney, Thomas, ed. *Essays of George Eliot.* London: Routledge and Kegan Paul, 1963.

Pratt, John C., and Victor A. Neufeldt, eds. *George Eliot's "Middlemarch" Notebooks: A Transcription.* Berkeley: University of California Press, 1979.

Rignall, John, ed. *Oxford Reader's Companion to George Eliot.* Oxford: Oxford University Press, 2000.

Semmel, Bernard. *George Eliot and the Politics of National Inheritance.* Oxford: Oxford University Press, 1994.

Shuttleworth, Sally. *George Eliot and Nineteenth-Century Science: The Make-Believe of a Beginning.* Cambridge: Cambridge University Press, 1984.

Welsh, Alexander. *George Eliot and Blackmail.* Cambridge, Mass.: Harvard University Press, 1985.

Wisenfarth, Joseph, ed. *George Eliot: A Writer's Notebook 1854–1879 and Uncollected Writings.* Charlottesville: University Press of Virginia, 1981.

Witemeyer, Hugh. *George Eliot and the Visual Arts.* New Haven: Yale University Press, 1979.

Articles

Arnold, Jean. "Cameo Appearances: The Discourse of Jewelry in *Middlemarch*." *Victorian Literature and Culture* 30 (2002), 265–88.

Austen, Zelda. "Why Feminist Critics Are Angry with George Eliot." *College English* 37 (1976), 549–61.

Beaty, Jerome. "History by Indirection: The Era of Reform in *Middlemarch*." *Victorian Studies* 1 (1957), 173–9.

Blake, Kathleen. "*Middlemarch* and the Woman Question." *Nineteenth-Century Fiction* 31 (winter 1976), 285–312.

Carroll, Alicia. "Vocation and Production: Recent George Eliot Studies." *Dickens Studies Annual* 28 (1999), 225–55.

Edwards, Lee. "Women, Energy and *Middlemarch*." *Massachusetts Review* 13 (1972), 223–38.

Graver, Suzanne. "Incarnate History: The Feminisms of *Middlemarch*." In *Approaches to Teaching Eliot's "Middlemarch."* New York: Modern Language Association of America, 1990.

Hardy, Barbara. "George Eliot for the Twenty-first Century; *Middlemarch* and the Poetry of Prosaic Conditions." *George Eliot Review* 32 (2001), 13–22.

Hertz, Neil. "Recognizing Casaubon." *Glyph* 6 (1979), 22–41.

Knoepflmacher, U. C. "*Middlemarch*: An Avuncular View." *Nineteenth-Century Fiction* 25 (1975), 53–81.

———. "*Middlemarch*: Affirmation through Compromise." In *Laughter and Despair: Readings in Ten Novels of the Victorian Era.* Berkeley: University of California Press, 1971.

Langland, Elizabeth. "Inventing Reality; The Ideological Commitments of George Eliot's *Middlemarch*." In *Nobody's Angels; Middle-Class Women and Domestic Ideology in Victorian Culture*. Ithaca: Cornell University Press, 1995.

Logan, Peter Melville. "The Story of the Story of the Body: Conceiving the Body in *Middlemarch*." In *Nerves and Narratives: A Cultural History of Hysteria*. Berkeley: University of California Press, 1997.

Lysack, Krista. "Debt and Domestic Economy: *Middlemarch's* Extravagant Women." *Nineteenth-Century Feminisms* 6 (fall/winter 2002), 41–73.

MacKillop, Ian, and Alison Platt. " 'Beholding in a Magic Panorama': Television and the Illustration of *Middlemarch*." In Robert Giddings and Erica Sheen, eds., *The Classic Novel; From Page to Screen*. New York: St. Martin's Press, 2000.

Martin, Bruce K. "Fred Vincy and the Unravelling of *Middlemarch*." *Papers on Language and Literature* 30 (winter 1994), 3–24.

Miller, J. Hillis. "Narrative and History." *ELH* 41 (fall 1974), 455–73.

———. "Optic and Semiotic in *Middlemarch*." *Harvard English Studies* 6 (1975), 125–45.

Paris, Bernard. "*Middlemarch* Revisited; Changing Responses to George Eliot." *PSYART: A Hyperlink Journal for the Psychological Study of the Arts* 4 (2000), n. p.

Ringler, Ellin. " '*Middlemarch*': A Feminist Perspective." *Studies in the Novel* 15 (spring 1983), 55–61.

Rischin, Abigail. "Beside the Reclining Statue; Ekphrasis, Narrative and Desire in *Middlemarch*." *PMLA* 111, 5 (October 1996), 1121–1132.

Shelston, Alan. "What Rosy Knew: Language, Learning and Lore in *Middlemarch*." *Critical Quarterly* 35 (winter 1993), 21–30.

Showalter, Elaine. "The Greening of Sister George." In *George Eliot: Critical Assessments,* vol. 4, ed. Stuart Hutchinson. East Sussex, England: Helm Information, 1992.

Staten, Henry. "Is *Middlemarch* Ahistorical?" *PMLA* 115, 4 (October 2000), 991–1005.

Sutphin, Christine. "Feminine Passivity and Rebellion in Four Novels by George Eliot." *Texas Studies in Language and Literature* 29 (fall 1987), 342–63.

Tambling, Jeremy. "*Middlemarch*, Realism and the Birth of the Clinic." *ELH* 57 (1990), 939–60.

Thomas, Jeanie. "An Inconvenient Indefiniteness; George Eliot, *Middlemarch*, and Feminism." *University of Toronto Quarterly* 56 (spring 1987), 392–415.

Tucker, John. "George Eliot's Reflexive Text: Three Tonalities in the Narrative Voice of *Middlemarch*." *Studies in English Literature* 31 (autumn 1991), 773–91.

Young, Kay. "*Middlemarch* and the Problem of Other Minds Heard." *Literature Interpretation Theory* 14 (2003), 223–41.

Index